Lonely Planet Publications
Melbourne | Oakland | L...

BATH -
→SALL...
P
-BATH PASS
30 Attractions
Roman BATH
x
x *x*
summer Solstace

Terry Carter &
Lara Dunston

Dubai

The Top Five

1 Burj Al Arab
Admire Dubai's iconic hotel (p146)
2 Sheikh Zayed Rd
Enjoy the fabulous architectural skyline (p56)
3 Souqs
Buy whatever you desire at Dubai's many markets (p120)
4 Dubai Creek
Cruise Dubai's city-splitting waterway (p47)
5 Bastakia Quarter
Wander around this traditional district (p52)

Contents

Published by Lonely Planet Publications Pty Ltd
ABN 36 005 607 983

Australia Head Office, Locked Bag 1, Footscray,
Victoria 3011, ☎ 03 8379 8000, fax 03 8379 8111,
talk2us@lonelyplanet.com.au

USA 150 Linden St, Oakland, CA 94607,
☎ 510 893 8555, toll free 800 275 8555,
fax 510 893 8572, info@lonelyplanet.com

UK 72-82 Rosebery Ave, Clerkenwell, London,
EC1R 4RW, ☎ 020 7841 9000, fax 020 7841 9001,
go@lonelyplanet.co.uk

The Authors

TERRY CARTER

Terry has lived in the United Arab Emirates (UAE) since 1998, when his wife, Lara, accepted a job offer in a country he'd never heard of. Eventually locating the UAE on a map and quite bored with looking at publishing schedules in Sydney, he quit his job and started packing. Over the past few years Terry and Lara have visited almost every country in the Middle East (war permitting) and are halfway through their second passports. Happily freelancing from Dubai, Terry has recently completed his Masters dissertation on representations of nationalism in the UAE media. Furthermore, he can recite the menu of most of Dubai's better restaurants from memory.

LARA DUNSTON

For the five years Lara's family toured Australia in a caravan, the young Lara marked the journey in her *Jacaranda Junior World Atlas*. For her undergraduate film degree she learnt about cinema by country: Russian avant-garde, Italian neo-realism, French new wave. This love of film and travel took Lara to live in Abu Dhabi for five years, after which, in 2003, she moved to Dubai to run the Dubai Women's College Communication Technology programme. Moving to Dubai, however, did not cure Lara's travel bug, it just meant a cheaper taxi ride to Dubai airport. Sadly, when friends visit Dubai, Lara creates a written itinerary for them each day, complete with instructions for the taxi driver.

PHOTOGRAPHER
PHIL WEYMOUTH

Australian born, Phil Weymouth and his family called Tehran, Iran, home from the late 1960s until the revolution in 1979. After studying photography in Melbourne, Phil returned to the Middle East in the mid-1980s to live and work as a photographer in Bahrain. Now based again in Melbourne, this assignment took Phil back to Dubai where he marvelled at how staggeringly fast the city changes. Despite this, it still retains much of its Arabic charm and, between snapping images, Phil enjoyed the warm hospitality of the people, watching the *abras* (water taxis) jockey for position on the Creek, and washing down lamb shwarma with hot sweet tea.

Introducing Dubai

In 1894 Sheikh Maktoum bin Hasher al-Maktoum, ruler of a fledgling Dubai, lured foreign traders to the city by offering a safe, tax-free port. Now, his entrepreneurial descendents are doing the same with tourists. Dubai currently draws in over five million travellers per year from all over the world. And it's easy to see why. Dubai is a flashy, fun, often surreal, yet uniquely Arabian experience. With year-round sunshine, stunning five-star beach hotels, dazzling shopping, extensive nightlife, and world-class events and sporting facilities – coupled with Bedouin hospitality and history – Dubai's cosmopolitan, yet easy-going, charm makes it the best introduction to the Middle East.

The audacity of the city's rulers is breathtaking. Running out of coastline to build new resorts? Build two artificial islands with 120km of new beachfront. Need better airline coverage for your city? Build up an award-winning airline in 15 years. Need to keep your name on the world stage? Host the world's richest horse race, international tennis and golf tournaments, and a month-long shopping festival. Need an iconic landmark that people will recognise worldwide? Up goes the world's tallest and most lavish hotel, built on one of the aforementioned artificial islands.

The optimism that fuels these projects is contagious and everyone comes to Dubai for a piece of the action. Pakistanis, Indians, Sri Lankans, the English, Canadians, Filipinos – they're all here, chasing money and opportunities that can transform their lives. The mix of cultures this creates gives Dubai a unique multilingual buzz. But the sound of the muezzin calling the faithful to prayers cuts through the noise; Islam is still at the core of Dubai's values and every neighbourhood has its mosque. The call to prayer is just about all that can get Emiratis off their mobile phones. The city is eerily quiet on Friday morning until the mullah gives his sermon. For 11 months of the year DJs spin the latest wax at hip clubs, but this stops for the fasting month of Ramadan.

While the only thing that may have changed about the Emiratis' national dress is the designer label now attached, it's still a potent link to Dubai's past. When you see the glistening buildings lining Dubai Creek and Sheikh Zayed Rd, or sip champagne at a gorgeous rooftop bar after sampling a degustation feast at a fine dining restaurant, you'll find it hard to reconcile this with the images of Dubai's past – even its recent past (p36). Dhows that still trickle into Dubai's Creek have been joined by flights from all over the world landing at Dubai's award-winning airport. Shoppers can still walk the souqs or visit Dubai's busy shopping centres, which have become tourist attractions in their own right. Even the searing summer temperatures and rainless months have been conquered with air-conditioned everything and fresh water extracted from the sea, while sun-starved Europeans flock in to soak up Dubai's endless sunny days.

While Dubai may lack the physical sense of history that other Middle East destinations, such as Marrakech and Cairo have, it makes up for it in an eagerness to please and a willingness to cater to your every whim. Such is the nature of the fabled Bedouin hospitality. But while proud of its heritage and traditions, Dubai doesn't dwell too much on the past – it's too busy working towards its future. With the entrepreneurial flair that's clearly hereditary in the Al-Maktoum family, you wouldn't bet against Dubai having a bright one.

TERRY & LARA'S TOP DUBAI DAY

Our friends arrive in Dubai already jet lagged – a five-movie flight. We ply them with champagne and Iranian caviar and send them off to bed. Late start the next morning, straight to **Dubai Museum** (p53). They love it. They think it's fascinating and adore the kitsch mannequins. Taxi to the **Marina Seafood Market** (p84) at the Jumeirah Beach Hotel for lunch. Our guests are just stunned by the awesome view of the **Burj Al Arab** (p57) hotel as we take the golf buggy out to the restaurant – fresh seafood, good wine, perfect weather and one of the best views in the world.

In the taxi on the way home the phone starts ringing. Message: *House party. Jumeirah tonight.* Message: *New club night @ Terminal.* Perhaps we'll check these out after dinner. We walk along the Creek and catch the *abra* (small boat) to Deira. Our friends quickly learn how to play the gold-souq haggle, zigzagging between the shops. The sun sets as our *abra* crosses back over the Creek. Before they have a catnap, our guests request more 'cool Arabian stuff' for tonight. We work the phones and score a booking at **Tagine** (p85). It's now 7pm. First stop **Bahri Bar** (p91) where the view across the water is superb. Our table at Tagine is excellent – right near the musicians. Outside for

Essential Dubai

- **Bastakia Quarter** (p52) The restored residential area of Dubai.
- **Burj Al Arab** (p57) Dubai's architectural icon that also happens to be a hotel.
- **Deira Gold Souq** (p50) The place to haggle over some gold chains.
- **Dubai Creek** (p54) *Abras* still crisscross the traditional heart of Dubai.
- **Dubai Museum** (p53) Trace the changes of this fast-evolving city in this fascinating museum.

sheesha (water pipe) in the courtyard, then our friends are keen to push on. A drink at *The Thousand and One Nights* fantasy that is the **Rooftop Bar** (p93) then it's off to **Sho Cho's** (p94) where the DJ already has the outdoor crowd moving. There's a line forming at **Boudoir** (p95) and it's only 11pm. We make a move. Looks like another late start tomorrow.

City Life

City Life

DUBAI TODAY

Dubai thinks it's pretty damn good. You want to know why? Check out photos from 40 years ago in the **Dubai Museum** (p53) – just Creek and desert. Now it's a modern oasis where you can visit the world's first 'seven star' hotel in a Porsche Cayenne, or relax in a corporate box at the planet's richest horse race while clutching some Veuve Clicquot. You did know that The Palm resort is visible from outer space, didn't you? David Beckham can't wait to move in – he wrote a cheque for his villa on the spot.

Dubai is also needy and always desperate for attention. It's almost as if Dubai thinks that if the world turns away for a second, the enormous wealth will disappear, the buildings will dissolve into sand and the expats will take their bat and ball and go home.

The leaders of Dubai have handled the transformation of this small trading town into a regional business and tourism hub with aplomb. When the Al-Maktoum family and other members of the Bani Yas tribe left Liwa for Bur Dubai (see p41), it's almost as if they knew this was their destiny. Each successor has built on the achievements of the last, with no small amount of entrepreneurial skill, daring and vision. These Arab alchemists have come up with a formula that is unique to Dubai, and instilled in its people a sense of optimism and a 'can do' spirit coupled with an expectation of success.

While everyone who comes to live in Dubai in some way shares in its success, there is always an underlying feeling of being the 'hired help', which of course everyone is. While buying property in Dubai now allows expats to have an open-ended residency visa, it's not citizenship – and even if it was, how much of a say would you have in a society based on tribal affiliations and no elections?

Deira (p48)

For many expats, the wealth they have accumulated in Dubai infuses them with a form of affection for the place. Others feel a sense of disconnectedness and resentment, voiced through a commonly heard statement that 'sure it's great here, but the place would fall apart if it wasn't for us expats'. Another popular expat saying used to be, 'just wait until the oil runs out, then we'll see what happens'. The oil in Dubai *is* running out, but Dubai is virtually finished with its oil-dependent days and the noise of the disgruntled expat sounds increasingly like a plea for recognition of their contribution rather than a statement of defiance.

This notion of the expats doing all the work, however, is not lost on the Emiratis. In Dubai especially, where Emiratis make up only 22% of the population, this is particularly pertinent. An Emiratisation policy to place Emiratis in jobs has met with limited success, especially in the private sector where, in Dubai, Emiratis comprise only 1% of the workforce. There is a perception in the private sector that Emiratis want too much money for their level of qualification and expect promotion without merit. Ironically, recent reports have shown that most Emiratis respond well to working in these multicultural workplaces when they are given a chance.

The major stumbling block is money. The cheap labour that keeps the wheels of Dubai turning is a double-edged *khanjar* (traditional curved dagger). Why train locals to do jobs such as plumbing when you can hire someone to do it for one tenth of what an Emirati would expect – and what Emirati would be willing to attend college to learn such a trade?

The cheap labour affects Dubai in other ways. Many workers are cheated out of money, often not being paid for months, or are underpaid and overworked against the terms of their employment agreement. On the other hand, these workers are often employed illegally or try to abscond. In a recent six-month amnesty, 100,000 workers left the United Arab Emirates (UAE), but authorities consider this to represent only 30% of the total figure of illegal workers. Given that the expat workers ratio of men to women is 7:3, there's also the question of the growing prostitution trade in the city. In an area of Bur Dubai the recent installation of streetlights was seen by many as a signal for street prostitution to move somewhere less open, but it's simply improved the shopping experience for the clients. Even the hippest clubs have Eastern European girls trying to ply their trade. Despite the best efforts of the police, the drug scene is also burgeoning.

There does, however, appear to be a sense of balance in Dubai, both within the city and with its relationship with the rest of the world. Dubai today is friends with the West and, for progressive Arabs, a shining example of a modern Arab city, but for increasingly conservative branches of Islam, it is seen as far too liberal. How Dubai manages to balance all these factors is just as important as keeping up its spectacular growth. Given the track record of Dubai's leaders over the past few years, it would be unwise to bet against them. That's what makes Dubai so exciting today – like an Arabian thoroughbred, it's just getting into its stride.

Hot Conversation Topics

The malls, the cafés, the clubs and pubs are all alive with conversation. Here's what people are talking about:

- Traffic – can it possibly get any worse?
- Is Dubai really hip yet?
- Celebrity sightings – was that Naomi Campbell?
- More visiting pensionable performers. Why do we only see UB40, Blondie and Bryan Adams?
- Real estate – where to live and who's bought what.
- There's another mall/offshore island/indoor ski resort/huge resort being built?
- What ever happened to the light rail project?

CITY CALENDAR

Dubai's city calendar takes increasing advantage of the cooler months. December to March are now so busy that locals are almost relieved when the Dubai World Cup ends. For information on Dubai's public holidays, see p177.

JANUARY & FEBRUARY
DUBAI FASHION WEEK

With aspirations of joining Paris, Milan, New York and London as one of the world's leading fashion capitals, Dubai has included Fashion Week on its social calendar. Just two weeks after launching their spring/summer *haute couture* collections in Paris, the very best fashion houses, such as Christian Dior, Ungaro, Givenchy and Christian Lacroix, come to Dubai for five days.

DUBAI INTERNATIONAL JAZZ FESTIVAL

Held during the Shopping Festival, this event is staged over three nights at Dubai Media City. The festival showcases a diverse array of musical offerings, including jazz, funk, Afro and Latin.

DUBAI MARATHON
www.dubaimarathon.org

The event offers a full marathon, a 10km run and 3km fun run. While those in Dubai during the hotter months might think this is madness, the January date means the temperature is quite pleasant. We're still not sure running through the Shindagha Tunnel is a great idea though.

DUBAI SHOPPING FESTIVAL
www.mydsf.com

Running for a month from mid-January, this festival is not just about shopping, it's about

Top Five Quirky Events

- **Concerts** Any live event involving has-been rock stars playing the hits to boost their retirement fund or a visiting diva down on her luck looking for a captive audience – yes, that's you Whitney and Mariah.
- **Diwali Festival** Only the Indian expats can pronounce the names of the different days of the festival or know what it's about, but the food's good, there're lots of pretty lights and yes, I'd love some more biryani.
- **Dubai International Jazz Festival** Memo: We'll call it a 'jazz' festival instead of just a music festival because it sounds, well, more sophisticated. But we can't really have too many jazz artists because no-one will turn up. And we'll have a style of music called 'diva' – you know, women singing ballads while wearing evening gowns.
- **Dubai Shopping Festival's Global Village** There's nothing like watching a Chinese magician in Dubai performing in front of some Somalis eating Lebanese food.
- **Wooden powerboat racing** Open only to UAE nationals, this sport combines the traditional art of wooden boat building with the noise and pollution resulting from bolting a couple of outboards on the back and driving like there's no tomorrow.

shopping for stuff from all around the world at the 'Global Village'. The hotels are full, there's live music and performances, fireworks every night and, in keeping with the global village theme, spectacular traffic jams that must have been imported from Los Angeles, starting every day around 4pm and lasting well into the night.

DUBAI TENNIS CHAMPIONSHIPS
www.dubaitennischampionships.com
Held over two weeks from late February, the championships consist of a Women's Tennis Association (WTA) event followed by an Association of Tennis Professionals (ATP) one. While the women and men slug it out from the baseline, we kinda miss Anna Kournikova getting knocked out of the tournament early in the week and then being spotted all over town.

MARCH
DUBAI DESERT CLASSIC
www.dubaidesertclassic.com
The Dubai Desert Classic lures some of the best golfers in the world to Dubai to partake in one of the world's richest golf tournaments. Just as celebrity-mad Dubai stalked Anna Kournikova, Tiger Woods is similarly obsessed over in Dubai and was offered a reported US$3 million to turn up in 2004. His best golf of the tournament, however, was when he hit some balls off the helipad at Burj Al Arab.

DUBAI WORLD CUP
www.dubaiworldcup.com
The Dubai International Racing Carnival, running from February through to the end of March, culminates in the Dubai World Cup, the world's richest horse race with prize money of a dizzying US$6 million and a total purse of over US$15 million. While there's no betting, many of Dubai society's women take a punt in wearing some of the silliest hats this side of the Melbourne Cup.

SHARJAH CUP
So it's not actually in Dubai, but the Sharjah Cup, usually held in March or April, is a firm fixture on Dubai's sporting calendar. Participating cricket teams change every year, but there are three competing nations each time, one of which is India or Pakistan. The stadium holds up to 22,000 fanatical supporters – a match between India and Pakistan held here is quite an event.

JUNE
DUBAI SUMMER SURPRISES
www.mydsf.com
Similar to the Dubai Shopping Festival, this event is a more family-oriented affair and has been successful in attracting Gulf State visitors who would normally sit out the heat somewhere more pleasant than Dubai in summer. One of the key attractions is the room rates – much cheaper than at other times of the year.

OCTOBER
UAE DESERT CHALLENGE
www.uaedesertchallenge.com
This desert rally starts off in Abu Dhabi and finishes in Dubai. The UAE Desert Challenge is held over four days, covers some challenging terrain, and attracts car, truck and motorbike riders.

DECEMBER

DUBAI INTERNATIONAL FILM FESTIVAL

Aimed at the multicultural local community and international visitors, the goal of this international film festival is to build cultural bridges and promote understanding, tolerance and peace. The five-day festival will showcase contemporary and classical global cinema, showing some 80 features and 30 shorts. And in true Dubai style there will be nightly red-carpet events at the Madinat Jumeirah Arabian Resort.

CULTURE

IDENTITY

Recent estimates put Dubai's population at just over 1.1 million, a giant leap from 183,200 in 1975. These statistics apply to the whole of the Dubai emirate, though most of the population lives in the city of Dubai. The population has been growing by as much as 6% a year and authorities are planning for a population of two million by 2010. Roughly 220,000 people are Emiratis; the expatriate community makes up the rest of the population – one of the most multicultural in the world.

Dubai is a tolerant and relaxed society, with its cultural life firmly rooted in Islam. Day-to-day activities, relationships, diet and dress are dictated very much by religion. Gender roles are changing, with women wanting to go into the workforce before marriage, but overall traditions are still adhered to; men engage with the outside world and women rule the roost in domestic life.

While there is only a limited amount of 'bricks and mortar' representing traditional Arabic and Bedouin life in Dubai, the cultural identity of Emiratis remains strong. The physical representations of the past still exist in the form of the old buildings in **Bur Dubai** (Map pp212-13), along the waterfront near the souq and in Deira around **Al-Ahmadiya School** (Map pp208-9). But to get an idea of traditional culture, you need to visit the Dubai Museum or venture out of Dubai to some of the villages around the East Coast and to Al-Ain, where life appears not to be too far removed from the way it was before federation.

Disregard comments you may hear about the local culture in Dubai being just a 'shopping culture'. Although popular, shopping is just a pastime and a social activity. Emirati cultural

Heritage Village (p54)

Man in traditional attire walking past a modern building

identity is expressed through poetry, traditional song and dance. If you are lucky enough to be invited to a wedding, it's a great way to see these cultural traditions in action.

Dubai has been very active over the last few years in preserving and publicly displaying many of the local traditions. The **Dubai Museum** (p53) and the **Heritage Village** (p54) in Shindagha display traditional village life, as does the **Heritage Village** (p156) in Hatta. Expensive restoration work is being carried out on traditional turn-of-last-century houses in the Al-Ahmadiya district of Deira, in the Bastakia Quarter and the Shindagha area of Bur Dubai. The aim of such work is not just to attract and entertain tourists, it is also designed to educate young Emiratis about their culture and heritage.

One matter of great concern to the authorities is the trend for Emirati men to marry foreign women. One reason for this is the prohibitive cost of a traditional wedding, plus the dowry that the groom must provide – it's cheaper and easier to marry a foreign woman. There's also a suggestion that as Emirati women have become better educated, they are less willing to settle down in the traditional role of an Emirati wife. This issue is discussed in great depth in the Arabic press. In a culture where women who are unmarried by the age of 24 are

Population Breakdown

The majority of expats (about 60%) are from India, supplying the city with cheap labour, although there are also a large number holding professional positions. Most of the labourers and men in low-prestige positions (taxi drivers, hotel cleaners etc) come from the southern Indian state of Kerala and many are Muslims. There are also lots of workers from the states of Tamil Nadu and Goa. In contrast, most of the Indians in office jobs or managerial positions are recruited by agencies based in Mumbai, and many come from that city. In addition, all of the leading Indian mercantile communities – Jains, Sindhis, Sikhs and Marwaris – are represented here. These communities are sometimes collectively called the Banians or Traders.

About 12% of expats are from other Arab countries (mainly Lebanon, Syria, Jordan and Egypt). There's also a substantial Iranian community. The first wave of Iranians built the Bastakia neighbourhood in the 1930s. They were mostly religiously conservative Sunnis and Shiites from southern Iran. After the 1980 Islamic revolution, a more affluent, often Western-educated, group of Iranians settled in Dubai. There is also a growing community of Filipino expatriates, as well as some Chinese, Indonesian and Vietnamese residents. Western expats make up about 3% of the population, once predominantly British but now also strongly represented by people from Ireland, Germany and France.

perceived as being 'on the shelf', or even as a slight on the family's honour, the growing number of single women is a hot subject indeed. The rising divorce rate is another topic that attracts considerable concern.

The UAE Marriage Fund, set up in 1994 by the federal government to facilitate marriages between UAE nationals, grants up to Dh70,000 to each couple to pay for the exorbitant cost of the wedding and dowry. It also promotes mass weddings, which allow nationals to save most of the marriage grant for a down payment on a house and other living costs. These have reduced the rate of intermarriages between Emirati men and foreign women to a degree, but many Emirati women feel that there are not enough 'good men' to go around; in other words, it is hard to find a husband who will accept his wife's desire to have kids and a career.

LIFESTYLE

There are as many different lifestyles being played out in Dubai as there are grains of sand on Jumeirah Beach. Disposable income plays a big part in how people live in Dubai. At the top end of the pay scale is the

Top Five Books

- *Dubai, A Collection of Mid-twentieth Century Photographs* by Ronald Codrai. An important document of everyday life in the preoil days of the seven sheikhdoms before they united, providing a rare look at a traditional way of life that is fast disappearing.
- *Dubai Life & Times: Through the Lens of Noor Ali Rashid* by Noor Ali Rashid. A pictorial history of Dubai over the last four decades by the royal photographer.
- *Dubai Tales* by Mohammad al-Murr. A collection of charming short stories, written by one of the UAE's best known writers, provides an intimate insight into the lives and values of the people of Dubai.
- *Father of Dubai: Sheikh Rashid bin Saeed al-Maktoum* by Graeme Wilson. A terrific photographic and narrative tribute to the founder of modern Dubai.
- *Mother Without a Mask: A Westerner's Story of her Arab Family* by Patricia Holton. This chronicle of a British woman's experience living with a wealthy Emirati family offers a rare insight into the realm of Arab women.

professional and wealthy business class. Good salary package or income, nice car (Mercedes or BMW), a large villa with a maid or two and a lifestyle that allows them to travel overseas for two months a year to escape the heat of summer. Housewives left with little to do at home spend much of their time with other women in similar circumstances. It's fair to say these women keep the cosmetics and spa industries alive and the coffee shops ticking over during the day. These expats are generally Western, but there are plenty of Indians and Iranians that fall into this category.

There is another category of professional expat – the academics, health professionals, media and IT people – who earn much the same as they would back home in gross terms, but with no tax, free housing, good holidays and other benefits, such as free schooling and health care, they come out way ahead in financial terms. These expats are also generally Western, but there's a large number of Indians working in the IT field. Depending on how many children they have, some families have a full-time or part-time maid or nanny. Some are here to put away as much money as possible to pay off a place back home, while others enjoy the lifestyle and often leave without saving a cent, but having had a great time.

Dubai has a huge service sector and traditionally workers come from India, Pakistan and the Philippines, but now there are workers coming from other Asian countries as well. Working as line cooks, waiters and in supermarkets, these expats stand to make much more money in Dubai than at home, usually working six days a week and staying in relatively cheap accommodation with several others from the same company. Their one day off is generally spent with friends or emailing home. Many of the Pakistani and Indian men have organised cricket matches as well as meeting places where they catch up on news from home.

There is a huge number of maids employed in Dubai – check the classifieds of *Gulf News*. Indian, Pakistani and Sri Lankan live-in maids are generally paid between Dh500 and Dh800 a month, usually living in a tiny room in a villa or a large apartment. While the money earned is one tenth of a Western professionals' starting money, it's still much more than unskilled work pays back home. Depending on the family, some of these maids become an integral part of the family structure, forming close bonds with the children.

For around the same money Indians, Pakistanis and workers from other Arab countries go about the hazardous business of construction. These men usually work six or six and a half days a week on 12 hour shifts and live in compounds provided by the construction companies. While conditions have improved, the heat is still oppressive and the pressure to complete buildings in Dubai is enormous.

FOOD

Local cuisine in Dubai is mainly based on Middle Eastern dishes and largely borrowed from other countries in the region, in particular Lebanon, Syria and Iran. The diet of the Bedouin who inhabited the area that is now Dubai consisted only of fresh fish, dried fish,

Karama Shopping Centre (p129)

dates, camel meat and camel milk. Traditional Emirati cuisine doesn't lend itself to tantalising interpretations of these ingredients.

Muslims do not eat pork, as it is haram (forbidden by Islam). Sometimes, as an alternative to pork bacon, supermarkets sell beef bacon and turkey bacon. Dishes containing pork generally only appear on the menus of top-end restaurants and are marked as such, as are dishes using alcohol in the cooking process or the sauce. Meat consumed by Muslims must be halal, meaning religiously suitable or permitted. The animal must be killed by having its throat cut and the blood drained out before it is butchered. This is why much of the red meat slaughtered and sold locally is very pale in colour.

The range of cuisines offered in Dubai is wide, but mainly falls into several categories. Besides Middle Eastern, you'll find plenty of European, Indo-Pakistani and Asian or Far Eastern eateries.

The most common of Middle Eastern food you'll see is Lebanese (see the boxed text below). Lebanese restaurants are found all over Dubai and cover all price ranges. All Lebanese dishes are served with pickles, piles of Arabic bread and a big plate of fresh salad. The Lebanese have food covered – you can grab their version of fast food, the shwarma, when you're in a hurry, or linger for hours over mezzes and mixed grills. Throw in a belly dancer and some *sheesha* (water pipe) and you have the makings of a great night out.

Though there are similarities with Lebanese cooking, Iranian (Persian) food has its own style and flavours (see the boxed text on p16). The Iranians are big on spicy rice dishes and a favourite in Iranian cooking is the buttery crust left at the bottom of the pan after rice is cooked. Anyone who doesn't serve this part of the rice dish to guests is considered either a bad cook or a bad host.

Iranian food is usually served with a plate of lettuce, cabbage, tomato and onion, with a minty yogurt sauce on the side. Naan (Iranian bread) is baked in several different ways, but the most common variety in Dubai is known as *lavash* – it is thin, square and somewhat elastic.

Lebanese Food Lingo 101

Lebanese food is delicious and available everywhere in Dubai. Here are some of the most popular dishes you'll see.

Street Food

felafel – deep fried balls of chickpea paste served on flat bread

shwarma – found at the front of Lebanese and other restaurants, it's the cone shaped pressed meat on a vertical spit. There's usually lamb and chicken and it's wrapped in flat bread with a little sauce and salad. Look for the vendors that are busy.

Restaurant Starters

baba ghanooj – char-grilled eggplant with tahini, olive oil, garlic and lemon juice

fattoosh – salad of lettuce, tomato, cucumber, fried Arabic bread, and a lemon, garlic and olive-oil dressing

hummus – chickpea and garlic puree, sometimes served with lamb pieces

kibbeh – deep-fried balls of minced meat, pine nuts, onion and cracked wheat

mezze – the term given to the selection of dip-style starters

tabbouleh – finely chopped parsley, tomato, cracked wheat and mint

Restaurant Main Courses

kebab – pieces of grilled meat or fish on a skewer

kofta – grilled skewers of spicy minced lamb

shish tawooq – spiced pieces of char-grilled chicken

To try a little of everything for your main course, order a 'mixed grill', which will include all of the meats mentioned above (except fish).

Persian Plates

Iranian food is very different in flavour to Lebanese food. The following dishes make an excellent introduction to this wonderful cuisine.

baghleh polow – rice with dill, broad beans and chicken or mutton

bakhtari kebab – kebab served with grilled capsicum

berenj – spicy rice dishes, usually topped with nuts and raisins

chelow kebab – on every Persian menu, *chelow* is rice cooked separately from the other ingredients and it's topped with a grilled kebab

chelow kebab barj – a variation where the kebab is thinner than usual

chelow kebab makhsoos – a variation where the kebab is thicker than usual

istanboli polow – rice with haricot beans and chicken or mutton on top

koresh – meat stew with vegetables

lari kebab – marinated kebab cooked in yogurt

zereshk polow – rice mixed with barberry and chicken

FASHION

The inaugural 2004 Dubai Fashion Week was much anticipated by Dubai fashionistas, who were out in full force. Dubai invited the best Parisian fashion houses to show their full *haute couture* collections. Just two weeks after launching their spring/summer ranges in Paris, Dior, Ungaro, Givenchy and Lacroix flew the whole lot over, along with supermodels, to Dubai for five days. The extravagantly theatrical shows were a resounding success with Dubai's rich but not so famous falling for the magic. A good thing, because Dubai has plans to establish a 'Fashion City' to attract the fashion houses here to do business, and a fashion institute to teach the creation of couture.

Emirati women are over the moon. Not only are they addicted to designer wear, but also there are a few young, emerging Emirati designers. Look out for the designs of Hind al-Mehrairbi, a youthful fusion of East meets West. Her first show featured long skirts and figure-hugging

Henna

Henna decoration is an oriental tradition dating back to Neolithic times. The leaves of the henna shrub *(Lawsonia inermis)* have been dried, ground into powder and turned into paste for at least 6000 years. In central Turkey in 4000 BC women painted their hands in homage to the mother goddess. This tradition spread through the eastern Mediterranean region where the henna shrub grows wild. The paste is applied and left to stain the skin (in any autumn colour from brown to red). Women decorate their hands, nails and feet, usually for a special event, such as a wedding, and it stays on for about six weeks.

A few nights before a wedding, brides-to-be are honoured with *layyat al-henna* (henna night). This is a women-only affair, part of a week of festivities and events before the wedding ceremony. At this party the bride-to-be is anointed from head to toe with expensive perfumes and oils, her hair is washed with jasmine and frankincense perfumes, and her hands, wrists, ankles and feet are decorated with henna. How well the henna pattern lasts is said to be an indication to the mother-in-law of what kind of wife the bride will make. If she's a hard worker, the henna will penetrate deeper into the skin of her hand and remain longer. The henna is applied in intricate, often floral patterns. On henna night, the friends and relatives of the bride-to-be share a feast of special foods, and sing and dance. It's also a night for the trousseau – silks, jewellery and perfumes given as gifts – to be displayed.

There are many beauty salons in Dubai that do henna decorations for clients; just look for signs with painted hands on them. You'll find a number of salons around the Deira souqs and in Karama. Some are more popular than others – generally the ones that do the latest and most original designs (henna patterns go in and out of vogue also). Tourists can get their henna done in the Arabian Treasures *majlis* at **Deira City Centre** (Map pp210-11). In addition, many bigger hotels now have henna 'stalls'.

Mannequins

long-sleeve tops in bold bright colours, the midriff slightly exposed. Islamic calligraphy, henna-hand imprints and Arabian symbols cut from colourful gold-threaded Indian fabrics were positioned in cheeky places such as the buttocks or thigh.

Most older Emirati women do still wear traditional dress under their *abeyya* and *shayla*, and will sometimes put on a colourful *kandoura* (dress-shirt) when relaxing at home, in the desert or on the family farm, and always during Ramadan. It is also still customary for women to get henna done (see the boxed text on p16) and it's not uncommon to see a modern Emirati girl dressed in Gucci with henna-patterned hands and feet. Older women tend to wear henna more often on their nails, toes and fingertips. They also wear the *kandoura* under the *abeyyas* and *shaylas*, and it's not at all uncommon to see older women wearing a black or gold burka over their face, whether they're on the street or in the shopping mall.

SPORT

The traditional Emirati sports of horse, camel and boat racing have been supplemented by the myriad expats who bring their own sports to the region. Even during the fiercest heat of summer you'll see people

Private Parades

When you're out shopping you're likely to see groups of elegant national women laden with shopping bags. You might wonder what they do with these expensive clothes when all you see is the black national dress. When women are at home or in the private company of other women, they don't necessarily wear their *abeyya* (full-length black robe) and *shayla* (headscarf). Local girl, Latifa al-Falasy may be a communication technology student by day, but she's also a 'student of fashion' and loves to shop. And not only in Dubai – she travels to London every summer, where she buys from the latest collections. When asked why she has a passion for fashion, she replied, 'Why wouldn't I? For the same reasons other women do!'

Latifa's top five designer brands:

- Chanel
- Christian Dior
- Louis Vuitton
- Miu Miu
- Cartier

Latifa's favourite local brands (for the best *abeyyas* and *shaylas*):

- My Fair Lady
- Hanayan
- Al Bander
- Khanji
- Tribune

17

playing golf or partaking in a social game of cricket in an empty car park. Just about any sport you can think of has a small group of dedicated enthusiasts finding a way to in-dulge in their favourite activity despite the heat and relative lack of facilities.

Clearly the best time to play or watch sport in Dubai is during the winter months when all of Dubai's sport-lovers make the most of the marvellous weather. Tennis and golf are extremely popular as are all brands of football, but water sports are more suited as a year-round activity. Scuba diving, sailing and windsurfing are all popular and the new water sport on the block, kite surfing, is growing quickly, gaining new aficionados. For more on these sports see p111.

MEDIA

The media is booming in Dubai – if the number of Porsches, Ferraris, BMWs, and Mini Coopers in the Dubai Media City car park is anything to go by. Dubai's media has come a long way since the 1969 opening of Dubai Television. Since its establishment in 2001, with its mission 'freedom to create', Media City has very rapidly become the Middle East media hub Sheikh Mohammed bin Rashid al-Maktoum envisaged it would be. CNN, Reuters, MBC, CNBC, Al-Arabiya, Arabian Radio Network, Lowe, and dozens of advertising agencies, newspapers, magazines and production companies have moved their regional headquarters here, working alongside scores of freelance writers, producers, directors, graphic artists, web designers, photographers, musicians, technicians and animators. The city's annual international Ibda'a (Creativity) Awards for media students is bringing talent here from as far afield as South Africa and Australia. Winners receive internships with local media companies and Media City continues to grow.

LANGUAGE

Arabic is the official language of Dubai while English is the language of business, though it competes with Hindi and Urdu as the lingua franca. You will have little trouble making yourself understood, although when you venture out into rural areas you will find that

What You Won't Read

Reading the headlines of the local papers each day becomes reassuringly familiar. A sheikh has said something wise, had a successful meeting or received a message of congratulations and hardly a day goes by without a call for Arab unity in the opinion and editorial columns. But there's plenty you won't read about. Local newspapers and magazines, both in Arabic and English, follow a careful policy of self-censorship. For expatriate journalists who break the rules, the next question they'll be asking is whether their seat is aisle or window.

In an effort to avoid that hastily arranged flight home, journalists avoid criticising the government or anyone in authority, from the sheikh down to motorcycle policemen. There can be no reporting of a crime without the police permitting it, no coverage of a court case without a briefing from the court and certainly no reporting of a civil commotion, disturbance or protest. If there is a major local or regional disturbance, journalists have to wait for the government to give the go-ahead to report it. Sometimes this comes days after the event, such as the Iraqi invasion of Kuwait in 1990, and sometimes it never comes at all. The news 'angle' is usually the reaction of the most senior official responsible, for example, 'police chief warns polluters', rather than 'polluters threaten wildlife'.

While Qatar's Al-Jazeera satellite TV station has revolutionised Arab TV, with its hard-hitting news reports, and media companies such as Reuters and CNN operate freely out of Dubai Media City, the local papers remain a criticism-free zone. Still, the classified sections are a great place to sell that 'expat returning home' Porsche or advertise your sister as a potential marriage candidate (see the boxed text on p14).

English is not as widely spoken or understood. Signs in Dubai are generally in Arabic and English and you'll find that telephone automation systems (for government departments and banks) allow you to choose between the two.

Knowing the Iranian language, Farsi, will win you some fast friends. Hindi, Urdu and Malayalam (the language of Kerala in India) are all reasonably useful because of the large number of Indian and Pakistani expats you will come in contact with.

For some useful words in Arabic see the Language chapter on p187.

ECONOMY & COSTS

OH YOU WHO BELIEVE! EAT NOT UP YOUR PROPERTY AMONG YOURSELVES IN VANITIES, BUT LET THERE BE AMONGST YOU TRAFFIC AND TRADE BY MUTUAL GOODWILL.

Quran 4:29

Dubai is the second-richest emirate in the UAE, after Abu Dhabi. It has used its modest oil resources to build a global trading base, with stunning results. About 70% of the UAE's nonoil GDP is generated in Dubai, and about 90% of Dubai's GDP is not oil-based. Dubai's reserves of oil and gas were never huge, and recent reports indicate that Dubai's oil industry will start to wind down by 2010. Dubai has prudently used its limited oil and gas revenue to create the infrastructure for trade, manufacturing and tourism.

Some analysts believe Dubai has expanded too far, too fast, and that its economy is heading for trouble. Others, including the *Economist* magazine, believe the city has a sufficiently sturdy economic base.

Dubai's main exports are oil, natural gas, dates and dried fish. The Emirate's imports are primarily minerals and chemicals, base metals (including gold), vehicles and machinery, electronics, textiles and foodstuffs. The re-export trade (see the boxed text on p43) in Dubai makes up about 80% of the UAE's total re-export business. Dubai's re-exports go mainly to Iran, India, Saudi Arabia, Kuwait and Afghanistan. Dubai is also the home of a huge dry-dock complex, one of the Middle East's busiest airports and duty-free operations, the UAE's biggest airline and large free-trade zones at Jebel Ali, 30 minutes from the city centre, and at Dubai airport. Attracting foreign business to its free-trade zones has been one of Dubai's greatest economic achievements in the last 20 years. Companies are enticed with the promise of full foreign ownership, full repatriation of capital and profits, no corporate tax for 15 years, no currency restrictions and no personal income tax for staff.

The Dubai Internet City and neighbouring Dubai Media City have been equally successful in adding a new high-tech information and communication stratum to the city's economy as well as gaining credibility by attracting the big media players, such as CNN, to base their Middle East operations in Dubai.

Dubai's tourism industry has also exploded. The city's tolerance of Western habits, profusion of quality hotels, long stretches of beach, warm winter weather, shopping incentives and desert activities have helped it become the leading tourist destination in the Gulf. For Emirati citizens all this prosperity translates into the kind of benefits that much of the rest of the world only dreams of: free health care, free education, heavily subsidised utilities and, in some cases, free housing.

Dubai's per capita income is estimated to be about Dh60,000 per annum. This is far above the average wage of a professional expat and, when you consider the fact that

How Much?

- **Abra ride** 50 fils
- **Beer at a five-star hotel** Dh20
- **CD from Virgin Megastore** Dh55
- **Round of golf (18 holes)** Dh300
- **Fresh juice cocktail** Dh4
- **Gulf News newspaper** Dh2
- **Movie ticket** Dh30
- **Night at the 'seven-star' Burj Al Arab hotel** Dh6000
- **Short taxi ride** Dh15
- **Street shwarma** Dh4

Hawala: the Business of Trust

Imagine a money transfer system with minimal or no fees and quick delivery, which is available to people in the poorest countries in the world. This is *hawala* and Dubai is one of its key centres.

Hawala is an Arabic term for a written order of payment. It works like this. You hand over your dirhams and the contact details of the recipient to your neighbourhood *hawala* trader. In return you get a code – say, a letter and four numbers. Then you ring up the recipient and give them the code. The trader contacts the people in his network. The next day, maybe two days later, the *hawala* trader's partner hands over the money, sometimes delivering it to the door of the recipient. The commission taken by the *hawala* traders might be as little as 1% or 2%, even zero if they can make a little profit on exchange-rate differences.

Some newspaper reports say as much of 90% of wages remitted to developing countries from the UAE were sent via this system until recently. Sending Dh100 to India via a bank would yield Rs1200, while via a *hawala* trader it yields Rs1280. The smaller the amount to be sent, the bigger the difference is between bank rates and *hawala* rates. It's a huge benefit to workers who can only afford to send home small amounts.

The *hawala* system has existed among Arab and Muslim traders for centuries as a defence against theft. It's a uniquely Islamic system, completely dependent on trust and honour. *Hawala* traders hardly ever cheat their customers, but if they do the punishments are said to be abrupt and severe. Their reputation is crucial to their business.

The *hawala* system developed in Dubai through the gold smuggling business in the 1960s. Once the gold was sold in India or Pakistan, the traders couldn't get the money back to Dubai. They found their solution in the growing numbers of expatriate workers. The workers gave their wages to the gold traders in Dubai, and the gold traders in India paid their relatives. Thus the books balanced.

Today the system is under pressure. The US claims *hawala* is being used to transfer money to terrorists. What they don't say is that *hawala* is also used to transfer money to people who would find it impossible to receive it any other way, because they're illiterate, they don't have a bank account, or don't live in a village with a bank. In Dubai's open economy there used to be no restrictions on currency trading and no specific laws against *hawala* trading, but the authorities in the UAE have moved to set up a registration and reporting system for brokers. Without regulation in every country participating in the system, this will just move the problem somewhere else other than Dubai.

many unskilled expat labourers earn Dh500 to Dh1000 per month, you get an idea of the kind of salary and benefits that a national takes home. Still, there is one hurdle in the economy that Dubai is seeking to overcome. Dubai is highly dependent upon expat labour and, at the same time, its citizens spend a great deal of money. The government has made some attempt to 'Emiratise' the economy by placing nationals in the public workforce and imposing local employee quotas on private companies.

Many private companies are reluctant to hire nationals, believing that it will result in a drop in profits and efficiency. There is no doubt that Dubai will be dependent on foreign labour and expertise for a long time to come, which means that much of the money generated in the workforce is leaving the country.

GOVERNMENT & POLITICS

Power rests with the ruling family, the Al-Maktoums (see the boxed text on p37). There are no political parties or general elections in Dubai. Though the UAE has a federal government, over which Sheikh Zayed bin Sultan al-Nayan of Abu Dhabi presides, each of the rulers is absolutely sovereign within his own emirate. The UAE is, nevertheless, a rare example of Arab unity – a concept much discussed at meetings of Arab rulers.

The degree of power that the seven emirs cede to the federal government has been hotly debated in government circles since the founding of the UAE. Dubai has fought hardest to preserve as much of its independence as possible and to minimise the power of the country's federal institutions. Along

Did You Know?

The term 'emirate' is derived from the term 'emir' which means ruler, but the rulers of the emirates in the UAE are generally known as sheikhs – which is pronounced 'shake', *never* 'chic'.

with Ras al-Khaimah, it maintains a legal system separate from the federal judiciary.

Politics in the UAE tends to be rather opaque, but the relative interests of the various emirs are fairly clear. Abu Dhabi is the largest and wealthiest emirate and has the biggest population. It is, therefore, the dominant member of the federation and is likely to remain so for some time. Dubai is the second-largest emirate by population and wealth, with an interest in upholding its free-trade policies and a pronounced independent streak. One sign of this is Dubai's relation to the Organization of Petroleum-Exporting Communities (OPEC), the cartel of the world's major oil-producing countries. Officially the UAE is a member of OPEC, but in practice Dubai has opted out, while Abu Dhabi has stayed in. Thus, if Abu Dhabi agrees to a cut in production in line with OPEC, there's some tension if Dubai raises its output and Abu Dhabi's has to fall further to compensate. The other emirates are dependent on subsidies from Abu Dhabi, though the extent of this dependence varies widely.

The forum where these issues are discussed is the Supreme Council, the highest legislative body in the country. The council, which tends to meet informally, comprises the seven emirs. New federal laws can be passed with the consent of five of the seven rulers.

Wusta

This translates loosely as 'influence high up'. Never underestimate the power of *wusta* in Dubai, it's a very desirable thing to have. It can be especially useful when you're trying to get through tedious and protracted administrative procedures, such as registering a car. A little *wusta* with the traffic police is very handy indeed.

Many businesses employ agents whose *sole* role is to speak to the right people in the bureaucracy to get paperwork processed in a trouble-free manner. Most Westerners get a little outraged at the thought of a select few receiving favours and special treatment because of powerful contacts. *Wusta* is an accepted part of life in Dubai and it's not challenged like its Western equivalents (favouritism, bias and nepotism) are.

Streetscape

The Supreme Council also elects one of the emirs to a five-year term as the country's president. In December 2001 Sheikh Zayed was elected to his sixth term as president, a position he seems likely to hold for life. Some commentators see problems ahead when Sheikh Zayed (born c 1915) dies. As he is the UAE's first and only president, the succession issue for the federation has never arisen before.

There is also a cabinet and the posts within it are distributed among the emirates. Most of the federal government's money comes from Abu Dhabi and Dubai so members of these governments hold most of the important cabinet posts.

The cabinet and Supreme Council are advised, but cannot be overruled, by the Federation Council of Ministers, a 40-member consultative body whose members are appointed by the emirs. Abu Dhabi and Dubai hold almost half of the council's seats, and all the council's members come from leading Emirati merchant families.

Within Dubai, the Dubai Municipality is effectively the local government for the Emirate, handling everything from economic planning to rubbish collection. Above the municipality is Sheikh Maktoum's private office, called the Diwan or the Ruler's Office.

The Majlis

Majlis translates as 'meeting place' or 'reception area'. The *majlis* was a forum or council where citizens could come and speak to their leaders and make requests, complaints or raise any issues. In Dubai the *majlis* system was preserved until the 1960s. In its domestic sense, a *majlis* is a reception area found in all older buildings in Dubai (such as Al-Fahidi Fort, now the Dubai Museum, and the Heritage House in Al-Ahmadiya). Its Western cousin is probably the lounge room. The *majlis* is still an important room in an Arab household and is usually the domain of the male members of the family. It's a place where they can get together and talk without disturbing the women of the house. Some traditional houses have a separate *majlis* for women.

ENVIRONMENT
CLIMATE

For information on Dubai's climate see p174.

THE LAND

Dubai sits on the Gulf, in the northwest region of the UAE. This city is the capital of the emirate of the same name, which is the second-largest of the seven emirates which comprise the UAE. The emirate of Dubai is 3885 sq km and the constantly expanding city is roughly 35 sq km. Dubai Creek, which extends 12km inland from the coast, divides the city in two.

Prior to settlement, this area was flat sabkha (salt-crusted coastal plain). The sand mostly consists of crushed shell and coral and is fine, clean and white. The sabkha was broken only by clumps of desert grasses and a small area of hardy mangroves at the inland end of the Creek. Photographs of the area from the early 20th century show how strikingly barren the landscape was.

East of the city, the sabkha gives way to north–south running lines of dunes. The farming areas of Al-Khawaneej and Al-Awir, now on the edge of Dubai's suburbia, are fed by wells. Further east the dunes grow larger and are tinged red with iron oxide. The dunes stop abruptly at the gravel fans at the base of the rugged Hajar Mountains (see Hatta on p156), where there are gorges and waterholes. A vast sea of sand dunes covers the area south of the city, becoming more and more imposing as it stretches into the desert, known as the Empty Quarter, that makes up the southern region of the UAE and the western region of Saudi Arabia. North of Dubai, along the coast, the land is tough desert scrub broken by inlets similar to Dubai Creek, until you reach the mountainous northern emirates.

For Dubai residents, the weather is a common topic of conversation. In the cooler months everyone wants to spend time outside enjoying the moderate temperatures and clear skies. For visitors, this is the best time of year to visit and it's no surprise that this is when Dubai's city calendar (p9) is busiest.

July and August are the months when anyone who has the means leaves Dubai for cooler climes. For those left behind, venturing outside during the middle of the day is an experience that can only be compared to sticking your head in a fan-forced oven at 200° Celsius. But residents and visitors get by – jumping from air-conditioned accommodation to air-conditioned taxi to air-conditioned destination.

GREEN DUBAI

Other than the sand and dust you would expect in an arid desert environment, Dubai is a very clean city, compared with others in the region, although air pollution from the ever-growing traffic is becoming an issue and the Creek suffers from marine pollution.

In contrast to Abu Dhabi's emphasis on the 'greening of the desert', Dubai's efforts have been more modest. There are a number of well-established parks and gardens around the city, and some major roads are lined with palm trees, shrubs, flowers and manicured lawns, but Dubai has none of the vast forestry projects that characterise Abu Dhabi emirate.

Although the public is much better educated about littering than a few years ago, you will still see rubbish left on beaches, in parks or thrown out of car windows. As a result, an enormous number of workers are employed to make sure the rubbish on the street doesn't stay around to sully the city's image, and the municipality slaps out Dh500 fines for littering. Dubai generates one of the highest per capita volumes of waste in the world, and the Emirates Environmental Group has opened a number of recycling centres around the city.

Because of the proximity of Dubai's oil industry to the city, there is a high risk of oil spills off the coast. Over the years the damage caused by these spills has prompted a concerted effort by government agencies to monitor and control marine pollution, not least because they threaten the city's vital desalination plants. Oil companies are required to spend money on the protection of the coast.

Local Environmental Organisations

The Federal Environmental Agency legislates on environmental issues and encourages communication on these issues between the emirates. There are also a number of Non-Governmental Organisations (NGOs) concerned with the environment.

Dubai Natural History Group (☎ 349 4816) This volunteer group organises public lectures and field trips, and gives members access to a small lending library of natural history publications. Annual membership costs Dh50.

Emirates Diving Association (☎ 393 9390; www.emirates diving.com) This association is an active participant in local environmental campaigns, with an emphasis on the marine environment.

Emirates Environmental Group (☎ 331 8100; www.eeg -uae.org) This group organises educational programmes in schools and businesses as well as community programmes, such as clean-up drives.

Skyline, Sheikh Zayed Road (p56)

FLORA & FAUNA

In Dubai's parks you will see indigenous tree species such as the date palm and the neem, and a large number of imported species, including eucalypts. The sandy desert surrounding the city supports wild grasses and the occasional date-palm oasis.

In the salty scrublands along the coast, the desert hyacinth emerges in all its glory after the rains. It has bright-yellow and deep-red dappled flowers.

Decorating the flat plains that stretch away from the foothills of the Hajar Mountains, around Hatta, are different species of acacia. These are flat-topped, rather scraggly, incredibly hardy trees. The ghaf also grows in this area; this big tree looks a little like a weeping willow. It is able to survive because its roots stretch down for about 80m, allowing it to tap into deep water reserves. The lower foliage of the ghaf is usually trimmed flat by grazing camels and goats.

As in any major city, you don't see much wildlife. Urbanisation, combined with zealous hunting, has brought the virtual extinction of some species. These include the Houbara bustard, the Arabian oryx (also called the white oryx), the caracal and the striped hyena. The sand cat and Gordon's wildcat are types of cat that have adapted to desert life and are under threat because of cross-breeding with domestic tabbies.

On the fringes of the city, where the urban sprawl gives way to the desert, you may see a desert fox, sand cat or falcon if you are very lucky. Otherwise, the only animals you are likely to encounter are camels and goats. The desert is also home to various reptile species, including the desert monitor (which grows up to a metre long), the sand skink, the spiny tailed agama and several species of gecko. The only poisonous snakes are vipers, such as the sawscaled viper, which can be recognised by their distinctive triangular heads. There are even two remarkably adapted species of toad, which hibernate for years burrowed deep in wadis between floods.

The city is a hot spot for bird-watchers; because of the spread of irrigation and greenery the number and variety of birds is growing. Dubai is on the migration path between Europe, Asia and Africa, and more than 320 migratory species pass through in the spring and autumn, or spend the winter here. The city's parks, gardens and golf courses sustain quite large populations, and on any day up to 80 different species can be spotted. One new urban settler is the common mynah, which arrived in the 1970s from India and now exists in large numbers. Species native to Arabia include the crab plover, the Socotra cormorant, the black-crowned finch lark and the purple sunbird.

Artificial nests have been built to encourage flamingos to breed at the **Dubai Wildlife & Waterbird Sanctuary** (also known as Khor Dubai Wildlife Sanctuary, see p54), at the inland end of Dubai Creek. In addition to flamingos, the sanctuary is also home to ducks, marsh harriers, spotted eagles, broad-billed sandpipers and ospreys.

The waters off Dubai teem with around 300 different types of fish. Diners will be most familiar with the hamour, a species of groper, but the Gulf is also home to an extraordinary range of tropical fish and several species of small sharks. Green turtles and hawksbill turtles used to nest in numbers on Dubai's beaches, but today their nesting sites are restricted to islands.

URBAN PLANNING & DEVELOPMENT

With one of the fastest growing populations in the world, Dubai has its share of urban planning challenges. To house this growing population Dubai grows steadily upward with huge residential towers, inland with new housing estates and creates a new coastline or two when it runs out of natural coastline (see the boxed text on p137). While Dubai has finally approved a light rail system in principle, Dubai's serious traffic problems will plague it for many years to come. Planning in this regard appears to involve the municipality creating new roads between two points while private companies develop projects that span the two. While developers are quick to build malls, other forms of public spaces – such as parks – are neglected, or left to the developers to incorporate into their projects.

Art &
Architecture

Art & Architecture

While Dubai's architectural landscape has reached a high level of sophistication and found a balance between its obsession with towers and incorporating pan-Arabian influences, the visual arts are at an exciting crossroads. New gallery spaces are affording local and resident artists a chance to exhibit their work. While there are myriad works of literature in Arabic, sadly little of them have been translated to English – although many would state that the act of translation robs the words of their beauty and power. While cinema may be in its infancy in Dubai, some of the student work being produced reveals film makers with a unique vision and real stories to tell. Traditional dance remains a popular form of expression and traditional Arabic popular music tops the charts, yet the music scene in Dubai has offered up some interesting hybrids of traditional Gulf music and wider contemporary Middle Eastern influences.

ARCHITECTURE

Visitors to Dubai will immediately be struck by its stunning architecture. The incongruous blend of traditional Arabian architecture with modern constructions straight out of science fiction make the city an amazing sight. A boat ride along the Creek reveals many of the city's architectural treasures. Moving from the wind-tower houses in the **Bastakia Quarter** (p52) of Bur Dubai to the pointed dhowlike roof of the **Dubai Creek Golf & Yacht Club** (p112), it's hard to believe it's the same city. These modern constructions sit well with the traditional architecture of the cosmopolitan city, mirroring other juxtapositions in Dubai – East and West, classic and contemporary. It is impossible to compare these disparate architectural styles, simply because they are so different. Much recent architecture, however, such as the Madinat Jumeirah complex (see the boxed text on p137), is doing a fine job of melding the two and hopefully this is an indication of things to come.

Emirates Towers (p145), Sheikh Zayed Rd

Top 10 Notable Buildings

- **Burj Al Arab** (p146) Dubai's rulers wanted a landmark to rival the Eiffel Tower or Sydney Opera House and the Burj Al Arab (Arabian Tower) is like no other building. Completed in 1999, it is set on an artificial island about 300m from the shore, near the southern end of Jumeirah Rd in Umm Suqeim. The 60-floor, sail-shaped structure is 321m high, including the thin spire on top. The hotel has 300 two-storey suites, a 200m-high lobby and an underwater restaurant, among other facilities. A bar, restaurant and helipad extend from side to side at the top of the building. A translucent fibreglass wall shields the desert sun during the day and serves as the screen for a light show at night. The design is supposed to evoke a sail of an ultramodern catamaran. The interior design has to be seen to be believed – everything that looks gold is gold.

- **Dubai Chamber of Commerce & Industry** (Map pp208-9) Next door to the National Bank of Dubai, this triangular building is blanketed in sheets of blue glass. From some angles the building takes on a one-dimensional appearance, like a great featureless monolith.

- **Dubai Creek Golf & Yacht Club** (p112) When you cross the bridges over the Creek, you will notice the pointed white roof of the clubhouse set amid artificial, undulating hillocks. The idea behind this 1993 UK design was to incorporate a traditional element into the design – the white sails of a traditional Arab dhow.

- **Dusit Dubai** (p144) Sheikh Zayed Rd has many modern skyscrapers, but none as eye-catching as this one. The 153m-high building has an inverted 'Y' shape – two pillars that join to form a tapering tower. It's supposed to evoke the hands-joined Thai gesture of greeting, appropriate for this Thai hotel chain – although it also resembles a tuning fork stuck into the ground.

- **Emirates Towers** (p145) Dubai's tallest buildings are currently the highest in the Middle East and Europe, and some of the tallest worldwide, although they'll soon be outgrown by the new Burj Dubai. Designed in an ultramodern internationalist style, the twin, triangular, gunmetal-grey towers on Sheikh Zayed Rd soar from an oval base. The taller of the two towers (355m) houses offices, while the second tower (305m) is a hotel. This is balanced by the curvilinear base structure. The curved motif is repeated in the upper storeys of the buildings.

- **Emirates Training Building** (Map pp210-11) No, you're not about to get wiped out by an aircraft that's off course. This building, on Al-Garhoud Rd at the Deira entrance to the Al-Garhoud Bridge, is designed to look like the front end of an aeroplane. It's gimmicky and eye-catching, but isn't ageing particularly gracefully.

- **Etisalat Building** (Map pp208-9) Recognisable by the giant golf ball that perches atop all Etisalat headquarters, this building, on the corner of Al-Maktoum and Omar ibn al-Khattab Rds, was completed in 1990. The ball represents the world encompassed by the power of global communications. At night it sparkles as little lights come on all around it.

- **Jumeirah Beach Hotel** (p147) This long S-shaped construction is intended to represent a wave, with the Gulf sea as its backdrop. The glimmering façades of the Jumeirah Beach Hotel and its close neighbour the Burj Al Arab are achieved through the use of reflective glass and aluminium. The two structures combined – a huge sail hovering over a breaking wave – symbolise Dubai's maritime heritage. The vast lobby features a mural stretching the full height of the building, with Dubai at the base and the sun at the very top.

- **National Bank of Dubai** (Map pp208-9) This shimmering building, off Baniyas Rd, Deira, overlooking the Creek, has become one of the quintessential symbols of Dubai. Completed in 1997, it looks like a long, thin D-shape. The bronze windows reflect the activity on the Creek and at sunset, when the light is just right, it is a beautiful sight.

- **One&Only Royal Mirage** (p148) This opulent Arabian-style hotel on Al-Sufouh Rd is supremely elegant and stylish. The Moroccan-like palace features low-rise mud walls and battlements, protecting an elegant Persian-influenced garden, which features waterways, courtyards and terraces. Thirteen hundred date palms give the illusion of an oasis. The interior references Arabic design elements, such as pendant lights and quiet alcoves, with intricate woodwork and mosaic flooring influenced by Islamic geometric designs.

- **Port Rashid Customs Authority** (Map pp212-13) There are no prizes for speculating correctly on the concept behind this design. The Port Rashid Customs Authority, on Al-Mina Rd, looks like the hulls of two enormous dhows from a distance. The bows extend to sit like gargoyles on either side of the entrance to the building. The two hulls run down the side of the building and the offices sit between them.

TRADITIONAL ARCHITECTURE

Dubai's traditional architecture was influenced by the demands of the environment, the teachings of Islam and the social structure of the town. There were essentially four types of building – domestic (residential houses), religious (mosques), defensive (forts and watch-towers) and commercial (souqs). Readily available materials, such as gypsum and coral from offshore reefs and from the banks of the Creek, were used. **Sheikh Saeed al-Maktoum House** (p55) in Shindagha is a fine example of a construction using these. Limestone building blocks were also used and mud served to cement the stones together. Mud constructions, however, suffered badly in the heat and had a very limited lifespan, sometimes only a few years. The dimensions of buildings were, to a degree, governed by the use of timber. The length of roof beams, imported from India or East Africa, was determined by the maximum size that could be loaded onto a dhow.

If you wander through the lanes surrounding the **Deira Spice Souq** (p120) and behind the **Al-Ahmadiya School** (p49) in Deira you will notice that the alleyways are narrow and the buildings are close together. Houses, souqs and mosques were built this way to provide maximum shade so that inhabitants could move around the town in comfort, protected from the harsh sun. There were two types of traditional house – the *masayf* was the summer house (incorporating a wind tower) and the *mashait* was the winter house (incorporating a courtyard).

Wind-Tower Houses

Barjeel (wind towers) are the Gulf's unique form of nonmechanical air-conditioning. In Dubai, scores of original wind towers still exist, traditionally rising 5m or 6m above a house. The tower is open on all four sides to catch the breezes, which are channelled down around a central shaft and into the room below. In the process, the air speeds up and is cooled. The cooler air already in the tower shaft pulls in, and subsequently cools, the hotter air outside through simple convection. The towers work amazingly well. Sitting beneath a wind tower, you'll notice a distinct drop in temperature and a consistent breeze even when the air outside feels heavy and still.

The wealthy Persian merchants who settled in Dubai around the turn of the 20th century were the first to build a large number of wind towers in the city, largely in the **Bastakia Quarter** (p52), Bur Dubai. In some houses the tallest wind tower was above the master bedroom, while smaller towers cooled the living rooms. The merchants brought red clay from Iran, which they mixed with manure to make *saruj*. This was baked in a kiln and used to build the foundations of the wind-tower house. Other materials included coral rock and limestone for the walls and plaster for decorative work. The walls were built as thick as 60cm, so the house could be extended upwards if the family expanded. Chandel wood from East Africa, palm-frond matting, mud and straw were used to build the roofs.

Courtyard Houses

Houses in Dubai were traditionally built around a central courtyard. The courtyard, known as *al-housh* in Arabic, was considered the heart and lungs of a house. Today they still provide many homes with light, fresh air, space for a garden, a place for entertaining and somewhere for children to play. All the rooms of the house surrounded the courtyard and all doors and windows opened onto it, except those of the guest rooms, which opened to the outside of the house. A veranda provided shade, kept sun out of the rooms at certain times of the day, and was usually the place where the women did weaving and sewing. For great examples of a courtyard house, visit the **Heritage House** (p50) in the Al-Ahmadiya district in Deira. In the **Bastakia Quarter** (p52) are several wind-tower houses that have been built around a central courtyard – **XVA hotel** (p56) and the **Majlis Gallery** (p55), near the Al-Fahidi Roundabout, are good examples.

Barasti

Barasti describes both the traditional Gulf method of building a palm-leaf house and the completed house itself. *Barasti* houses are made from a skeleton of wooden poles (date palm trunks) onto which *areesh* (palm leaves) are woven to form a strong structure through which air can still circulate.

They were extremely common throughout the Gulf in the centuries before the oil boom, though few examples of this type of house survive today. Those that do are usually fishermen's shacks and storage buildings in rural and coastal areas of the UAE. Local families, however, will often build a *barasti* house in their backyard to remind their family of their heritage. They were relatively easy to build and maintain since, unlike the mud-brick houses you find in the oases around Al-Ain and Buraimi, their construction does not require water. The circulation of air through the palms also made *barasti* houses much cooler than mud-brick structures during the summer. The courtyard in the **Dubai Museum** (p53) and the **Heritage Village** (p54) in Shindagha both contain examples of *barasti* houses. You can also see *barasti* constructions at the **Majlis Ghorfat Um-al-Sheef** (p59) on Jumeirah Rd. For a detailed description of how a *barasti* house is constructed see Geoffrey Bibby's book *Looking for Dilmun*.

Mosques

Fundamentally simple structures, mosques are made up of a few basic elements. The most visible of these is the minaret, the tower from which the call to prayer is broadcast five times a day. Virtually every mosque in the world has a minaret; many have several. Minarets can be plain or ornate. The first minarets were not built until the early 8th century, some 70 years after the Prophet Mohammed's death. The idea for minarets may have originated from the bell towers that Muslim armies found attached to some of the churches they converted into mosques during the early years of Islam. The more minarets on a mosque, the more important it is. No mosque has more than seven minarets, the number on the Grand Mosque in Mecca.

A mosque must also have a mihrab, a niche in the wall facing Mecca, indicating the qibla, the direction believers must face while praying. Mihrabs are thought to have been introduced into Islamic architecture around the beginning of the 8th century, and like minarets they can be simple or elaborate. The minbar, a pulpit chair traditionally reached by three steps, dates from the Prophet Mohammed's lifetime. In addition, a mosque needs to have a water supply so that worshippers can perform the wudu (ritual washing) that is required before they begin praying. Neighbourhood mosques in Dubai are visited five times a day for prayers, with worshippers travelling further afield to the larger mosques for Friday prayers.

The **Jumeirah Mosque** (p59) is based on the Anatolian style, identified by a massive central dome. Other mosques in Dubai are based on Iranian and Central Asian models, which have more domes covering different areas of the mosque. Shiite mosques are notable for their exquisite green-and-blue faïence tile work covering the façades and main dome. One stunning example is the **Iranian Mosque** (p57) on Al-Wasl Rd. The multidomed **Grand Mosque** (p54) in Bur Dubai is a variation on the Anatolian style. Other mosques, such as the **Bin Suroor Mosque** (Map pp212–13) in Shindagha, are small and boxlike.

Window detail, Grand Mosque (p54)

MODERN ARCHITECTURE

Dubai's relentless building boom has lured top architects from around the world who want to be part of the city's metamorphosis into a postmodern metropolis. This has resulted in an eclectic influence in the design and architecture of the city. There is enough wealth in Dubai to fund the most ambitious of projects and, unlike Abu Dhabi where all architecture must have Islamic features (such as archways), there are no such restrictions in Dubai.

About 90% of Dubai's architecture can be described as cosmopolitan or international and is built using concrete, steel and glass. Because there was concern these materials absorb heat and transfer it to other parts of the construction – causing damage over a period of time – high-tech, state-of-the-art materials are now being used that have great heat resistance. Most large-scale building projects are designed by architects from Europe, Australia and the Middle East, although there are some emerging Emirati architects.

In the realm of interior architecture and furniture design, Emiratis are bringing creativity and flair to the fore. High-profile sheikhas Mai and Wafa al-Qasimini, from the highly creative Sharjah royal family, have accepted several exciting commissions, including a purpose-built educational building and auditorium in Sharjah, offices in Emirates Towers, and the restoration of Afghanistan's 150-year-old Bagha Bagha Palace in Kabul into a boutique hotel. Faisal al-Mutawa, meanwhile, uses abstract ideas and natural materials to create his ground-breaking furniture – large saucer-shaped chairs, abaca panels and unusual steel-framed sofas, coffee tables, lamps and vases.

VISUAL ARTS

Dubai's visual arts scene is at an exciting turning point. The established galleries, such as the **Majlis Gallery** (p55), **Total Arts** (p60) and the **Green Art Gallery** (p57) are continually hosting innovative exhibitions, and new and unusual spaces are opening up, mostly in the Bastakia Quarter. **XVA hotel** (p56) has a gallery that holds regular exhibitions, and is starting an artist-in-residence programme. Royal photographer Noor Ali Rashid is soon opening a photographic gallery. The **Hilton Dubai Creek** (p138), in Deira, occasionally hosts photography and art exhibits. The 9714 team have put on some fun mixed media events in bars and clubs, combining installations, performance art and music, and are showing innovative photography and arts at their new lifestyle concept store, **Five Green** (p128).

Total Arts' (p60) Dariush Zandi has curated eclectic exhibitions of ground-breaking photography, painting and video by artists from Iran, Pakistan, France, Belgium and the US. In an attempt to address post-9/11 Muslim stereotypes, Pakistani photographer Mansoora Hassan's self-portraits have her holiday-snaplike in her burka in front of well-known US monuments, such as the White House. Curator Sunny Rahbar puts together some of the more innovative shows, which are a breath of fresh air – 'Killing two birds with one stone…', an exhibition of painting and photography by Mike Manzoor and Wael Hamadeh was recently shown at the Fairmont hotel.

Top Five Photography Books

- *A Vanished World* by Wilfred Thesiger – these portraits of tribal peoples taken over decades of travel earned Thesiger worldwide recognition as a photographer. During five years in Arabia from 1945–50 he captured on film his Bedouin companions in their harsh desert home with great sensitivity.
- *Dubai, A Collection of Mid-twentieth Century Photographs* by Ronald Codrai – Codrai visited Dubai in 1946 and stayed 35 years, taking some amazing pictures of Dubai life, from the birth to the maturity of this city.
- *Dubai Life & Times: Through the Lens of Noor Ali Rashid* – a pictorial history of Dubai over the last four decades by the royal photographer Noor Ali Rashid. The photographs are absolutely stunning and very candid.
- *The Emirates by the First Photographers* by William Facey & Gillian Grant – these extraordinary images taken over the last 60 years of the 20th century tell a remarkable story of a state that has grown from the sand.
- *Under the Spell of Arabia* by Mathias Oppersdorff – a collection of photographs depicting the still-traditional life of the 1970s, a world of tribesmen, fishermen, artisans and even soldiers.

Although most of the art shown in the long-established galleries has primarily been produced by expats, more and more locals are starting to get exhibited and the work itself is more exciting. In the past many of the themes adopted by expats reflected the history and culture of Dubai: family life, traditional pastimes, souq life, Bedouin heritage and seafaring. Although this kind of work is still done, more artists are experimenting in abstract and mixed media forms. There has also been an increase in patronage over the years, often taking the form of commissions from sheikhs, wealthy families, hotels, large corporations and government departments, but more frequently extending to the personal support of an artist. A patron of many exhibitions is the writer and chairman of the Dubai Cultural Council, Mohammad al-Murr.

A few Emirati artists have gained well-deserved attention from the international art community, including Sheikha Hessah (the eldest child of Sheikh Maktoum), who was trained by renowned Bangladeshi artist Tina Ahmed, Sheikhas Azza al-Qasimi and Sawsan al-Qasimi, Safia Mohammed Khalfan and Khulood Mohammed Ali. Abdul Qader al-Rais is considered to be the torchbearer of the artistic movement in the Emirates. Abdul Rahim Salem, chairman of the Emirates Fine Arts Society, is also a successful artist who was born and bred in Dubai. His strikingly modern paintings use bold colour and are unusual in that he doesn't resort to the stereotypical Arabian themes that are so common in the work of other Dubai artists.

Much of the credit for the invigoration of the visual arts scene can go to Sheikha Hoor al-Qasimi, Director of the Sharjah International Biennale, who excited art lovers with a daring and inspirational 6th biennale featuring some thought-provoking work by 118 artists, including Shadi Ghadirian, Tarek al-Ghoussein and Tony Chakar. The **Sharjah Art Museum** (p154),

Top Five Art Museums & Galleries

- **Green Art Gallery** (p57) Local and international artists inspired by Arabia.
- **Majlis Gallery** (p55) This beautifully restored Arabian house can prove more distracting than the art inside.
- **Sharjah Art Museum** (p154) The only real art museum, it houses a permanent collection of contemporary art, Orientalist painting, and hosts the cutting-edge Sharjah International Biennale.
- **Sultan bin Ali al-Owais Cultural Foundation** (p51) This new centre for Arabic culture and intellectual activity houses an exquisite calligraphy collection.
- **Total Arts** (p60) Galleries in this large courtyard space mainly feature Middle Eastern artists.

Majlis Gallery (p55)

headed by the Abdul Rahim Salem, also exhibits some work by local artists although the bulk of its collection comes from overseas. A tremendous effort has been made by the Sharjah Ministry of Culture to encourage local artists, both Emiratis and resident expatriates, to come together and practice their art at the Bait Obeid al-Sharasi artists' studios in Sharjah.

LITERATURE

Although there's a great deal of literature in Arabic, unfortunately little of it is available in English. Of renowned author Mohammad al-Murr's 12 published collections of short stories, only two have been printed in English. Despite this, there are some English translations that are well worth reading. In *Heirloom: Evening Tales from the East*, former Iranian expat, now UAE citizen, Marian Behnam retells folktales she recalls from the 1920s to the 1940s, many translated from Bastaki, her mother tongue.

The lack of English translations could change through a number of initiatives, some of which are student-led projects from the postsecondary institutions where both English and Arabic are studied. Zayed University has published an impressive anthology of fiction and poetry, while the communications students at Dubai Women's College have recently started a writing club. Interestingly, young women are driving this literary activity; perhaps Dubai will soon see an Adhaf Souief (the Egyptian author of numerous works, including *The Map of Love*) or Hanan al-Shaykh (the well-known Lebanese author) emerge. The Abu Dhabi Cultural Foundation also announced national literary grants for Emiratis interested in travel writing, either researching or translating the work of early Arab travellers, or writing about their own country or foreign adventures.

It's curious that there aren't more expatriates documenting their travels and experiences living in the multicultural melting pot of postmodern Dubai where, on a daily basis, their lives are touched by the traditional and hyper-modern, the familiar and the foreign, the global and the local. American Patricia Holton's *Mother Without a Mask* is one of only a few books that provide a rare insight into Emirati culture and everyday life. On the other hand, there is a burgeoning children's literature scene, with a spate of delightful illustrated books published recently, including Julia Johnson's 4th illustrated book *One Humpy Grumpy Camel*. This counting book contains wonderful watercolours and rhymes to tell the story of a lost camel looking for his caravan. Along with her *A is for Arabia* book, you'll have a terrific educational souvenir for kids.

Arab Poetry

Nothing touches the heart of a Gulf Arab like poetry. Poetry dominates Arabian literature and Arab cultural, intellectual and everyday life.

The Quran is regarded as divine poetry, but even before Islam the shrine of the Kaaba at Mecca was bedecked with banners embroidered with poems. These poems, the *Muallaqat* (Hung Ones), are still studied at schools today.

In Bedouin culture a facility with poetry and language is greatly prized. A poet who could eloquently praise his own people while pointing out the failures of other tribes was considered a great asset. Modern poets of note from the UAE include Sultan al-Owais, some of whose poems have been translated into English, and Dr Ahmed al-Madani, who wrote in the romantic *baiti* style. Palestinian resistance poets such as Mahmood Darwish and Samih al-Qasim are popular, though traditionalists complain that they have broken with the 16 classical meters of poetry developed by the 8th-century Gulf Arab scholar Al-Khalil bin Ahmed. There are currently about 50 well-known male poets in the UAE who still use the forms of classical Arabic poetry, though they often experiment by combining it with other styles. There are also some well-known female poets, most of who write in the *tafila* prose style.

Nabati (vernacular poetry) is especially popular. Sheikh Zayed, the president of the UAE, and Sheikh Mohammed bin Rashid al-Maktoum, Dubai's crown prince, are keen writers in this tradition. The Jebel Ali Palm Island project features small islands shaped out of Sheikh Mohammed's poetry. Many Arabic-language newspapers and magazines publish pages of *nabati* poetry.

Emiratis spontaneously recite poetry with their friends, during social occasions and public events, and even in shopping centres. Young people publish their own poetry, particularly romantic poems, on websites and student magazines, and produce documentaries about the Emirati passion for poetic words.

CINEMA

There has never been an Emirati feature film and there is no film industry in the UAE, although some exciting developments have been under way. Five years ago there seemed to be only a few people in the UAE interested in developing a home-grown film culture, and sowing the seeds by nurturing aspiring young filmmakers, mostly from the Higher Colleges of Technology. Along with educators from the communication technology departments at these colleges, Dubai local Masoud Amralla al-Ali can be given a great deal of credit for developing the UAE's future filmmakers by establishing the Emirates Film Competition, which inspires young people by showing innovative

Dubai International Film Festival

This festival, running for the first time in 2004, is part of a grand plan to develop Dubai as a regional film hub. This includes incentives for major players to move their base here, the promotion of Dubai as a location and the creation of a film institute. The five-day festival will showcase contemporary and classical global cinema, showing some 80 features and 30 shorts. Programmes include Arabian Nights, Operation Cultural Bridge, Bollywood Meets Hollywood, Cinema from the Subcontinent, Contemporary World Cinema and Arabian Shorts.

short films from the Middle East and around the globe, and supporting local talent by showing their videos and providing decent cash prizes for the best. Awards have gone primarily to the young women from the Abu Dhabi and Dubai Women's Colleges, who have produced some well-crafted dramas, experimental shorts and documentaries with strong local narratives about their everyday life, and to a couple of independent male videomakers. Hani al-Shaibani is the most promising of these videomakers, receiving a lot of well-deserved attention for his short video, *Jawhara*, which dealt with alcoholism. Other talents to watch out for include Mariam bin Fahd, currently studying film at Leeds University, and Azza al-Zarouni and Rehab Omar Ateeq, whose shorts *Blue* and *The Car or The Wife?* have screened at scores of film festivals. Many of the young women are now working in television, waiting impatiently for a film industry to develop.

They may not have long to wait. Dollywood was a term coined to describe the future Film City development underway by Dubai Media City, which includes the construction of state-of-the-art studios and production facilities. The plan is to establish Dubai as a regional film-production hub. Lebanese and Indian music videos have been shot here for some time, and Bollywood movies have recently been filmed here.

MUSIC & DANCE
DANCE

Traditional song and dance are inspired by the environment – the sea, desert and mountains. Contact with other cultures through Dubai's trading history has brought many influences to the UAE shores. Music and dance are performed spontaneously at weddings, social occasions and family gatherings, and at various places around the city on National Day (2 December). You may be lucky to see such a performance if you're exploring an Emirati neighbourhood and come across a wedding tent, otherwise you will have to visit the Heritage Village (p54). A good time to catch some local action is during the Dubai Shopping Festival or Summer Surprises (p10) when there are a variety of performances throughout the night. Women should make an effort to visit on a ladies' night when they will get the rare opportunity to hear local women singing.

One of the most popular dances is the *liwa*, which is performed to a rapid tempo and loud drumbeat. It was most likely brought to the Gulf by East African slaves and is traditionally sung in Swahili. The *ayyalah*, is a typical Bedouin dance, celebrating the courage, strength and unity of the tribe. The *ayyalah* is performed throughout the Gulf, but the UAE has its own variation, which is performed to a simple drumbeat. Anywhere between 25 and 200 men stand with their arms linked in two rows facing each other. They wave walking sticks or swords in front of them and sway back and forth, the two rows taking it in turn to sing.

It is a war dance and the words expound the virtues of courage and bravery in battle. There is a display on video of this dance in the **Dubai Museum** (p53).

The instruments used at traditional musical celebrations in Dubai are the same as those used in the rest of the Gulf. The *tamboura*, a harplike instrument, has five strings made of horse gut, which are stretched between a wooden base and a bow-shaped neck. The base is covered with camel skin and the strings are plucked with sheep horns. It has a deep and resonant sound, a little like a bass violin.

A much less sophisticated instrument is the *manior*, a percussion instrument that is played with the body. It is a belt made of cotton and decorated with dried goats' hooves. It is wrapped around the player who keeps time with the beat of the *tamboura* while dancing. The *mimzar* is a wooden instrument a little like a small oboe, but it delivers a higher pitched sound, which is haunting and undeniably Middle Eastern.

An unusual instrument and one that you'll often see at song and dance performances is the *habban*, the Arabian bagpipes. Made from a goatskin sack, it has two pipes attached. The sack retains its goat shape and the pipes resemble its front legs. One pipe is used to blow air into the sack and the other produces the sound. The *habban* sounds much the same as the Scottish bagpipes, but is shriller in tone.

The tabla is a drum, and has a number of different shapes. It can resemble a bongo drum that is placed on the floor, or it can be a *jaser*, a drum with goatskin at both ends, which is slung around the neck and hit with sticks.

CONTEMPORARY MUSIC

Much of the more interesting contemporary Arab music, such as Oryx, Blue Bedouin and Shoo Abalak (see the boxed text this page) has been produced at Dubai Media City and released by either Virgin-Capitol or EMI Arabia. The fusion of sounds is often the result of the diverse nationalities of the musicians. For example, Ahmed Ghannoum's band consists of a Syrian singer, Lebanese guitarist, French bassist, Sri Lankan pianist, two percussionists from India and Africa and a South African harpist. He describes his music as a cross between chill-out, house, garage, jazz and bossa nova with an Arabic thread.

The *local* live music scene, in contrast to the expat rock bands and lounge singers who perform in hotels, bars and clubs, is just starting to take off, with occasional one-off performances in smaller venues, recording studios and private homes. Nirvana-like Sandwash, a group of American University of Dubai students, have formed a music consortium, Sound Society, to promote UAE musicians. Pakistani-Indian band Abstrakt Collision play a mix of jazz, funk and pop, and recently self-released their debut album *In the Meantime of Tomorrow*.

The music you're most likely to hear on the radio, however, is *khaleeji*, the traditional Gulf style, recognisable to those familiar with Arabic pop music. Popular singers include Ahlam, Ali Burroghr and Mohammed Nasser, who had a huge hit with 'Ya Bint'. Newcomer Dubai-born Yaseer Habeeb also sings in the *khaleeji* genre. The first UAE national to have a major hit in Europe and the Middle East, he operates his own recording studio and recently released his second album, *Sadoh*.

For more information on concerts and live music events, see p97.

Top Five Arabian CDs

- *Blue Bedouin* – Hussain al-Bagali's 'blissful and chilled-out beats from the desert' with songs called 'Desert Groove', 'Jumeirah Sunset' and 'King of Satwa', is Dubai's answer to Café del Mar.

- *From Maghreb to Mashreq* – features 'Ya Bint', the hit of Mohammed Nasser, one of the UAE's biggest stars.

- *Oryx* – Dubai expats Palestinian Bashar Abed Rabbo and German Dirk Heibel have produced a cool CD that combines tunes from ambient Arabian instrumentals to electronic dance music, mixed with Arabic chants.

- *Shoo Abalak* (translation: What's on your Mind?) – Ahmed Ghannoum's debut album sets Arabic lyrics to Latino rhythms, bossa nova beats and tabla.

- *Yaseer Habeeb* – 'Elama', from UAE national and Dubai native Yaseer Habeeb's self-titled debut album, was a huge hit in Europe and the Middle East.

History

History

THE RECENT PAST

Since oil was first discovered in Dubai in 1966, the speed of Dubai's growth began accelerating at a pace that has not yet slowed down. This was to change life in Dubai forever. Sheikh Rashid bin Saeed al-Maktoum, known as the 'father of modern Dubai', was ready for the change and when exports of oil began in 1969, infrastructure projects such as Port Rashid were well underway. Just as the phenomenal wealth generation was beginning, significant political change was in the air.

In 1968 Britain announced its departure from the region and an attempt was made to create a state that included the Trucial States (today's United Arab Emirates), Bahrain and Qatar. While talks collapsed and both Bahrain and Qatar moved onwards to their own independence, the leaders of Abu Dhabi and Dubai strengthened their commitment to creating a single state. After many meetings and much persuasion by Abu Dhabi's leader, Sheikh Zayed bin Sultan al-Nayan, the federation of the United Arab Emirates (UAE) was born on 2 December 1971. The UAE consisted of the emirates of Dubai, Abu Dhabi, Ajman, Fujairah, Sharjah and Umm al-Qaiwain, with Ras al-Khaimah joining in 1972. The UAE remains to this day the only federation of Arab states in the Middle East.

Under the agreement, the emirs approved a formula whereby Abu Dhabi and Dubai (in that order) would carry the most weight in the federation, but which would leave each emir

Heritage House (p50)

c 3000 BC	c 2500 BC
The Magan civilisation dominates the world's copper trade	Agriculture develops with the cultivation of the date palm

The Al-Maktoum Dynasty

The ruling family of Dubai has successfully managed to blend its private interests with politics. As in all the Gulf states, the family maintains the Arabian tradition of the *majlis*, in which any Emirati man can approach the ruler to discuss any matter.

The current ruler of Dubai is Sheikh Maktoum bin Rashid al-Maktoum. He's also vice president and prime minister of the UAE. Sheikh Maktoum's second brother, Sheikh Hamdan, is the deputy ruler of Dubai and the federal minister of finance and industry. Their uncle, Sheikh Ahmed bin Saeed al-Maktoum, is the chairman of Emirates Airlines.

Sheikh Mohammed, the third brother, is the crown prince of Dubai and the defence minister of the UAE. He is the best known of the ruling family and is constantly in the public eye as a result of his public policies, his instrumental involvement in pushing ahead some of the most ambitious projects, and one of his passions – horse racing.

Horse racing is a hobby of all the members of the ruling family and they are well respected in the international equestrian community. Sheikh Maktoum owns the largest racing stables in the world; Sheikh Hamdan is known as a leading breeder of racehorses and Sheikh Mohammed owns several champion racehorses.

Among the women of the family, Sheikha Hessah bint Maktoum al-Maktoum, the eldest daughter of the ruler, is a well-known artist whose vibrantly coloured abstract paintings have been exhibited in Paris and London.

largely autonomous. Sheikh Zayed of Abu Dhabi became the supreme ruler (or president) of the UAE and Sheikh Rashid of Dubai became vice president.

Since 1971 Dubai has been one of the most politically stable cities in the Arab world. This does not mean, however, that political life in the UAE has been devoid of controversy. Border disputes between the emirates continued throughout the 1970s and '80s, and the degree to which 'integration' among the seven sheikhdoms should be pursued has been the subject of constant debate.

In 1979 Sheikh Zayed and Sheikh Rashid sealed a formal compromise under which each gave a little ground on his respective vision of the country. The result was a much stronger federation in which Dubai remained a bastion of free trade, while Abu Dhabi imposed a tighter federal structure on the other emirates. Rashid also agreed to take the title of prime minister as a symbol of his commitment to the federation.

Sheikh Rashid, the driving force behind Dubai's phenomenal growth, died in 1990 after a long illness and was succeeded as emir by the eldest of his four sons, Sheikh Maktoum bin Rashid al-Maktoum. For several years prior to Rashid's death Maktoum had been regent for his father in all but name, and has continued to follow in his father's footsteps.

Understanding that the oil wealth would not last indefinitely, Sheikh Maktoum has pursued a policy of promoting Dubai whenever and wherever possible, to the point where oil-related revenues now account for less than 10% of Dubai's income. The crown prince and third son of the dynasty, Sheikh Mohammed bin Rashid al-Maktoum has also been a vigorous and inspiring figure on the Dubai scene and has contributed an enormous amount to Dubai's profile.

By the mid-1990s, the Dubai Desert Classic (p10) had become a well-established stop on the annual Professional Golfer's Association tour; and the first running of the world's richest horse race, the Dubai World Cup (p10), placed the city firmly on the world sporting map. The idea of keeping Dubai on the world stage is behind the world-class tennis tournaments, boat racing, desert rallies and the Dubai Air Show (one of the four largest in the world) put on by the city.

These events, along with other 'firsts', such as the world's first seven-star hotel, the **Burj Al Arab** (p146), have had a huge impact on the profile of Dubai and in turn tourism, transforming it from a stopover to being a darling of travel magazines around the world.

The history of Dubai reads like a tale of rags to riches, a chronicle that has witnessed a small coastal hamlet transform into a major commercial hub – a Hong Kong of the Gulf.

c 700 AD	1580
The Umayyads introduce Arabic and Islam to the region	Marco Polo describes Dubai as a prosperous town

Top Five Books on the History of Dubai

- *Arabian Destiny* by Edward Henderson – this wry memoir by a British colonial official includes some perceptive observations of the society he's lived in: Dubai hasn't simply changed since the 1950s, it has become a different place altogether.
- *The Emirates of Yesteryear* by Ronald Codrai – an important document of everyday life in the preoil days in the seven sheikhdoms before they united. The photos taken in the 1940s and 1950s provide a rare look at a traditional way of life that is fast disappearing.
- *Father of Dubai: Sheikh Rashid bin Saeed al-Maktoum* by Graeme Wilson – a terrific photographic and narrative tribute to the founder of modern Dubai.
- *The Merchants: the Big Business Families of Saudi Arabia and the Gulf States* by Michael Field – a brief sketch of the rise of Dubai as a trading centre and the role played by its powerful tribal relationships.
- *Seafarers of the Emirates* by Ronald Codrai – this remarkable record of the last years of a traditional life related to the sea recreates the lives of the pearl divers and merchants, ship builders and seafarers – most of the photos were taken in Dubai in the middle of the 20th century when the UAE was on the threshold of radical change.

The end of this growth, or even a slowdown, doesn't appear likely and it's hard to think of anywhere else in the world that has developed at such a frenetic pace and in such a short space of time.

FROM THE BEGINNING
EARLY SETTLEMENT

This part of Arabia has been settled for millennia. Archaeological remains found in Al-Qusais, on the northeastern outskirts of present-day Dubai, show evidence of human remains as far back as 8000 BC, after the end of the last ice age.

Up until 3000 BC the area supported nomadic herders of sheep, goats and cattle. These early inhabitants camped on the coast and fished during winter, and moved inland with their herds during summer. The first signs of trade emerge with the discovery of pottery from Ubaid (in present-day Iraq) dating back to 5000 BC. Agriculture developed with the cultivation of the date palm around 2500 BC, which not only provided food and a range of materials for building and weaving, but also shelter for smaller plants grown for food.

Archaeological evidence also suggests that this area, together with present-day Oman, was closely associated with the Magan civilisation during the Bronze Age. It is thought that the Magans dominated the ancient world's copper trade, exploiting the rich veins of copper in the hills throughout the Hajar Mountains and especially near Sohar, in Oman. It is also likely that they traded pearls in Mesopotamia (present-day Iraq) and with the Indus Civilisation, in present-day Pakistan.

All records of the Magan civilisation cease after the 2nd millennium BC and some historians have speculated that the desertification of the area hastened its demise; others have argued that its importance may have been diminished by the growing reliance on iron over copper for the manufacture of weapons and tools.

There is little archaeological evidence of occupation during the Iron Age and the next major habitation of the area appears to have been by the Sassanian empire. Archaeological excavations at Jumeirah, about 10km south of Dubai Creek, have revealed a caravan station dating from the 6th century AD, which is thought to have links with this empire. The Sassanids were a dynasty who ruled in Persia from 224 to 636 and wielded power over the

1833	1841
The Al-Maktoum family arrives in Bur Dubai from Bani Yas	The Al-Maktoum power base extends to Deira

region from about the 3rd century AD until the Umayyads, a Damascus-based Islamic dynasty, uprooted them in the 7th century. Archaeologists believe that the buildings at Jumeirah were restored and extended by the Umayyad dynasty, making it the only site in the UAE to span the pre-Islamic and Islamic periods.

The Umayyads brought with them the Arabic language and joined the region with the Islamic world. Christianity had made a brief appearance in the region in the form of the Nestorian sect, members of which had a monastery on Sir Bani Yas Island, west of Abu Dhabi, in the 5th century. It was the arrival of Islam, however, that shaped the future of the region. The early Islamic period, from the 7th to the 14th century, hasn't been well documented in the UAE. It is known that during this period the area was loosely under the control of the Umayyads and their successors the Abbasids. After the Baghdad-based Abbasid dynasty went into decline, the centre of power in the Islamic world shifted to Cairo, leaving the UAE isolated on the periphery. In

Dubai Museum (p53)

History – From the Beginning

the absence of centralised control, the tribes of the Arabian Peninsula asserted themselves in the hinterlands, while the coastal regions were dominated by trading ports such as Julfar, near present-day Ras al-Khaimah, and Hormuz, an island in the Strait of Hormuz.

In the early Islamic period, the Gulf experienced a boom in maritime trade due to its location on the major trade routes between the Mediterranean Sea and the Indian Ocean. Trade soon became the backbone of the local economy as ships travelled as far as China, returning laden with silk and porcelain.

Returning Fire

The origins of the brief 1940 war between Dubai and Sharjah stem from a complicated struggle within the Al-Maktoum family. Sheikh Saeed bin Maktoum al-Maktoum, the ruler of Dubai, was challenged in the 1930s by his cousin, Mani bin Rashid, who at one point practically controlled Deira while Sheikh Saeed held onto Bur Dubai. Sheikh Saeed gained the upper hand and sent his cousin into exile in 1939. Mani bin Rashid and his followers then settled in Sharjah, too close to Dubai for Sheikh Saeed's comfort. Sheikh Saeed asked Sheikh Sultan of Sharjah to exile Mani bin Rashid, but Sheikh Sultan refused on the grounds that it compromised the traditions of Arab hospitality. After much fruitless diplomacy, a desultory war broke out in January 1940 between Dubai and Sharjah, all of 23km apart. The British tried to quell the war by restricting the importation of firearms and ammunition. The rival forces then resorted to using ancient muzzle-loading cannons. The soldiers were sometimes able to recover the cannonballs fired at them and to fire them back.

While the war was on, Imperial Airways, a forerunner of British Airways, would still refuel its flying boats on Dubai Creek and send the passengers over to the fort at Sharjah for lunch. For this operation a truce was called, and the passengers would pass through the battlefront without, in most cases, realising anything odd was afoot.

When the ammunition and gunpowder had nearly run out, the rival sheikhs began negotiating again. Mani bin Rashid died peacefully soon after and the matter was put to rest with him.

1894	1930
Exemption for foreign traders declared	Dubai's pearling trade collapses

Books: Arabs & the Arab World

Dubai may get only the briefest of mentions, but these books will give you a solid understanding of the peoples and the region in which Dubai is now a central focus.

- *A History of the Arab Peoples* by Albert Hourani – a bestseller when first published, this superb book covers politics, culture, society, economy and thought.
- *Arabia and the Arabs: From the Bronze Age to the Coming of Islam* by Robert G Hoyland – drawing from inscriptions, poetry, histories and archaeological evidence, the author explores the main cultural areas of Arabia, from ancient Sheba in the south, to the deserts and oases of the north.
- *Arabian Sands* by Wilfred Thesiger – the English explorer recounts five years spent with the Bedouin of the Arabian peninsula in the Empty Quarter in the 1940s. Thesiger, who lived as a Bedouin, wearing their dress, walking barefoot and adopting the same ritualistic patterns of life, describes unimaginable hardships as if they were minor inconveniences, and mourns a vanishing way of life as he tells how the Bedouin traded in their camels for 4WDs.
- *The Arabs* by Peter Mansfield – this must-read book considers the Arabs themselves, their characteristics, aspirations and future, covering the pre-Islamic nomads of Arabia, the life of the Prophet Mohammed and the rise of Arab power, to the modern Arab renaissance built from oil.
- *Archaeology of the United Arab Emirates* by Daniel T Potts, Hassan al-Naboodah and Peter Hellyer – a collection of papers from an international conference on UAE archaeology.
- *From Trucial States to United Arab Emirates* by Frauke Heard-Bey – an insight into a society in transition written by a leading scholar on the UAE and long-term expatriate of the Emirates.
- *The Middle East: 2000 Years of History* by Bernard Lewis – an expansive survey of the civilisations of the region that focuses on how history has shaped the identity of the Middle East.
- *Sheikhdoms of Eastern Arabia* by Peter Lienhardt & Ahmed al-Shahi – an insight into how oil wealth altered Arabia, tribal structure, gender relations and the complex relationship between the ruling sheikhs and their subjects.
- *Struggle and Survival in the Modern Middle East* by Edmund Burke III (ed) – this book of biographies of ordinary men and women includes a chapter on Ahmad, a Kuwaiti pearl diver, and his difficult life.
- *Travellers in Arabia* by Robin Bidwell – Arabia as experienced by its earliest tourists, Burckhardt, Burton, Palgrave, Philby, Stark, Cox and Thesiger.
- *United Arab Emirates: A New Perspective* by Ibrahim al-Abed & Peter Hellyer – these essays by leading UAE scholars cover archaeology, the coming of Islam, the Islamic period, tribal society, the Trucial States, formation of the federation, economic development, industrialisation, the environment, cultural development and poetry.
- *The United Arab Emirates AD 600 to the Present* by Aqil Kazim – this detailed and dense academic read covers the historical, economic and social transformations that have taken place in the country.

The West was first to hear about the settlement in Dubai from two Italian explorers: Gasparo Balbi and Marco Polo. In 1580 Marco Polo described Dubai as a prosperous town, largely dependent on pearl fishing.

EUROPEAN PRESENCE

Attracted by the lucrative trade routes with India and the Far East, in the late 16th century Portugal became the first European power to take an interest in this part of the Gulf coast. Its occupation of the area lasted until the 1630s and eventually extended as far north as Bahrain. The arrival of the well-armed Portuguese was a disaster for the Muslim traders. The Portuguese wanted a monopoly on trade routes between Europe and India and they tolerated no rivals. Local trade dried up to the extent that many coastal settlements were practically abandoned, and the tribes took refuge in oases far from the coast, such as Liwa and Al-Ain. The two cannons on display at the **Dubai Museum** (p53) are the only evidence of the Portuguese presence in the area.

1940	1951
War breaks out briefly between Dubai and Sharjah	Trucial States Council founded

The French and the Dutch subsequently infiltrated the area in the 17th and 18th centuries, both aspiring to control the trading routes to the east. The British were equally intent on ruling the seas in order to protect the sea route to India, and in 1766 the Dutch finally gave way to Britain's East India Company, which had established trading links with the Gulf as early as 1616.

Throughout this time Dubai remained a small fishing and pearling hamlet, perched on a disputed border between two local powers – the seafaring Qawasim of present-day Ras al-Khaimah and Sharjah to the north, and the Bani Yas tribal confederation of what is now Abu Dhabi to the south. The region was also affected by the rivalries between bigger regional powers – the Wahhabi tribes of what is now Saudi Arabia, the Ottoman Empire, the Persians and the British.

THE TRUCIAL COAST

At the turn of the 19th century, Dubai was governed by Mohammed bin Hazza who remained ruler of Dubai until the Al-Bu Fasalah, a branch of the Bani Yas tribe from Abu Dhabi, came to dominate the town in 1833, severing it from Abu Dhabi. The Bani Yas were the main power among the Bedouin tribes of the interior. Originally based in Liwa, an oasis on the edge of the desert known as the Empty Quarter (Rub' al-Khali), in the south of the UAE, they engaged in the traditional Bedouin activities of camel herding, small-scale agriculture, tribal raiding and extracting protection money from merchant caravans passing through their territory. At the end of the 18th century, the leader of the Bani Yas moved from Liwa to the island of Abu Dhabi on the coast.

About 800 people from this tribe settled by the Creek in Bur Dubai under the leadership of Maktoum bin Butti, who established the Al-Maktoum dynasty of Dubai, which still rules the emirate today. For Maktoum bin Butti, good relations with the British authorities in the Gulf were essential to safeguard his new and small sheikhdom against attack from the larger and more powerful sheikhdoms of Sharjah to the north and Abu Dhabi to the south.

Beautiful Gems, Hard Lives

Images of the heyday of pearling are laced with romanticism. But for those who dived the depths to collect the pearls, it was a life of hardship and the rewards were no match for the dangers involved. Most of the divers were slaves from East Africa and the profits of the industry went straight to their master, the owner of the boat.

The only equipment the divers used was a rope tied around the waist, a turtle-shell peg on their nose and leather finger gloves to protect their hands from the sharp coral and shells. At certain times of the year they would wear an all-over muslin bodysuit to protect them from jellyfish stings. The best pearls were found at depths of up to 36m and divers would be under the water for around three minutes. To reach this depth divers used a rope weighted with a stone that was tied to the boat and thrown overboard.

The pearl-diving season lasted from May until September. On the ship there would be divers, men responsible for hauling up the divers after each dive, a cook and boys employed to serve food and water and open the oyster shells. Each boat also had a singer, the *naham*, whose job was to lead the crew in songs or lighten their mood by singing to them. Many of the songs were about lucky men who had become rich through diving and the joys of returning home after the diving season.

Back on shore pearl merchants would grade the pearls according to size by using a number of copper sieves, each with different sized holes. The greatest market for pearls was originally India, but in the early 20th century the UK and the US became keen buyers of this fashionable jewel. The discovery of the means to make artificial pearls in the early 20th century triggered the demise of the industry.

The **Dubai Museum** (p53) and the **Diving Village** (p54) feature wonderful and significant displays on the pearling industry.

1958	1966
Sheikh Rashid officially becomes ruler of Dubai	Oil discovered in Dubai

Heritage House (p50)

In 1841 the Bur Dubai settlement extended to Deira on the northern side of the Creek, though throughout the 19th century Dubai largely remained a tiny enclave of fishermen, pearl divers, Bedouin, and Indian and Persian merchants. The Indian and Persian (now Iranian) merchants still give much of the Creek its character today.

Things began to change, however, around the end of the 19th century. In 1892 the British, keen to impose their authority on the region and protect their empire in India, extended their power through a series of so-called exclusive agreements under which the sheikhs accepted formal British protection and, in exchange, promised to have no dealings with any other foreign power without British permission. As a result of these treaties or truces, Europeans took to calling the area the Trucial Coast, a name that was retained until the 1971 federation.

At the end of the 19th century, Sharjah, the area's main trading centre, began losing its trade prosperity to Dubai. In 1894 Dubai's ruler, Sheikh Maktoum bin Hasher al-Maktoum, permitted tax exemption for foreign traders and the free port of Dubai was born – something that exists to this day. Around the same time Lingah (now Bandar-e Langeh), across the Strait of Hormuz in Iran, lost its status as a duty-free port, and the Al-Maktoum family made a concerted effort to lure Lingah's disillusioned traders to Dubai while also managing to convince some of Sharjah's merchants to relocate.

At first the Persians who came to Dubai believed that it would just be a temporary move, but by the 1920s, when it became evident that the trade restrictions in southern Iran were there to stay, they took up permanent residence.

More good news for the town came in the early 20th century when the Al-Maktoums, probably with the assistance of the Persian traders, prevailed on a British steamship line to switch its main port of call in the lower Gulf from Lingah to Dubai. This gave Dubai regular links with British India and the ports of the central and northern Gulf – Bahrain,

1969	1971
Oil production begins	The UAE is established

Kuwait, Bushehr and Basra. Dubai's importance to Britain as a port of call would remain in place for half a century, marking the beginning of Dubai's growth as a trading power and fuelling the prosperity that would soon follow.

THE EXPANDING CITY

By the turn of the 20th century, Dubai was well established as an independent town, with a population of about 10,000. Deira was the most populous area at this time with about 1600 houses, inhabited mainly by Arabs but also by Persians and Baluchis who came from parts of what are now Pakistan and Afghanistan. By 1908 there were about 350 shops based in Deira and another 50 in Bur Dubai, where the Indian community was concentrated. To this day the **Bur Dubai Souq** (p120) shows a strong Indian influence and is home to the only Hindu temple in Dubai.

The development of Dubai as a major trading centre was spurred on by the collapse of the pearling trade, which had been the mainstay of Dubai's economy for centuries. The pearling trade fell victim both to the worldwide depression of 1929 and to the Japanese discovery, in 1930, of a method by which pearls could be cultured artificially. Sheikh Rashid concluded that the pearling industry was almost certainly finished and started to look for alternative forms of revenue. This chain of events heralded a new era in Dubai's trade – re-exporting (see the boxed text below). The rise of this trade was spurred on by WWII and continued to flourish thereafter.

The next key event in Dubai's expansion occurred in 1939 when Sheikh Rashid bin Saeed al-Maktoum took over as regent from his father, Sheikh Saeed, but only formally succeeded to the leadership when his father died in 1958. He quickly moved to bolster the emirate's position as the main trading hub in the lower Gulf. At about the same time, the rulers of Sharjah made the costly mistake of allowing their harbour to silt up, while in Dubai Sheikh Rashid was fast improving facilities along the Creek. In January 1940 war broke out briefly between Dubai and Sharjah – see the boxed text on p39.

In 1951 the Trucial States Council was founded, bringing the leaders of what would become the UAE together. The council comprised the rulers of the sheikhdoms and was

The Re-export Trade

Dubai's economy is built on trade, especially the re-export trade, which started around the time of the collapse of the pearling trade in the 1930s. Its merchants imported goods, which they then sold on to other ports. In practice, this involved smuggling, especially of gold to India. The goods entered and exited Dubai legally; it was the countries at the *other* end of the trade that looked on it as smuggling.

WWII also played a role in the growth of the re-export trade. The war brought much trade to a standstill and this was compounded by a shortage of basic food supplies. The British government supplied the Trucial sheikhdoms with plenty of rice and sugar. Dubai merchants bought these goods cheaply and, finding themselves oversupplied, shipped them off to the black market in Iran.

It was around this time that modern Dubai began to take shape. During the 1950s Sheikh Rashid became one of the earliest beneficiaries of Kuwait's Fund for Arab Economic Development, which loaned him money to dredge the Creek (it had become badly silted up, reducing the volume of Creek traffic) and to build a new breakwater near its mouth. The project was completed in 1963 and gold smuggling took off like a rocket, using the trade networks built up through the pearling business. India had banned gold imports after 1947 to stabilise its currency, which sent the price of gold in India soaring. In 1967 the price of gold in Dubai was US$35 an ounce, while in India it sold for US$68 an ounce. The gold trade peaked in 1997 when 660 tonnes of gold left Dubai.

Dubai's days as a smuggler's paradise are not over. The trade now supposedly focuses on Iran; dhows take cargo such as VCRs and Levi's jeans to Iranian ports and return laden with caviar and carpets.

1979	1985
Sheikh Rashid declared prime minister of the UAE	Emirates Airlines is established in Dubai

Modernisation & Development

Oil was first discovered near Dubai in 1966 and oil exports began three years later. A building boom had, however, already begun along the Creek well before Dubai struck oil. Even after oil revenues began coming in, trade remained the foundation of the city's wealth, though oil has contributed to trade profits and encouraged modernisation since its discovery.

The first bank, the British Bank of the Middle East, was established in 1946, and when Al-Maktoum Hospital was built in 1949 it was the only centre for modern medical care on the Trucial Coast until well into the 1950s. When Sheikh Rashid officially came to power in 1958 he set up the first Municipal Council. He also established a police force and basic infrastructure, such as electricity and water supply.

Until the early 1960s the only means of transport in town was donkey or camel. As is still the case today, *abras* (water taxis) were used to transport people across the Creek. Construction of the airport began in 1958 and the British Overseas Airways Corporation (BOAC) and Middle East Airlines (MEA) launched regular flights to Dubai soon after. Roads and bridges appeared in the early 1960s.

The ambitious UK£23 million Port Rashid complex was begun in 1967 after it became obvious that the growing maritime traffic could no longer be managed by the current facilities. It was completed in 1972.

The mid-1970s saw the beginnings of a massive programme of industrialisation that resulted in the construction of Jebel Ali Port, said to be the largest artificial port in the world, and the adjacent industrial centre, which was to become a free-trade zone.

All of these developments brought to life Sheikh Rashid's vision of Dubai as one of the Middle East's most important commercial hubs.

the direct predecessor of the UAE Supreme Council. It met twice a year under the aegis of the British political agent in Dubai.

The end of the war, India's independence and the decline of the British Empire saw the end of Britain's presence in the region and prompted the establishment of the UAE. Before withdrawing from the region, the British set in motion the means by which the borders that now make up the UAE were drawn. Incredibly this involved a British diplomat spending months riding a camel around the mountains and desert asking village heads, tribal leaders and Bedouin which sheikh they swore allegiance to. The British withdrawal and the discovery of oil accelerated the modernisation of the region. For more on modernisation and development, see the boxed text above.

1990	1994
Sheikh Maktoum becomes ruler of Dubai after Sheikh Rashid passes away	Sheikh Mohammed appointed Crown Prince of Dubai

Neighbourhoods

Neighbourhoods

Dubai has plenty of suburb names, but not many of them are in common usage and reciting them is always met with a blank stare from taxi drivers. So we've condensed large areas of Dubai into four main areas. These areas are where you'll be spending the lion's share of your time and the names are the most commonly used by Dubai residents. Once you have these areas firmly entrenched in your mind, you're well on the way to being a local.

Originally the action in Dubai was centred on the Creek, with traders crisscrossing the calm waters between Deira and Bur Dubai. The Deira definition we are using includes Al-Garhoud, the area near the airport. There are three ways to cross the Creek south to Bur Dubai other than using the *abras* (water taxis). There is the Al-Shindaga Tunnel close to the open sea, followed inland (east) by the Al-Maktoum Bridge, followed by the Al-Garhoud Bridge. At certain times of day you may notice stationary cars seemingly for miles on either side of these crossings. It's not a traffic jam – this is so people have time to make phone calls and touch up their make-up.

Our Bur Dubai definition takes in the area immediately south of the Creek, from the sea to the Al-Garhoud Bridge, the heritage district of Bastakia and the busy residential area of Karama. From the Bur Dubai area we head southwest on two fronts towards Jebel Ali. The first area, Sheikh Zayed Rd, runs inland but parallel to the coast. This area starts at the Trade Centre roundabout, south of Karama, and finishes at Interchange No 1. There are many hotels and eateries along this strip.

The last area we identify is Jumeirah. Jumeirah Rd runs parallel to the coast about a block inland from the sea. We start our coverage of this area at the Dubai Marine Beach Resort and proceed down the coast. There are actually three Jumeirah areas (logically named 1, 2, 3), followed by Umm Suqeim (1 and 2).

Large dhow, Dubai Creek

ITINERARIES

One Day

Dubai's city has historically centred around the Creek, so with only one day, start right on the waterfront near the **UK embassy** (p176). Take in the very modern Dubai Creek skyline over in Deira while walking to the **Bastakia Quarter** (p52) to check out the restored houses. Head to the excellent **Dubai Museum** (p53) to get a historical perspective of Dubai. After that, stroll to **Sheikh Saeed al-Maktoum House** (p55) for the architecture and the old photographs of Dubai. Then to the **Heritage Village** (p54) and a late lunch of traditional Middle Eastern dishes at **Kan Zaman** (p79). After lunch take an *abra* across to Deira, checking out the dhows and life on the Creek. Follow your nose into the **Deira Spice Souq** (p50) and if you want some more history head to the **Al-Ahmadiya School** (p49) and **Heritage House** (p50) or straight up to the **Deira Gold Souq** (p50). If the shopping bug bites visit **Deira City Centre** (p49) for the shopping and social scene. A trip to Dubai is incomplete without seeing the **Burj Al Arab** (p57) and a five-star beach hotel, so kill two birds with one stone with a drink at the **Bahri Bar** (p91) at the **Mina A'Salam** (p148). For dinner, if you feel like hanging out back on the Creek and it's not too hot, head to **Fatafeet** (p79) for a feast and *sheesha* (water pipe). For a taste of Morocco head to **Tagine** (p85) and straight outside to the **Shisha Courtyard** (p90).

Top Five for Children

- Al-Mamzar Park (p49)
- Deira City Centre (p49)
- Dubai Museum (p53)
- Jumeirah Beach Park (p58)
- Wild Wadi Waterpark (p60)

Three Days

As you have more time you could spread out the above itinerary over two days and include a drink at the **Burj Al Arab** (p57), a sunset **dhow cruise** (p47) and perhaps playtime at **Wild Wadi** (p60) for the kid in all of us. Try some shopping and a cheap meal at **Karama** (p75). Perhaps dine at the Hilton Dubai Creek's **Glasshouse** (p72) or, for some true fine dining, try its more famous sister, Gordon Ramsay's **Verre** (p74). A night out clubbing is a must in Dubai so head to **Sho Cho's** (p94), followed by neighbouring **Boudoir** (p95). A trip to **Sharjah** (p153) should be included, especially for those who want to do more shopping or check out the art scene. A trip to the desert is also a must and the easiest way is to take a **desert safari** (p151). Given all the misinformation in the media about Islam and Arabs, take the **Jumeirah Mosque** (p59) tour and don't be shy – ask some questions.

One Week

If the desert safari has whetted your appetite for more scenery, get out of town by checking out the Excursions chapter (p149). This includes East Coast destinations **Khor Fakkan** (p158) and **Fujairah** (p158), as well as the oasis city of **Al-Ain** (p162) and the peaceful retreat of **Hatta** (p156). On your final day do your last-minute shopping. Pick up that **carpet** (p122) you can't stop thinking about and then head for a dinner with a view, either at **Eauzone** (p83) or **Zheng He's** (p85). While **The Palm** (p137) might be visible from space, it's also visible from the **Rooftop Bar** (p93), where you can chill, Arabian style, and see the lights from Dubai's next jaw-dropping resort.

ORGANISED TOURS

For desert safari tours see p151.

Creek Cruises

COASTLINE LEISURE Map pp208-9

☎ 398 4867; in front of Sheraton Dubai Creek; tour Dh35

With plenty of scheduled cruise times, these one-hour guided dhow tours of the Creek are good value. They depart daily at 11.30am, 1.30pm, 3.30pm, 5.30pm and 7.30pm.

DANAT DUBAI CRUISES Map pp212-13

☎ 351 1117; Al-Seef Rd, Bur Dubai; sundowner cruise adult/child Dh65/45

Take the Afternoon Sundowner Cruise, which goes past the Heritage district before entering the Gulf for sunset. The cruise boards at 5pm and returns at 6.30pm.

Rise above It All

If you *really* want to see all of Dubai, and better the views from Emirates Towers or the Burj Al Arab, take a 10-minute helicopter tour over Dubai city. Leaving from central Dubai, the flight goes over the Creek and Port Rashid, giving you a great view of the spectacular architecture. You can also organise individually tailored flights to other regions of the UAE.

Contact **Arabian Adventures** (Map pp206-7; ☎ 343 9966; www.arabian-adventures.com; 1-4 people Dh975; ☽ Sat).

Bus Tours

BIG BUS COMPANY Map pp214-15

☎ 324 4187; www.bigbustours.com; Wafi City; adult/child/family Dh120/75/315

Adding to Dubai's often surreal sights are eight open-topped London double decker buses plying two routes (city and beach) between 9am and 5pm every day. The ticket is an all day affair and you can get off and on at any one of 19 well-positioned stops. The ticket includes free entry to Dubai Museum, Sheikh Saeed al-Maktoum House and a Wafi City discount card. The buses leave from Wafi City on the hour and half hour, and there's a running commentary in English.

WONDER BUS TOURS Map pp212-13

☎ 359 5656; www.wonderbusdubai.com; BurJuman Centre; adult/child/family Dh95/65/290

An even more surreal sight awaits you at the BurJuman Centre with the amphibious Wonder Bus. Twice a day up to 44 souls can take this bus down to the Creek, enter the water, cruise up and down the Creek, and then head back to the BurJuman Centre. The trip takes two hours. The head trip, figuring out exactly why Dubai needs this attraction, could take somewhat longer.

City Tours

Both these companies are reliable long-standing tour operators in the UAE.

ARABIAN ADVENTURES Map pp206-7

☎ 343 9966; www.arabian-adventures.com; Emirates Holidays Bldg, Interchange No 2, Sheikh Zayed Rd, Dubai; tour Dh110, children under 14 free

Owned by Emirates Airlines, Arabian Adventures has a half-day tour covering Jumeirah Rd, Jumeirah Mosque, Dubai Museum and the Gold and Spice Souqs in Deira. It also has half-day shopping tours of the Gold and Spice Souqs and Karama for the same price.

NET TOURS & TRAVELS Map pp214-15

☎ 266 8661; www.nettoursdubai.com; Al-Bakhit Centre, Abu Baker al-Siddiq Rd, Hor al-Anz; tour Dh95

The tour route covers Jumeirah Mosque, the Creek, Bastakia Quarter, Dubai Museum and the textile market in Bur Dubai Souq, and includes an *abra* ride across the Creek to the Spice and Gold Souqs.

DEIRA

Eating p71; Shopping p125; Sleeping p138

Along with Bur Dubai, Deira is the heart of old Dubai. Trading has been going on here for centuries and, riding an *abra* across to Deira from Bur Dubai, you can feel the old, represented by dhows juxtaposed against the breathtaking modern skyline. Here you can stroll down the Creek to the Dhow Wharfage area, with its amazing array of goods waiting to be loaded onto the ancient dhows or – for avid shoppers – head into the souqs, where the smell of the Spice and Perfume Souqs await and the scales and calculators of the gold merchants are ready for bargaining.

Close to the Gold Souq is Dubai's first school, Al-Ahmadiya School, and Heritage House. All of these attractions are located in a small radius and while the Deira Fish Markets should be visited in the morning, the rest are best done in the late afternoon, especially in the hotter months. It's a great idea to either hire an *abra* or do a cruise (p47) to see the sunset. Alternatively, time your walk along the Dhow Wharfage for sunset.

AL-AHMADIYA SCHOOL Map pp208-9

☎ 226 0286; Al-Khor St, near Gold House; admission free; ☒ 7.30am-7.30pm Sat-Thu, 2-7.30pm Fri

This school, the oldest in Dubai, is behind the Heritage House in the souq area of Deira and has recently been fully restored. The classrooms lead off a central courtyard and inscriptions from the Quran sit above each doorway. The school was built by a philanthropic pearl merchant in 1912 and was attended by Sheikh Rashid bin Saeed al-Maktoum, the prime mover behind the development of modern Dubai. By the middle of last century the building fell into disrepair and it wasn't until the early 1990s that restoration work began. There are now guides and touch screens on hand to take you through the tour of both the school and the **Heritage House** (p50).

The small area around the school is home to a number of traditional houses that have been restored of late, including some courtyard houses made of gypsum, sea rock, coral, wood (from East Africa) and the trunks of date palms. This is a great opportunity to see some of Dubai's traditional architecture.

AL-MAMZAR PARK Map pp206-7

admission/car Dh5/30; ☒ 8am-9.30pm Sat-Wed, 8am-10.30pm Thu, Fri & public holidays, women & children only Wed

This park covers a small headland on the northern outskirts of Dubai, at the mouth of Khor al-Mamzar (across this inlet lies Sharjah). It has plenty of open space and a wooden castle for kids to play on. There are beaches, jet skis for hire, a swimming pool, children's play areas, barbecues and kiosks. Lifeguards are on duty between 8am and 6pm on at least one of the small beaches. At the northern tip of the park there are 15 **chalets** (☎ booking office 296 7948; ☒ 9am-10pm), which can be hired for the day. Each has a kitchen, bathroom, barbecue and small sitting room. The chalets can be booked weeks in advance for weekends. The five big chalets cost Dh200 each per day to hire, the 10 smaller ones Dh150 each per day. Bookings are taken once you've paid (cash only).

Wednesday is for women and children only, unless there is a special event, in which case it's open to everyone.

DEIRA CITY CENTRE Map pp210-11

☎ 295 1010; Al-Garhoud Rd, near Dubai Creek Golf & Yacht Club; ☒ 10am-11pm

What's so special about this shopping centre, which is crowded when others have tumble-

Deira Highlights

- The **souqs** (below) are fantastic. Smell the spices, grab a fresh mango juice and get ready to test your nerve against the gold traders.
- A **Dhow Wharfage** (p50) walk is a trip back into Dubai's past. Marvel at how the laden dhows manage to stay afloat when there's a truck, several cars and a warehouse's worth of electrical goods on deck.

weed rolling through them? It attracts a cross-section of Dubai's residents that you'll rarely see elsewhere. New arrivals setting up with a trip to Ikea. Extended Emirati families filling several shopping trolleys at Carrefour. Newly tanned tourists grabbing pan-Arabian souvenirs or getting henna applied. Young Arab guys in Western dress checking out the new dance releases at Virgin before watching the latest action movie at the nearby cinema complex. Indian families wheeling a new flat-screen TV down to their car. American servicemen, thankfully armed with nothing more than bad haircuts and short pants, comparing prices of digital cameras. Young Emirati girls, in groups of three, clearing a perfume-wafting path to Zara for a new 'day' wardrobe, while their older brothers sit with friends at Café Havana chatting – not to each other, but to someone at the other end of the ever-present mobile phone.

Go on Friday afternoon to watch, go some other time to shop.

DEIRA COVERED SOUQ Map pp208-9

off Al-Sabkha Rd

Compared with just 20 or 30 years ago, not much of the old covered souq remains, but it still operates in the early morning and in the evening from around 5pm to 8pm. The souq sells just about everything, though it has more of an Indian feel than an Arabic one. Textiles, spices, kitchenware, walking sticks, *sheesha*, clothes and a lifetime's supply of henna (as well as henna patterns) are all available here.

DEIRA FISH MARKET Map pp208-9

Al-Khaleej Rd

Arrive late in the morning and you'll smell it before you see it, but this fish market is worth a visit. Mainly regional fish is sold here and while the presentation isn't exactly Tokyo, merchants will scale and fillet the fish – as

Display, Al-Ahmadiya School (p49)

well as carry your bags around the market for a small fee.

DEIRA GOLD SOUQ Map pp208-9
on & around Sikkat al-Khail St, btwn Suq Deira & Old Baladiya Sts

Deira Gold Souq is probably the largest such market in Arabia, attracting customers from all over the Middle East and the subcontinent. If you don't spot the glittering gold in the windows you'll recognise this souq by the wooden lattice archways at the entrances.

DEIRA SPICE SOUQ (OLD SOUQ)
Map pp208-9
Al-Sabkha Rd

The Spice Souq is a wonderful place to wander around and take in the smells of spices, nuts and dried fruits. The spices are mainly found at the souq's eastern end, nearest the Creek. There are sacks brimming with frankincense, dried lemons, ginger root, chilli and cardamom, to name but a few. Other shops in this souq sell tacky trinkets, kitchenware, shoes, rugs, glassware and textiles.

DHOW WHARFAGE Map pp210-11
Baniyas Rd

It's great to stroll along the Creek, west of the *abra* dock, to the Dhow Wharfage area. Dhows bound for every port from Kuwait to Mumbai dock here to load and unload all sorts of cargo. You'll see tyres, air-conditioners, jeans, kitchen sinks, cars, trucks and probably just about anything you can imagine. A testament to how safe Dubai is, the goods often sit on the wharves for weeks without a problem. While you're in the area check out some of the architecture behind you. The **National Bank of Dubai**, easy to pick because of its curved gold glass 'sail', was designed by Carlos Ott, who also designed the Opera La Bastille in Paris, as well as the **Hilton Dubai Creek** (p138).

HERITAGE HOUSE Map pp208-9
☎ 226 0286; Al-Khor St, near Gold House;
⏰ 7.30am-7.30pm Sat-Thu, 2-7.30pm Fri

This restored traditional house, situated next to Al-Ahmadiya School in the souq area of Deira, was built in 1890 and was once home to a wealthy Iranian merchant. It differs from the old houses in the Bastakia Quarter, on the other side of the Creek, as it has no wind towers. The house is characterised by many wooden shutters at street level and a balcony railing along the roof. Once inside, you find yourself in a large courtyard surrounded by rooms, with a veranda at one end.

As you move around the courtyard you will pass a *majlis* (meeting room), a cattle pen, a kitchen, bedrooms, ladies' *majlis* and a bride's room. This last room was where a young bride-to-be would prepare for her wedding day with the help of other women of the harem. It is decorated with mattresses, pillows and Persian rugs.

MUSHRIF PARK Map pp206-7
admission/car Dh2/10; ⓨ 8.30am-10.30pm Sat-Wed, 8.30am-11pm Thu, Fri & public holidays

This is the largest of Dubai emirate's parks and is on the eastern outskirts of the city, about 15km from the centre. Except for a core area with irrigation-fed greenery, most of the park is rolling scrubland and dunes. The biggest attraction here is the **World Village**, a miniature reconstruction of buildings from around the world, including a Dutch windmill, Tudor cottages and Thai stilt houses. Kids are welcome to crawl around the models. Another cute feature is the Smurf statues scattered around. There are camel and pony rides, a miniature train (Dh2 per ride), swimming pools (separate ones for men and women) and barbecues. Dubai's new zoo will be located here – *in sha' Allah* (God Willing). To get here, continue along Airport Rd, past the airport, until it becomes Al-Khawaneej Rd. You will see signs for the park.

PERFUME SOUQ Map pp208-9
Deira Gold Souq, Sikkat al-Khail St

At the eastern end of the Gold Souq is a small perfume souq. While it's really just a group of shops, it sells a staggering range of Arabic and European perfumes. The European perfumes are a mixture of designer originals and copies. The Arabic perfumes are much stronger and spicier. It's worth buying some of the Arabic perfumes for the kitsch packaging alone.

SHRI NATHJE JAYATE TEMPLE
Map pp212-13

Also called the Krishna Mandir (mandir is Hindi for temple), you may recognise this temple by the racks for shoes outside. It's usually closed outside prayer times (at 6.30am, 8.30am, 10.15am, 5pm and 6pm). These last for about half an hour and are accompanied by some spirited bhajans (devotional songs). Visitors are welcome, as long as you take off your shoes and don't take photos. Leaving the temple by its front door, head back, take a left, go under an old archway, then turn left into a narrow lane. Along here you will notice vendors selling Hindu religious paraphernalia – baskets of fruit, garlands of flowers, gold-embossed holy images, sacred ash, sandalwood paste and packets of bindis (little pendants Hindu women stick to their foreheads). You may also notice lots of shoes at the base of a flight of stairs. This is the way up to the **Sikh Gurdwara** (Map pp208–9). You must cover your head before entering the Sikh shrine (there are headscarves in a box near the stairs). Inside is a copy of the Sikh holy book, the Guru Granth Sahib, covered by a canopy.

SULTAN BIN ALI AL-OWAIS CULTURAL FOUNDATION Map pp208-9
☎ 224 3111; Al-Rigga Rd, Deira; ⓨ 9am-1pm & 5-7.30pm

Al-Owais, as it's locally known, is a cultural centre aimed at promoting Arab and Islamic culture. The shiny postmodern building hosts changing exhibitions of calligraphy, Islamic art and photography, as well as performances, and has a beautiful theatre and Arabic-language library.

Neighbourhoods – Bur Dubai

BUR DUBAI
Eating p75; Shopping p127; Sleeping p142

If you do only one touristy thing in Dubai, make it a visit to the Creek. Dubai's waterfront epitomises the city's personality, and the best way to see any great trading port is from the water. Instead of booking a cruise (see p47), you can hire an *abra* for an hour or so from any of the *abra* stations on the Creek. For around Dh40 (for the whole boat) the captain should take you to Al-Maktoum Bridge and back. For Dh60 he ought to extend that route to include a trip to the mouth of the Creek and back. These prices take a bit of bargaining to achieve. If he tries to charge Dh100, walk away. The shorter trip takes just over half an hour, the longer one takes 45 to 60 minutes.

The heritage and Bastakia areas provide a slice of life from the days when wealthy merchants resided in Bur Dubai. The area is steadily being redeveloped and restored, and it's also a wonderful place for an afternoon stroll – stop for *sheesha* at **Fatafeet** (p89) for a real Dubai experience. Further back from the Creek, past what is called Golden Sands, is Karama, home to run-down apartment blocks housing expat workers. There's a real community feel to the place, plus great shopping and cheap eats (p78) here.

Bur Dubai Highlights

- A visit to **Dubai Museum** (p53) should be high on the list of any Dubai visitor: it's not only an interesting museum, it makes visiting the rest of Dubai's sights more impressive when you see what it looked like circa 1956.
- The **Sheikh Saeed al-Maktoum House** (p55) has been wonderfully restored and holds a unique collection of early photographs of Dubai.
- The re-creation of traditional Bedouin and coastal villages at the **Heritage & Diving Villages** (p54) are wonderful – especially in the cooler months.

AL-BOOM TOURIST VILLAGE
Map pp206-7
next to Al-Garhoud Bridge

This is really just a nice place for a coffee and *sheesha* in traditional *barasti* (palm-leaf house) surroundings, or to have a meal at the Fish-market Floating Restaurant. This enormous restaurant dhow is permanently moored here. The rest of the 'village' is just made up of function rooms which are quite a sight when there's a wedding on. The *sheesha* café livens up in the evenings.

ALI BIN ABI TALEB MOSQUE
Map pp212-13
Ali bin Abi Talib St

Located at the rear of the fabric souq, it's not-able for its sensuous, bulbous domes and gently tapering minaret. While its outline is best admired from Baniyas Rd in Deira, on the opposite side of the Creek, the detail of the exterior is quite beautiful and needs to be seen at close quarters to be appreciated.

BASTAKIA QUARTER Map pp212-13

This district, on the waterfront east of the Bur Dubai Souq and the Diwan, features a number of traditional old wind-tower houses. Built at the turn of the 20th century, these houses were once the homes of wealthy Persian merchants lured to Dubai by its relaxed trade tariffs. Most came from the Bastak district in what is now southern Iran, hence the name Bastakia.

The quarter has been declared a conserva-tion area and restoration work is being car-ried out. As you wander through the narrow, peaceful lanes you can easily imagine the life of the early merchant residents. Notice the original carved wooden doors that remain on some of the houses.

Wind towers (p28) were a traditional form of air-conditioning whereby cool air was fun-nelled down into the house. Some of the wind-tower houses have been fully restored and are private homes. If you pass one of the houses under restoration ask the workmen if you can have a look around. One restored house is home to the **Majlis Gallery** (p55), which is well worth visiting to see some local artwork. You can also visit **XVA** (p56), another wonderfully re-stored house that is a hotel, gallery and café.

CREEKSIDE PARK Map pp210-11
admission Dh5; ☻ **8am-11pm Sat-Wed, 8am-11.30pm Thu, Fri & public holidays, women & children only Wed**

This is the largest of Dubai city's parks, running for 2.6km from Al-Garhoud Bridge, on the Bur Dubai side, towards Al-Maktoum Bridge. It has children's play areas, dhow cruises, kiosks, restaurants, an amphitheatre and beaches (though it's not advisable to swim in the Creek). It's one of the most scenic parks, in a delight-fully artificial way – fancy there being wood-lands in the middle of a desert city! The park also features a 2.5km-long cable-car ride (tick-ets Dh5), 30m above the shore of the Creek, but the ride does start to pall after a while. Another feature is the Al-Aflaj section, which has a reconstruction of a villa from Hatta, Du-bai's mountain enclave, and gardens watered with a *falaj* (traditional irrigation channel).

DIWAN Map pp212-13
Creekside

This impressive building, with its wind tow-ers, modern sculptures and black cast-iron fence, is home to the highest administrative body of the Dubai government, the Diwan. It also houses Sheikh Maktoum's office, which lends the building its other common name, the Ruler's Office.

Heritage & Diving Villages (p54)

DHOW-BUILDING YARD Map pp206-7
Jaddaf

On the Creek waterfront, about 1km south of Al-Garhoud Bridge in the Jaddaf district, is a yard where huge dhows are built in the traditional style – the planks are curved and fitted, one on top of the other, and then the frame is fitted on the inside. (In the West, the frame of a boat is generally built first and the planks are then fitted to it.) The enormous vessels are all built by hand, using just the most basic of tools – a hammer, saw, chisel, drill and plane. Teak, because it's so sturdy, and shesham are the most commonly used woods. Both are imported from Asia. These days dhows are powered by engines rather than sails.

To get to the dhow yard from the Bur Dubai side of the Creek, head along Al-Qataiyat Rd towards Al-Garhoud Bridge. Take the first exit to the right after the Dubai Police Club. Go past the nursery and turn left onto a gravel track just before the Dubai Docking Yard. Follow this track for about 700m as it bends around to the left and you will come to a string of dhow-building yards. You can't miss the enormous hulls of these dhows. If you are coming from the Deira side you will have to cross over Al-Garhoud Bridge then do a U-turn the next opportunity you have to get on the other side of the road.

DUBAI MUSEUM Map pp212-13

☎ 353 1862; Al-Fahidi St; adult/child Dh3/1; ⏲ 8.30am-8.30pm Sat-Thu, 3-9pm Fri

This fascinating museum occupies Al-Fahidi Fort, on the Bur Dubai side of the Creek next to the Diwan. The fort was built in the early 19th century and is thought to be the oldest building in Dubai. For many years it was both the residence of Dubai's rulers and the seat of government, before it became a museum in 1971.

The impressive front door came from the house of Sheikh Saeed al-Maktoum, grandfather of the current ruler. In the entrance is a display of aerial photographs showing the growth of Dubai over the years. As you enter the fort's courtyard, you will see a big tank which was used to carry fresh water on pearling boats. Several small boats are also in the courtyard, including a *shasha*, a small fishing boat made of palm fronds, still used by fishermen around Khor Kalba on the east coast of the UAE. There is also a *barasti* house with a wind tower. Enter during the hotter months and you can really feel the difference that the tower makes.

The hall along the right side of the courtyard has a display on the fort itself and another one featuring *khanjars* (traditional curved daggers) and other traditional weapons. The hall to the left of the courtyard has a video of traditional Emirati dances, a display of musical instruments and more weapons.

The tower at the far corner of the courtyard leads down to a large underground area where the rest of the museum's exhibits are. The first is a slick multimedia presentation of the city's fast development. Then you come to detailed re-creations of a typical souq, a home and a school, as they would have looked in the 1950s. These come complete with disturbingly lifelike dummies and hologramlike video projections. This is followed by a display about water and how it used to be conserved in the desert.

There is also an interactive exhibit on the flora and fauna of the UAE, a display of seafaring life and another on the archaeology of the area, including a complete grave from the Al-Qusais archaeological site. Another room features finds from the digs at both Al-Qusais and Jumeirah (2500 to 500 BC and 6th century AD, respectively).

To get to the museum, if you've come across the Creek by *abra*, walk inland from the dock

---

Dhows

Dhows are just as much a characteristic of Dubai now as they were centuries ago. The **Dhow Wharfage** (p50), set along the Creek, piled high with assorted goods from Iran, India, China and East Africa, gives the city an exotic flavour. Despite the glistening steel and glass buildings that now dominate the Creek waterfront, the dhows give the place an unmistakably oriental feel.

Dubai was once one of the most important dhow-building centres on the Gulf coast. The *al-galalif* (dhow builders) used basic materials and methods to construct the enormous vessels. The development of Dubai's maritime culture is reflected in the large number of different boats they constructed for different purposes. The larger dhows used for long-distance journeys were called *al-boom*, *al-bateel*, and *al-baglah*, and were up to 60m in length. Some of them have now been turned into cruise vessels and floating restaurants. The *sambuq* was a smaller boat, never more than 30m long, which was used mainly for fishing. It was characterised by its single mast and square stern, which had decorative wings protruding from it. *Baggara* (pearling boats) were larger and had no mast. The *abra* is still used to ferry people across the Creek.

for about 100m then turn left onto Al-Fahidi Rd. You'll see the museum on your left. Alternatively, head inland through the Dubai Souq and out the other end through the narrow streets and lanes and you'll eventually come to the museum. If you are catching a taxi, the Arabic word for museum is *mathaf*.

All displays in the museum have explanations in Arabic and English. Photography is not permitted and there is a gift shop just before you exit.

DUBAI WILDLIFE & WATERBIRD SANCTUARY Map pp206-7
Khor Dubai

Dubai's flamingo population can be found here at the southeastern end of the Creek. The flamingos are present in Dubai in the winter months and come from northern Iran. October to March are the best months for birdwatching, as Dubai is on a migratory path. For more on Dubai's bird life see p23. The sanctuary is difficult to stop at because there's no stopping at certain parts of the roads that are adjacent to the park and you will need binoculars to see the birds satisfactorily.

GRAND MOSQUE Map pp212-13
north of Dubai Museum

This multidomed mosque in Bur Dubai boasts the city's tallest minaret. While the mosque might appear to be a beautiful example of restoration work, it was in fact built in the 1990s. Maintaining the style of the original Grand Mosque, which dated from 1900 and was knocked down to make way for another mosque in 1960, its sand-coloured walls and wooden shutters blend in perfectly with the surrounding old quarter of Bur Dubai. As well as being the centre of Dubai's religious and cultural life, the original Grand Mosque was also home to the town's *kuttab* (Quranic school) where children learnt to recite the Quran from memory.

HERITAGE & DIVING VILLAGES
Map pp212-13
Al-Shindagha Rd; 7.30am-2pm & 3-9pm

These villages are on the Creek in the heart of the old Shindaga area. The **Heritage Village** (393 7151) re-creates traditional Bedouin and coastal village life, complete with *barasti* homes, a traditional coffeehouse and a small souq where you can buy freshly made *dosa* (a flat, grilled bread made of flour and water). There are also some traditional pottery and weaving workshops. The folks working here are very hospitable; it's well worth stopping by and chatting over a coffee. The other shops in the souq sell rather nice traditional handicrafts, Bedouin jewellery and pottery, as well as souvenirs from India, Africa and Asia.

There is also a small **museum** displaying artefacts and diagrams from archaeological sites at Al-Qusais, on the northeastern outskirts of town, Jumeirah, and Al-Sufouf, near Hatta. Finds from the Al-Qusais site (2500–550 BC) include human skeletons, bronze arrowheads, stone vessels, daggers, hooks, needles and pottery collected from around 120 graves. At Al-Sufouf, a circular collective tomb was discovered, much like the one at the **Hili Gardens & Archaeological Park** (p165) in Al-Ain. It suggests that this society belonged to the Umm an-Nar culture, which rose near modern Abu Dhabi. Little is known about it, except that it was probably part of the Bahrain-based Dilmun empire, which was then the ascendant power in the central and northern Gulf. More than 50 individual tombs were discovered, most of which were looted over the centuries. Finds from intact tombs include jars, jewels, beads and weapons.

The **Diving Village** (393 9390) has displays on pearl diving, once the livelihood of the city, and scale models of various types of dhows and pearling boats.

Grand Mosque (above)

You will notice some signs along the water-front here offering boat cruises for Dh100 per hour. If you want to take a boat ride it's better to make a deal with one of the many skippers who cruise up and down this area; you should only pay Dh40 for half an hour or Dh60 for one hour.

KARAMA SHOPPING CENTRE
Map pp214-15
Karama; 🕙 9am-10.30pm Sat-Thu, 9-11am & 4-10.30pm Fri

Karama is the district where the sales assistant you met on your last shopping excursion probably lives. Where does she go shopping? Karama Shopping Centre, which consists of two streets, running parallel, lined with shops selling luggage, clothes, jewellery and souvenirs (there seem to be lots of men whispering 'Rolex' and 'DVD' as you wander around). There are heaps of imitation goods here – if you like that kind of thing – but there's also some pretty kitsch stuff (see p124), as well as good souvenirs that are cheaper than in downtown Deira.

MAJLIS GALLERY Map pp212-13
☎ 353 6233; Al-Fahidi Roundabout; 🕙 9.30am-1.30pm & 4-7.30pm Sat-Thu

This gallery, in an old house in Bur Dubai's Bastakia neighbourhood, exhibits the paintings of local artists. There are also some handicrafts on display, such as cushion covers and bags, ceramics, glassware and sculpture. Most, but not all, of the paintings have some sort of local connection – Islamic calligraphy or desert

scenes for example. The owner has lived here for almost 20 years and has a wealth of knowledge of the local arts scene.

SHEIKH SAEED AL-MAKTOUM HOUSE Map pp212-13
☎ 393 7139; Al-Shindagha Rd; adult/child Dh2/1; 🕙 8.30am-9pm Sat-Thu, 3-10pm Fri

The house of Sheikh Saeed, the grandfather of Dubai's present ruler, has been restored as a museum of preoil times. It sits along the Creek waterfront, next to the Heritage and Diving Villages, on the Bur Dubai side in the Shindagha area. The 30-room house was built in 1896 during the reign of Sheikh Maktoum bin Hasher al-Maktoum. For many years it served as a communal residence for the Al-Maktoum family, in keeping with the Arabian tradition of having several generations living in separate apartments within the same house or compound. Sheikh Saeed lived here from 1888 until his death in 1958. The house was reopened as a museum in 1986 and houses an exhibition of photographs, mainly from the 1940s, '50s and '60s, documenting the history and development of Dubai. It is amazing to see how different the place looked only a few decades ago, making you realise just how quickly Dubai has developed from a sleepy Gulf fishing village into the leading metropolis of the region.

Some of the photographs date from the 19th century and there are fascinating shots of traditional life in Dubai taken in souqs and at celebrations such as Tawminah, the festival carried out on completion of the recitation of the Quran by school children. Traditional Bedouin life is also represented, and there are models of the different sorts of dhows used in Dubai. There is also a model of Bur Dubai from the 1950s.

There is a display of coins that were once used in the region, which were sometimes given unusual new names. Coins featuring Edward VII were known as umm salaah (bald headed). Until 1965 the Indian rupee (both the British Raj version and the Republic of India version) was the official currency, whereas between 1966 and 1973 Dubai and Qatar issued their own currency, called the riyal. The UAE dirham was adopted in 1973. There is a small display of postage stamps, too. Before the oil economy got going, the sale of stamps to overseas collectors was a handy little earner for the sheikhs of the future UAE.

The two-storey house, built around a court-yard, has a wind tower at each corner and is divided into four wings. Near the entrance is the main *majlis* and a room that was once set aside for the sheikh's clerk. The house is built of coral quarried from the Gulf and then covered with lime and plaster. Until recently this was a common building method along both the Gulf and Red Sea coasts of Arabia, and you can see more examples of it around Bastakia in Dubai and in the **Heritage Area** (p153) of Sharjah.

The gift shop sells souvenirs and is where you'll find a guide to the house.

XVA Map pp212-13
☎ 353 5383; xva@xvagallery.com; behind Basta Art Café, Al-Musallah Roundabout
One of Bastakia's recently restored residences features a central courtyard housing an art gallery and café. It's also a boutique hotel (p144) and a peaceful retreat from traffic chaos less than a block away.

SHEIKH ZAYED ROAD
Eating p80; Shopping p131; Sleeping p144
While everyone drives down this road in a hurry to get to Media City or Abu Dhabi, it's worth turning off and heading for a hotel with a view to check out the architecture on this strip. Several hotels have opened up here in the last couple of years and Sheikh Zayed Rd appears to be host to some free-form architectural jazz, where each new development riffs the last.

Neighbourhoods – Sheikh Zayed Road

EMIRATES TOWERS Map p218
☎ 330 0000; www.emiratestowershotel.com; Sheikh Zayed Rd
From some angles Emirates Towers look like strategically placed scalpel blades touching the sky and are the most satisfying design of the ambitious Jumeirah International group – at least until Madinat Jumeirah is finished. The taller of the two is the business tower – taller than the **Burj Al Arab** (p146) at 355m – and the shorter is the hotel. Take the glass lift up as far as it goes and then hop into the other lift to **Vu's Bar** (p94), giving you a fantastic view of the Sheikh Zayed metropolis. If you really like the view you can book a table at **Vu's restaurant** (p82).

Joining the two towers at ground level is the **Emirates Towers Shopping Boulevard** (p131).

NAD AL-SHEBA CLUB Map pp206-7
☎ 336 3666; www.nadalshebaclub.com; Nad al-Sheba district, 5km southeast of Dubai centre; morning stable tour adult/child Dh130/60; ⊙ 7am Sat, Mon & Wed Sep-Jun
Lovers of all things equine should not miss a chance to check out these world-class stables. The visit starts with a look at the morning training, followed by a guided tour around the thoroughbred training facilities. You'll enjoy an excellent breakfast at Spikes restaurant, then get to check out the Millennium Grandstand and walk through the Godolphin Gallery – an impressive trophy room. There are displays documenting the development of Godolphin Stables, but alas, no explanation as to why that Melbourne Cup win keeps eluding them!

SAFA PARK Map pp206-7
cnr Al-Wasl Rd & Al-Hadiqa St, Safa; admission Dh5; ⊙ 8am-11pm, women & children only Tue
This park stretches for 1km from Al-Wasl Rd to Sheikh Zayed Rd. It is one of the most colourful in Dubai and very popular with local residents. Cricket is played on the wide grassy expanses at weekends. One attraction is its small-scale models of famous landmarks from around the world, such as the Taj Mahal and the Colosseum. There is a lake where you can hire paddle boats, tennis courts, a soccer pitch, barbecues and an artificial waterfall.

From the Desert to the Derby

From the Desert to the Derby: Inside the Ruling Family of Dubai's Billion-Dollar Quest to Win America's Greatest Horse Race, by Jason Levin, doesn't just chronicle the Godolphin Stables as yet unsuccessful attempts to win the Kentucky Derby, it takes a fascinating and wide look at the thoroughbred scene in general. Interestingly, Levin explains how the stallions that started the thoroughbred breed in the United States were originally from the Middle East. It's full of race facts but is mostly an entertaining read of how this Dubai-based stable has sought to capture every Group 1 race in the world.

JUMEIRAH

Eating p82; Shopping p132; Sleeping p146

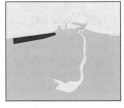

This stretch of coast is home to Dubai's busy beach resorts. It's a residential area too, and turning in either direction off Jumeirah Rd will allow you to have a snoop around some of the villas in the area. Many of the residents earn big money and there's usually a Mercedes and an expensive 4WD in the double driveways of these villas. The wives of these well-rewarded gentlemen have earned themselves a nickname – the Jumeirah Janes, similar to 'ladies who lunch'. To service the local residents there is an increasing number of cafés and shopping centres in the area and many residents believe this area is now the 'new Dubai centre'.

This stretch is home to some of the most remarkable construction projects on earth. The artificial islands of **The Palm** (see the boxed text on p137) can be seen from space and the image of the Burj Al Arab is associated with Dubai in the same way the Opera House is in Sydney. This being Dubai, there is more to come – but it's hard to imagine what could overtake the Burj's iconic status.

BURJ AL ARAB Map pp206-7

☎ 301 7000; www.burj-al-arab.com; Jumeirah Rd, Umm Suqeim

Built on an artificial island 280m offshore from the Jumeirah Beach Hotel, the 320m-high hotel is home to 202 suites – each with its own private butler. The hotel has a stunning exterior, taller than the Eiffel Tower, and a helipad resembling half of Star Trek's Starship Enterprise.

DUBAI ZOO Map pp216-17

☎ 349 6444; Jumeirah Rd; admission Dh3; ☼ 10am-6pm Wed-Mon

This zoo is rumoured to be closing its gates and a new one is planned to open next to Mushrif Park, on the outskirts of Dubai. This current zoo is a rather grim place; the animals are well cared for, but there just isn't enough room. The zoo was originally a private collection, but more and more cages and enclosures have been crammed in to accommodate the animals. If the sight and smell of animals in poor conditions upsets you, give this place a miss.

GREEN ART GALLERY Map pp216-17

☎ 344 9888; www.gagallery.com; 51 St, behind Dubai Zoo; ☼ 9.30am-1.30pm & 4.30-8.30pm Sat-Thu

This altruistic gallery focuses on local artists, regardless of nationality, and is committed to nurturing talent by educating artists about international art distribution and promotion. Exhibitions change regularly, and its website has information on opening nights and features selections from upcoming and past exhibitions.

Jumeirah Highlights

- The **Burj Al Arab** (p57) is Dubai's iconic landmark that doubles as a hotel.
- **Wild Wadi Waterpark** (p60) is one that doesn't look like a Lego set.
- **Jumeirah Beach Park** (p58) is the best place for an ocean dip outside the beach hotels.

IRANIAN MOSQUE Map pp216-17

Al-Wasl Rd

It's worth a quick drive to Satwa to see the stunning Iranian Mosque and, opposite it, the **Iranian Hospital**. The incredibly detailed design of the brilliant blue mosaic work is typical of Iranian buildings.

JUMEIRAH ARCHAEOLOGICAL SITE

This site is considered one of the biggest and most significant archaeological sites in the UAE. Remains found here date from the 6th century AD and can be seen in the small museum at the **Heritage Village** (p54) in Shinda-gha. The settlement is particularly interesting in that it spans the pre-Islamic and Islamic eras. Surrounded by modern villas and shopping centres, this was once a caravan station on a route linking Ctesiphon (in what is now Iraq) to northern Oman.

Remains at the site link it with the Persian Sassanian empire, the dominant culture in the region from the 3rd to the 6th century AD. The Sassanids were wiped out by Arab tribes, notably the Umayyad dynasty, with the coming of Islam in the 7th century. The Umayyads

1001 Nights at the Burj

1001 Arabian Nights at the Burj Al Arab, by Khuan Chew and Uschi Schmitt, is a glossy 160-page coffee-table book featuring more than 200 photos of the world's most jaw-dropping hotel. The photography is superb.

extended and restored many of the original buildings and the site continued to exist until at least the 10th century.

Excavations have revealed a series of stone walls that surrounded a souq with seven shops and a storage room. There are remains of a few houses, including a large courtyard house with decorative plaster work that was most likely the governor's palace (this kind of decoration can still be seen on restored houses in Dubai, such as in the Al-Ahmadiya district and along the waterfront in Bur Dubai).

There's no public access to the site. If archaeologists are working, you may be able to have a look inside, otherwise you will just have to peek through the fence.

To reach the site, head south down Jumeirah Rd and do a U-turn when you get to the Jumeirah Beach Park, just past the Jumeirah Beach Club. Take the first street on the right,

27 St, and continue straight to the end, then turn right; you will see a large fenced-in area about 50m along on your left.

JUMEIRAH BEACH PARK Map pp206-7

Jumeirah Rd; admission/car Dh5/20; 8am-11pm, women & children only Sat & Mon

This wonderful park fronts onto Jumeirah Beach and a walk on the grass is a real treat – it's a couple of degrees cooler than the beach. There is a children's play area, barbeques, picnic tables, walkways and kiosks. The stretch of beach is clean and lined with date palms for shade. Lifeguards are on duty between 8am and 6pm – keep in mind that unpatrolled beaches in Dubai can be dangerous due to strong currents. We recommend this beach for women who don't want to pay a small fortune to use one of the hotel beach clubs, but also don't want to risk unwanted male attention they may receive at other public beaches.

Next to the Dubai Marine Beach Resort & Spa, just off Jumeirah Rd, more or less opposite the Jumeirah Mosque, there is a stretch of **public beach** with facilities, including showers, shelters and toilets, and plenty of date palms. A little further away from town, north of the

Jumeirah Mosque (opposite)

The Five Pillars of Islam

Shahada The profession of faith: 'There is no god but Allah, and Mohammed is his Prophet'.

Salat Muslims are required to pray five times every day: at dawn, noon, midafternoon, sunset and twilight. During prayers a Muslim must perform a series of prostrations while facing the Kaaba, the ancient shrine at the centre of the Grand Mosque in Mecca. Before a Muslim can pray, however, he or she must perform a series of ritual ablutions, and if no water is available for this purpose, sand or soil may be substituted.

Zakat Muslims must give a portion of their income to help the poor. How this has operated in practice has varied over the centuries: either it was seen as an individual duty or the state collected it as a form of income tax to be redistributed through mosques or religious charities.

Sawm It was during the month of Ramadan that the Prophet Mohammed received his first revelation in AD 610. Muslims mark this event by fasting from sunrise until sunset throughout Ramadan. During the fast a Muslim may not take anything into his or her body. Food, drink, smoking and sex are banned. Young children, travellers and those whose health will not permit it are exempt from the fast, though those who are able to do so are supposed to make up the days they missed at a later time.

Haj All able Muslims are required to make the pilgrimage to Mecca at least once in their lifetime, if possible during a specific few days in the first and second weeks of the Muslim month of Dhul Hijja. Visiting Mecca and performing the prescribed rituals at any other time of the year is considered spiritually desirable. Such visits are referred to as *umrah* (little pilgrimages).

Jumeirah Beach Hotel, there is the **Umm Suqeim public beach**, which has hardly any facilities apart from a couple of rudimentary shelters. There are patches of beach between the hotels south of here, but they're quickly being filled up with more hotels and developments.

JUMEIRAH MOSQUE Map pp216-17
☎ 353 6666; Jumeirah Rd; admission free; ☽ 10am Thu & Sun

This is the best-known mosque in Dubai due to its size and elaborate design. While the best time to see it is at night when it is spectacularly lit up, this is one mosque in Dubai that you can visit. Under the auspices of the Sheikh Mohammed Centre for Cultural Understanding, the 'Open Doors. Open Minds' tour of the mosque is open to non-Muslims. As well as taking visitors through the architecture of the mosque, the visit is a chance for visitors to gain a better understanding of Islam (see the boxed text above) and UAE culture. There's a Q&A session that is a key part of the visit and it's best to prebook the tour so guides have an idea of the numbers, but you can turn up five minutes before and join the tour.

MAJLIS GHORFAT UM-AL-SHEEF
Map pp206-7
17 St; admission Dh1; ☽ 8.30am-1.30pm & 3.30-8.30pm Sat-Thu, 3.30-8.30pm Fri

It is unusual to find a traditional building still standing so far from the Creek, but this one,

south of Jumeirah Beach Park, has been well restored and is worth a visit. The two-storey building was built in 1955 and was attended in the evenings by Sheikh Rashid bin Saeed al-Maktoum. Here he would listen to his people's complaints, grievances and ideas. It was a place of open discussion and exchange. A former British political resident of Dubai, Donald Hawley, saw the *majlis* as 'an Arabian Camelot' and Sheikh Rashid as 'King Arthur'.

The *majlis* also provided a cool retreat from the heat of the day. It is made of gypsum and coral rock, traditional building materials of the Gulf, and the roof is made of *areesh* (palm fronds). The ground floor is an open area surrounded by columns and the floor above consists of a veranda on one side and the enclosed *majlis* on the other. The columns, windows and doors are all made of Indian teak. The *majlis* is decorated with cushions, rugs, a coffeepot, pottery and food platters, and is close to the way it would have looked in Sheikh Rashid's day. Windows surround the room and, in the summer heat, the breeze circulates freely around the house, keeping it relatively cool.

A garden of date palms and fig trees has been constructed around the *majlis*, and a traditional *barasti* café sits in one corner of the enclosure. The garden, with its *falaj*, needs to mature a little, but the sound of running water is very soothing and, though it's in the middle of a residential area, it's very peaceful. The *majlis* is just past the Jumeirah Beach Park.

TOTAL ARTS Map pp206-7

☎ 228 2888; www.courtyard-uae.com; Courtyard, Al-Quoz; 10am-1pm & 4-8pm Sat-Thu

The galleries in this unique courtyard space hold changing exhibitions of painting, calligraphy, mixed media, miniatures, rare Persian carpets and sculptures by local and Middle Eastern artists. The website has information on the artists and an online store – in case you like your purchase so much, you may want to buy more when you get back home!

WILD WADI WATERPARK Map pp206-7

☎ 348 4444; www.wildwadi.com; Jumeirah Rd; adult/child Dh95/75; ⏰ 11am-7pm Sep-May, 1-9pm Jun-Aug

Close to eight million litres of water are pumped through the 5-hectare park's various tunnels, tubes, slides, caves and pools daily. The 24 rides are all interconnected so that you can get off one and jump straight onto another. Some of the hairier rides reach speeds of 80km/h, while the Jumeirah Sceirah is the highest and fastest free-fall water slide outside North America. There are two Flowriders (stationary waves) as well as more sedate rides for younger kids and slightly nervous adults, and plenty of lifeguards on duty.

The design of the park, with its sand- and stone-coloured structures, is based around a legend in which the Arabic adventurer Juha and his friend Sinbad the Sailor are shipwrecked on a lush lagoon, beyond which lies a magical oasis. The design blends in with the natural surroundings fairly well. There are two restaurants and a few kiosks where you can buy food and drinks with a special credit card attached to your wrist. The balance is refunded when you leave. Towels and lockers can be rented for Dh5, and body boards and tubes are free. During summer there's a ladies-only day on Thursday.

Walking Tours

Walking Tours

While Dubai is a sprawling metropolis, the older parts of Bur Dubai and Deira are ideal for walking excursions. These areas are quite small and the features worth seeing are all fairly close together. Apart from these, the rest of Dubai's attractions are too spread out for a walking tour, so we've included one for Sharjah as it has a great heritage area and it's only – traffic willing – a short trip away.

Both the Dubai tours can be done within half a day, broken up with an *abra* (water taxi) ride and a stop for refreshment. If you are in Dubai when it is hot, you may want to do one walking tour in the early morning and the other in the early evening. The Sharjah tour should take a couple of hours and can be combined with a shopping trip.

BUR DUBAI

Start this walking tour midmorning, opposite the UK embassy on Al-Seef Rd. Stroll along the waterfront, admiring the modern architecture of Deira on the opposite side of the Creek. Note where **Fatafeet** (p79) is, as you may want to return to this excellent Egyptian/Lebanese restaurant one evening.

At the roundabout at the end of Al-Seef Rd, cross the road to the **Bastakia Quarter 1** (p52)

Walk Facts

Start Al-Seef Rd waterfront.

End Diving Village.

Distance 3km.

Duration Four hours (including museum visit).

Basta Art Café (p78)

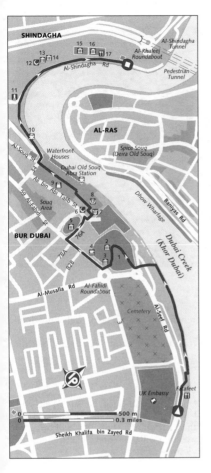

and spend time exploring the atmospheric narrow streets and admiring the beautifully restored courtyard houses. Here you'll find a number of attractions: a part of the original city walls; the **XVA hotel and gallery 2** (p56) where you can check out the art exhibition and appreciate the building's restoration; the **Majlis Gallery 3** (p55), which is housed in another restored wind-tower house; and the **Basta Art Café 4** (p78), where you can grab a quick cup of coffee or cold drink, depending on what time of year it is.

Head along Al-Fahidi St, in the opposite direction to Al–Fahidi Roundabout, until you arrive at the **Dubai Museum 5** (p53); the entrance to the museum is on 76A St. You can easily spend an hour here learning about the history, heritage and development of Dubai, and enjoying the kitsch dioramas.

After emerging from the museum, walk down 76A St to view the multidomed **Grand Mosque 6** (p54). When you visit the Sheikh Saeed al-Maktoum House (number 13 on this tour) you will see old photos of Dubai showing the original Grand Mosque.

Walk past the right side of the mosque and in the alley directly behind it is the Hindu **Shri Nathje Jayate Temple 7** (p51). You may notice lots of shoes at the base of a flight of stairs – this is the way up to the **Sikh Gurdwara 8** (p51).

From here continue through the narrow streets – you are now in the restored **Bur Dubai Souq 9** (p120). If you head towards the Creek, past the recently refurbished wooden stores, you will come to a lovely open area on the waterfront. You can look over to the Deira side and admire the restored wind towers that form part of the Spice Souq (Deira Old Souq), and watch the general activity on the Creek. Look to your left to see the renovated waterfront houses. Head back in the direction from which you came, turning right back into the souq. Wind your way northwards through the small streets lined with textile shops. Once you have wandered through the souq, you will come out at its western entrance. The **Bur Dubai abra station 10** should be ahead of you and to your right. On the corner you will see a small, nameless stand selling gorgeous curly-toed Aladdin slippers from Afghanistan and Pakistan. Walk past the *abras* and continue along the waterfront to the **Shindagha Tower 11**. Built in 1910, it differs from other watchtowers in the UAE in that it is square rather than round.

The tour now takes you further along this peaceful stretch of waterfront towards the mouth of the Creek. Soon you'll see the **Bin Suroor Mosque 12**, a tiny restored mosque originally built in 1930 and frequented by nearby workers. Next to this is the **Sheikh Saeed al-Maktoum House 13** (p55), once the residence of the ruling family of Dubai and now home to a magnificent collection of old black-and-white photographs of the city. The **Sheikh Juma al-Maktoum House 14**, nearby, is another noble old Shindagha house. Further along this part of the waterfront you will find the **Heritage Village 15** (p54) and the **Diving Village 16** (p54) where you can easily while away an hour or so. After an insight into Emirati traditional life, return to the

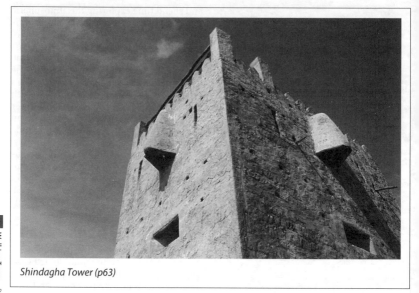

Shindagha Tower (p63)

waterfront and **Kan Zaman restaurant** 17 (p79), where you can enjoy a tasty Arabic lunch and watch the Creek life float by.

After a rest, you could head to the *abra* dock, cross the Creek and begin the walking tour of Deira, or save it for another day.

DEIRA

Begin at the **Sabkha abra station** 1, on the corner of Baniyas and Al-Sabkha Rds. Walk north along Al-Sabkha Rd and turn left onto Al-Suq al-Kabeer St, just past the Al-Khaleej Hotel, which is on your right. Turn right into 33B St then left onto 20D St. This will bring you into the hustle and bustle of Deira. As you head west you will pass shops selling goods such as textiles, clothes, rugs and luggage. This area is known as the **Murshid Souq** 2. You probably won't buy anything, but the ethnic diversity of the sellers and shoppers gives it a unique commercial verve.

When you get to Suq Deira St turn left and immediately right back on to Al-Suq al-Kabeer St. This brings you to the wooden entrance of the **Spice Souq** 3 (see the boxed text on p120) with its pungent aromas of cardamom, cloves and cinnamon. There's no set route you should take, just wander around and enjoy.

If you continue southwest you will eventually come out on Al-Abra St. Turn right

Walk Facts

Start Sabkha abra station and Al-Sabkha Rd.

End Naif Park.

Distance 3km.

Duration Two to three hours (excluding souq shopping).

then left onto Al-Ras St, the next main street. Walk until you get to Al-Hadd St and turn right. Al-Hadd St is lined with shops selling sacks of spices, nuts and pulses. At the end of this street turn right into Al-Ahmadiya St. About 50m along is the restored **Heritage House 4** (p50). Behind this is the equally well-restored **Al-Ahmadiya School 5** (p49).

Continuing along Al-Ahmadiya St, turn right into Old Baladiya St; ahead you will see the wooden latticed archway of the entrance to Dubai's famous **Deira Gold Souq 6** (see the boxed text on p120). When you come out at the other end (usually poorer than when you entered),

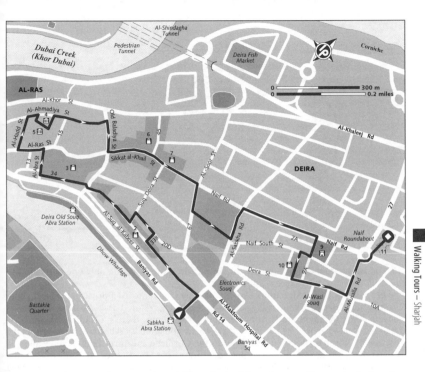

continue in the same direction along Sikkat al-Khail St and you will pass the **Perfume Souq 7** (p124), a string of shops selling Arabic and European perfumes. After passing through the Perfume Souq, you will see a roundabout. Turn right into 107 St where you will find trinket shops selling kitsch souvenirs.

Tucked behind the shops lining the east side (left side) of Al-Soor St is the **Deira Covered Souq 8** (p120), which sells everything from *sheeshas* (water pipes) to henna. Turn left and head through the souq. You will come out onto Al-Sabkha Rd, near the bus station. Turn left here then right into Naif Rd.

Follow Naif Rd and turn right into 9A St. As you round the corner you will see an **old fort 9** on your left, now a police station. Further along is **Naif Souq 10**. This small, covered souq is popular with women buying *abeyyas* (women's traditional full-length robes), headscarves, materials, perfumes and children's clothes. A walk through here will bring you to Deira St, on the souq's south side. Turn left into Deira St and walk to Al-Musalla Rd. Turn left into Al-Musalla Rd and on the next corner is **Naif Park 11**, which is a nice place to rest and end your Deira walking tour.

SHARJAH

Starting in the Heritage Area, the first stop is the **Al-Hisn Fort 1** (p153). After visiting here cross Al-Borj Ave and head across to Al-Borj Rd, which is one block west. Turn right and ahead of you is the **Sharjah Islamic Museum 2** and the **Sharjah Heritage Museum 3**, housed in a historic building that is the former home of the Al-Naboodah family. Behind the Heritage Museum is the **Majlis**

Walk Facts

Start Sharjah Heritage Area.
End Al-Majarrah Souq.
Distance 2km.
Duration Two hours.

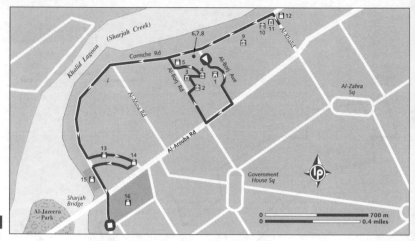

of Ibrahim Mohammed al-Midfa 4 – notice the round wind tower; it's the only one of its kind in the Gulf.

After visiting these attractions, make your way back onto Al-Borj Rd and head right, towards the water. On your right you'll see the lovely restored **Souq al-Arsah 5**. As well as housing some excellent crafts, souvenir and carpet shops, there's a traditional **coffeehouse 6** and **restaurant 7**, as well as a beautifully restored hotel, the **Dar al-Dhyafa 8**. Next stop is the noteworthy **Sharjah Art Museum 9**. Head out to the Corniche and turn right. You'll walk past Al-Borj Ave and the entrance is signposted on your right. A couple of doors down from the museum is the **Very Special Arts Centre 10**, which is both a workshop and a gallery for disabled artists, and the **Emirates Fine Arts Society 11**, which displays the works of local artists.

If you head back to the Corniche and keep walking east, you'll come across the gold-domed **Al-Majarrah Souq 12**, selling textiles, perfumes and clothes. From here, if you have time, you can walk back along the Corniche and visit the **Fruit & Vegetable Souq 13**, **Meat Souq 14**, **Fish Souq 15** and the **Central Market 16** (also known as the Blue Souq and famous for Omani silver jewellery, carpets and souvenirs).

Eating

Eating

The rich cultural mix of Dubai's population is echoed in the myriad choices of restaurants and coffee shops across the city. From the simplest Indo-Pakistani workers café in Karama to the gastronomic delights and décor of eateries at the One&Only Royal Mirage, Dubai offers a huge range of dining experiences.

You can start the day with a caffeine fix and a pastry at one of Dubai's long-standing cafés, such as Café Gerard in Jumeirah, grab some takeaway Indian finger food near the Gold Souq and dine at the latest restaurant overseen by Michelin-starred chefs.

There are hundreds of fast food outlets in Dubai. All the usual global brands are here, and a quick trip to a shopping mall food court should have all you need for a junk-food fix. But why not grab one of the best fast foods ever invented – the shwarma (strips of grilled meat or chicken on Lebanese bread). For more on food see p14.

Booking Tables

Generally speaking, you should always book tables at hotel restaurants, while for cheaper eateries this is not normally necessary. Restaurants usually want a mobile phone number when you book and the top-end restaurants will call you if you're late for a booking. Bookings for Wednesday and Thursday night, as well as Friday brunch (roughly the weekend in Dubai), are best made a couple of days in advance. There are an increasing number of 'gourmet' nights in Dubai, where a degustation menu is offered; check with the restaurant when making a booking.

Business Hours

Restaurant hours are generally from noon to 3pm and from 7.30pm to midnight, while the cheap eats are generally open from 9am to midnight. Most places are open seven days a week, with the exception being Friday lunch, when some of the smaller local eateries are closed. In the top-end restaurants, if you want to eat like a local resident, your booking should be for 8.30pm or 9pm (but of course you'll arrive late because of the traffic). For

Pyramids complex, Wafi City (p131)

Arabic/Lebanese restaurants that feature live music, an 11pm reservation is fashionable, as the entertainment usually continues until 3am.

How Much?

Street food such as a shwarma, costs around Dh5 and in local restaurants dishes, such as Indian curry, are about Dh8 to Dh10 (see the Cheap Eats listings in each neighbourhood section). At mid-range eateries expect to pay around Dh25 to Dh35 for a main course, while at the top end, prices are around Dh65 to Dh100. What really bumps the price of a meal into the stratosphere is alcohol. Alcohol can only be sold in restaurants/bars attached to hotels (in practice, three-star hotels or better) and some clubs, and the prices are pretty outrageous – expect to pay around Dh18 for a pint of beer or a glass of wine, and closer to Dh25 at a nightclub. Even the most ordinary bottle of plonk will set you back at least Dh85 a bottle. See the boxed text (p70) for recommendations that ease the pain of paying Dh100 for a Dh10 bottle of wine.

Self-Catering

Those interested in self-catering will find plenty of small grocery stores around Deira, Bur Dubai, Karama, Satwa and Rigga. They sell a good range of basic groceries, as well as a small selection of fruit and vegetables, although these are not always of the best quality.

For fresh fruit and vegetables the best place is the enormous **Fruit & Vegetable Market** (Map pp208-9) in Deira, near the Al-Shindagha Tunnel. Food is exported from here to Qatar, Oman and Bahrain. A huge range of fruit and vegetables is available, imported from Europe, Asia and the Middle East. Another part of the complex houses the Fish & Meat Market – collectively it's often called the **Shindagha Market** (☺ 7am-11pm). There are no fixed prices, so bargaining is the order of the day. Note that it is moving to the Abu Hail district (a suburb near the airport) in late 2004. Further up Al-Khaleej Rd, near Hamriya Port, the **Wholesale Market** (Map pp208-9; ☺ 7am-11pm) is even cheaper, but most sales are in bulk quantities. Again, haggling is the norm. The huge parking area is usually filled with trucks bringing in produce from Oman.

There are some great delicatessens around town where you can buy delicious treats; try **Goodies** (p129).

One of the biggest supermarket chains is the French-based Carrefour, which has branches at **Deira** (Map pp212-13) and **Deira City Centre** (Map pp210-11, see also p126). It's best to visit in the mornings for the wonderful seafood and to avoid the late afternoon and evening crowds. The North American Spinney's is the most popular supermarket with Western expats and stocks some brands the expats can't live without. There are branches on **Abu Baker Al-Siddiq Rd** (Map pp208-9) in Deira; on **Al-Mankhool Rd** (Map pp212-13), opposite Al-Rolla Rd; on **Sheikh Khalifa bin Zayed Rd** (Map pp212-13), near the corner with Kuwait St; on **Jumeirah Rd** (Map pp216-17); on **Al-Wasl Rd** (Map pp206-7) in Safa; and at **Mercato Mall** (Map pp216-17) on Jumeirah Rd. All are open from 8am to midnight daily.

Choithrams, catering for the Indian and Pakistani communities, has much the same stuff as Spinney's at considerably lower prices. Along with Spinney's, Choithrams sells pork products. You'll find Choithrams at the corner of **Al-Rolla** and **Al-Mankhool Rds** (Map pp212-13), next to Al-Khaleej Shopping Centre, and on **Al-Wasl Rd** (Map pp206-7), near Safa Park.

Safestway (Map pp206-7; Sheikh Zayed Rd), near Interchange No 1, has a better bakery and delicatessen section than Choithrams, but is a little out of the way for most people. Union Co-op Society has a good selection of cheap groceries, but no pork products. There is one branch on **Al-Wasl Rd** (Map pp206-7), near Safa Park, and a second on **Sheikh Khalifa bin Zayed Rd** (Map pp214-15) in Mankhool.

Tipping

Tipping is not compulsory and not necessarily expected, which may explain some of the comical 'service' that happens all too often in Dubai. A tip of up to 5% to 10% is generally the rule if you're happy with the service.

The Delicious Dozen

Dubai has only two alcohol importers, so the same wines pop up on wine lists all over town. Luckily, those available are a decent mix of Old and New World. We sat down with Dubai's best sommelier, Luca Gagliardi, from Gordon Ramsay's Verre, and came up with a dozen wines that should match just about every dish placed in front of you.

Alamos Chardonnay, Nicolas Catena

Argentina; around Dh185

Tasting notes Exotic fruit on the nose with a hint of oak. On the palate lots of pear, mango and pineapple aromas, and has a good length finish.

Try it with Drink it alfresco, or try it with tapas, fish with light sauces and pasta in creamy sauces.

Chateau d'Armajan des Ormes Sauternes

France, Bordeaux; around Dh95 per glass

Tasting notes Rich yellow-gold colour with aromas of peach, pineapple and honey on the nose. On the palate has medium sweetness with fruit aromas at the end. Long finish with good acidity.

Try it with Foie gras, instead of dessert, or with a creamy dessert, such as *crème brûlée*.

Domain Laroche Chablis

France, Bordeaux; around Dh250

Tasting notes Flinty nose with citrus and pineapple flavour. Dry on the palate with fresh fruit, mineral aromas and good acidity.

Try it with Fish with a cream or butter sauce and white meat dishes.

Evans & Tate Margaret River Shiraz

Australia, Margaret River; around Dh250

Tasting notes A bouquet of dense forest berries and spices, flavourful on the palate with great balance between the peppery aromas and the fruit – a big wine with a long finish.

Try it with Spicy meat dishes such as Indian tandoori, venison, marinated game, beef in wine sauces or barbecue.

Kanonkop Pinotage

South Africa; around Dh290

Tasting notes A smoky nose with complex flavours of black cherries, chocolate and bananas. Smooth and rich on the palate, it's a very balanced wine with flavour and silky tannins.

Try it with Duck dishes in sauces such as sherry vinegar, lamb with rich sauces, game dishes and on its own as an after-dinner drink.

Leeuwin Estate Prelude Vineyards Chardonnay

Australia, Margaret River; around Dh295

Tasting notes Peach and mango with a hint of vanilla on the nose. Well rounded with tropical fruit on the palate and a buttery note at the finish.

Try it with Seafood and fish in buttery sauce, white meats in light sauce, pasta and rice dishes.

Montes Alpha Cabernet Sauvignon

Chile; around Dh300

Tasting notes Full of blueberries and blackberries, with lots of tobacco and spices from the French oak on the nose. On the palate it's full of forest fruits, combined with cedar wood and chocolate.

Try it with Beef in rich sauces, complex casserole or barbecued meats.

Pinot Grigio 'Maso Lamm', Alto Adige, Della Staffa

Italy, Alto Adige; around Dh235

Tasting notes Oranges with hints of honey on the nose. Quite full bodied on the palate with ripe pear, apple and citrus aromas and a very dry finish.

Try it with Salads, seafood and fish, with olive oil and lemon dressing.

Sancerre Domaine Pascal Jolivet

France, Loire; around Dh320

Tasting notes Apple peel and earthy aromas on the nose. On the palate it's grassy with lots of grapefruit and has hints of mineral at the finish.

Try it with Seafood, fish with light sauces.

Scotchmans Hill Pinot Noir

Australia, Geelong; around Dh240

Tasting notes Aromas of cherry, game and toasted oak on the nose, with the flavour of strawberries and black cherry on the palate and a smooth, well-rounded finish.

Try it with Game dishes with light sauces, lamb, pigeon, Mediterranean dishes, Lebanese mezze and white meats in rich sauces.

Stonehedge Merlot

USA, California; around Dh195

Tasting notes Spices, ripe cherry and plum aromas with hints of mocha on the nose, warm and peppery on the palate, with smooth tannins and a note of chocolate and anise at the finish.

Try it with Mild Indian food, lamb chops in rich sauces, light red meat casseroles, English turkey with classic garnish.

Villa Maria Private Bin Marlborough Sauvignon Blanc

New Zealand, Marlborough region; around Dh175

Tasting notes Passionfruit and gooseberry nose with a lively and fresh palate, followed by crispy acidity and a note of lemongrass.

Try it with Great as an aperitif or with a cold seafood platter.

DEIRA

Deira is home to a wide range of the typical types of cuisine found in this colourful city. On top of this, a couple of Dubai's best eateries – Verre and the Blue Elephant – are located here. If you're travelling to Deira for dinner from one of the beach resorts (or even from Bur Dubai) remember to leave plenty of time to get to the restaurant, as the busy early evening traffic can really test your patience.

ASHIANA Map pp208-9   *Indian*
☎ 228 1707; Sheraton Dubai Creek, Baniyas Rd, Deira; mains Dh75; ☽ 12.30-3pm & 7.30pm-12.30am
Very popular with moneyed Indian expats, Ashiana is an attractive restaurant offering upmarket Indian ambience. Specialising in North Indian cuisine, there are wonderful tandoori and curry meat dishes on the menu, as well as excellent vegetarian options. Combine the wonderful food with the live sitar music and some cold beers, and it's probably worth the premium you pay over the nonlicensed Indian eateries.

BLUE ELEPHANT Map pp210-11   *Thai*
☎ 705 4660; Al-Bustan Rotana Hotel, Casablanca Rd, Al-Garhoud; mains Dh75; ☽ noon-3pm & 7-11.30pm
Quite simply the most refined Thai dining experience in town. While the Thai village interior (complete with fish-filled lake) borders on kitsch, the warm welcome and great menu removes any lingering doubts that this is the real thing. Settle down to a Royal Thai Banquet or just choose your favourites (including your choice of 'heat' level), safe in the knowledge that the kitchen delivers the goods. Good vegetarian options and particularly good value on buffet night. Book ahead.

CAFÉ CHIC Map pp210-11   *Fine Dining*
☎ 282 4040; Le Meridien Dubai, Airport Rd, Al-Garhoud; mains Dh75; ☽ 12.30-2.45pm & 8-11.45pm
With its elegant chocolate and tan interior and menu by two–Michelin star chef Michel Rostang, Café Chic should be a hit. But the food doesn't always live up to the surroundings or the chef's name, and the service is a little hit and miss. It's certainly respectable bistro food, but only the signature chocolate soufflé really rises to the occasion. Kudos

must go to the extensive wine list and ability to order a carafe of some drinkable wines – unusual in Dubai.

CASA MIA Map pp210-11 *Italian*

☎ 702 2506; Le Meridien Dubai, Airport Rd, Al-Garhoud; mains Dh50; ⏰ 12.30-2.45pm & 8-11.30pm

One of Dubai's most credible Italian experiences, Casa Mia is well known for fresh ingredients and great service. Set in the somewhat odd Le Meridien Village, you could dine alfresco, but the interior is more romantic given that it offers authentic surroundings. The beef carpaccio is a highlight of the starters, the fresh pastas and pizzas are excellent and, for those with a hearty appetite, the mains (secondi) are worth keeping room for. Delectable vegetarian options and a well-selected wine list make this a local favourite so book ahead.

CHINA CLUB

Map pp208-9 *Contemporary Chinese*

☎ 222 7171; InterContinental Dubai, Baniyas Rd; mains Dh50; ⏰ 1-3pm & 8-11pm

Secreted next to Yum! noodle bar, China Club is a partially hidden gem. A delicately beautiful interior with a variety of seating options (the booths are cool), the *mise en scène* is one of the best in Dubai. The quality of the produce is first-rate and while some of the more innovative dishes appear a little forced, the classics are excellent – try the Peking duck. The service is professional and attentive and there's a decent wine list on offer.

CREEKSIDE Map pp208-9 *Japanese*

☎ 207 1750; Sheraton Dubai Creek, Baniyas Rd, Deira; mains Dh50; ⏰ 12.30-3pm & 6.30pm-midnight

After a recent, enthusiastic pine make-over, this restaurant has attracted a loyal following with its outdoor seating and good-value theme nights. All the usuals are there – sushi, sashimi, noodles, teppanyaki and excellent tempura. Friendly and knowledgeable staff will help you work your way through the myriad choices. Bookings for theme nights are essential.

FISH MARKET Map pp208-9 *Seafood*

☎ 205 7333; InterContinental Dubai, Baniyas Rd; mains Dh100; ⏰ 1-3pm & 8-11.30pm

A popular seafood restaurant, it sports a suitably aquatic vista of the Creek that challenges the seafood for attention – anything that diverts your eyes from the unconsciously garish straw and cane interior is welcome. There is a wide supply of seafood, including live lobsters. You select your seafood, method of cooking and sauces and pay according to weight. The service is excellent and there's an apt wine list, but those who don't adore the fruits of the sea need not apply.

GLASSHOUSE

Map pp208-9 *Modern Global*

☎ 227 1111; Hilton Dubai Creek, Baniyas Rd; mains Dh50; ⏰ 12.30-3.30pm & 7-11.30pm

Living with a famous sibling is never easy. Having Verre, Gordon Ramsay's signature restaurant, living right across the hall would lead to a serious case of envy for most restaurants. In the case of Glasshouse, however, this open, modern brasserie has enough of its own personality and style to stand out on its own. A menu that houses old home-style favourites, such as bangers and mash, alongside salmon tandoori would be a disaster in less-safe hands, but here it's handled with aplomb. While the service isn't to the same standard as Verre, you can certainly dine here without furtive glances across the hotel at its more famous sister.

LA MODA Map pp208-9 *Italian*

☎ 205 7333; InterContinental Dubai, Baniyas Rd; mains Dh50; ⏰ 1-3pm & 8pm-2am

One of the first of Dubai's restaurants to have any real style, La Moda quickly became one of the city's most fashionable spots to be seen dining in. With its wood panelling and warm lights, it's a testament to the designers that it's only now starting to look a fraction tired. While it still attracts a loyal late-dining crowd, the food is respectable without breaking any new ground. Pizzas and risottos are reliable choices, and it's backed up with friendly service and a safe wine list. It gets lively late and it's a credible choice for a group dinner.

MINATO Map pp208-9 *Japanese*

☎ 222 7171; InterContinental Dubai, Baniyas Rd; mains Dh75; ⏰ 1-3pm & 8-11pm

The food of Minato far exceeds the cookie-cutter blandness of its traditional Japanese

Eating – Deira

restaurant interior. Book some seats at the tiny sushi bar or at a teppanyaki table for the best ambience and food. The fresh sushi and sashimi are of top quality and the chef is very knowledgeable (and entertaining). It has buffet deals on some nights, making it extremely good value, but remember to book.

MIYAKO Map pp208-9   *Japanese*

☎ 209 1222; Hyatt Regency Dubai, off Al-Khaleej Rd; mains Dh75; ☾ 12.30-3pm & 7-11pm

An excellent Japanese restaurant, Miyako impresses with a detailed menu and terrific Geisha-style service. The sushi and sashimi are first class – the tuna and salmon are arguably the best in Dubai. The beef hot pot is a treat, as is the perfect tempura. The teppanyaki performance by the chef matches the flavour.

MORE Map pp210-11   *Café*

☎ 283 0224; near Welcare Hospital, Al-Garhoud; mains Dh30; ☾ 7.30-12.30am

An eccentric and eclectic menu and interior set this café apart from the plethora of branded cafés in Dubai. While hearty soups and filling pastas are the safe choices, the fish or meat dishes are cooked in a number of diverse styles. A decent selection of vegetarian dishes, all-day breakfasts and great desserts make this a fine escape from the anonymous service and lacklustre menus of the chain cafés.

M'S BEEF BISTRO

Map pp210-11   *Steakhouse*

☎ 282 4040; Le Meridien Dubai, Airport Rd, Al-Garhoud; mains Dh75; ☾ 12.30-2.45pm & 7.30-11.45pm

This busy American-style steakhouse serves US and New Zealand beef and has become quite a favourite of Dubai's meat lovers. With starters such as carpaccio and tartare served as they should be and standards such as US tenderloin with Béarnaise sauce expertly cooked to order, it's quite the carnivorous feast. A good wine selection and fine service make this a wise choice for a meaty meal on this side of the Creek.

SEAFOOD MARKET

Map pp210-11   *Seafood*

☎ 282 4040; Le Meridien Dubai, Airport Rd; mains Dh100; ☾ 12.30-3pm & 7.30-11.30pm

One of the best of the select-your-seafood-and-tell-us-how-to-cook-it-style restaurants so popular in Dubai. The friendly staff is on hand to help you navigate the bewildering array of seafood on display and offer advice on how best to order its cooking method. While it's all good quality, the lobster warrants special mention and there's a good selection of white wine to accompany your choice.

SHABESTAN Map pp208-9   *Persian*

☎ 205 7333; InterContinental Dubai, Baniyas Rd; mains Dh75; ☾ 1-3pm & 8-11pm

For those new to the intricacies of Middle Eastern cooking, Shabestan offers a wonderful introduction to Iranian cooking. Select a table with Creek views or one of the intimate niches – perfect for groups – and sample the oven-fresh bread and the great Persian band while checking out the menu. While the selection of starters is recommended – especially for vegetarians, the highlight is the lamb; get a platter if there are more than two of you.

Let's Do Brunch…

Friday brunch is a very popular ingredient of the Dubai lifestyle and nearly everyone participates – keep in mind that Friday morning is the same as Sunday morning in Western countries. Shops and businesses are closed, so brunch is the perfect way to while away the hours until shopping recommences. For Thursday-night partygoers looking to ease that hangover and partake in a hair of the dog, to families sharing what is often their only day off together, there are plenty of venues across the city offering a relaxing and good-value feed. The brunches are all you can eat and bookings are essential. Here's a (very) short selection of the better brunch places.

Carter's (Map pp214-15; ☎ 324 0000; Pyramids, Wafi City; adult/child Dh65/30; ☾ 11.30am-3pm)

Cascades (Map p218; ☎ 332 5555; Fairmont; adult/child Dh95/45; ☾ 9am-3.15pm)

Colonnade (Map pp206-7; ☎ 348 0000; Jumeirah Beach Hotel; adult/child Dh130/65; ☾ noon-3.30pm) Alcohol included with adults' menu.

Pax Romana (Map p218; ☎ 343 3333; Dusit Dubai; adult Dh95, children under 12 free; ☾ noon-3pm) Alcohol included with adults' menu.

Vivaldi (Map pp206-7; ☎ 207 1717; Sheraton Dubai Creek; adult/child Dh70/35; ☾ 12.30-3.30pm)

SHAHRZAD Map pp210-11   *Persian*
☎ 209 1200; Hyatt Regency Dubai, off Al-Khaleej Rd; mains Dh75; ⏱ 12.30-3.30pm & 7.30-11pm, closed Sat

Steeped in *The Thousand and One Nights* ambience, Shahrzad is an excellent setting to sample fine Persian cooking. Gorgeous antiques, fountains, copper lamps, niches and live musicians set the scene for a memorable night (and Persian restaurants are always more fun at night). One of the first things you'll notice about this restaurant are the smells wafting from the kitchen, the *tanour* (bread oven) and the kebab grill fill the room with mouthwatering fragrances. The bread and hot starters are superb and mains are truly flavoursome; take the opportunity to try a traditional stew

as well as the obligatory kebabs. To cap off the experience try some *sheesha* (water pipe) and Iranian tea.

VERRE Map pp210-11   *Fine Dining*
☎ 212 7551; Hilton Dubai Creek, Baniyas Rd; mains Dh75; ⏱ 7pm-midnight

For confirmation that Dubai has 'arrived' as a world-class food destination, look no further than three–Michelin starred Gordon Ramsay's Verre. Ramsay's first foray outside the UK is a winner with its combination of beautifully presented contemporary cuisine and cool, minimalist surroundings. The floor staff are the best-drilled team in Dubai, the maître d' has Gallic charm to spare, the wine list has great

A Beautiful Body Needs a Good Soul

While Dubai's restaurant scene is increasing in sophistication, there's one thing that really bugs us – inconsistent dining experiences. Given that a good night out at a hotel restaurant can easily offset the money you saved by scoring that discount hotel room rate, we've omitted a few high profile eateries that don't live up to the hype.

One restaurant under no such threat is BiCE, the Italian trattoria at the Hilton Dubai Jumeirah. While consistently garnering great word of mouth, press reviews and awards, BiCE simply goes about its business serving up fresh, authentic Italian fare with effortless style. But why should this be so unusual? Manager of BiCE and passionate food, football and Ferrari lover Roberto Rella sees plenty of reasons why.

Roberto's head chef, Andrea, is Italian. While this shouldn't come as a surprise, behind the swinging doors at most Dubai restaurants – even the fine dining ones – you'll find chefs who had never cooked the type of cuisine they're asked to prepare before coming to Dubai. Roberto explains that it's not enough to learn to make dishes by rote, you have to have a passion for food and understand the philosophy behind the cuisine that you're making.

When checking out the kitchen, a staffer carrying a huge tray of fresh focaccia smiles proudly when we sample it. It's perfect. But as we cast our eyes around the kitchen we notice something else. It's six in the evening, the hungry hordes that have been happily splashing around in the hotel pool will be coming through the doors in an hour's time. The kitchen is calm. Benches are clean. Freshly sliced vegetables are arranged and ready to be roasted for tonight's service. It's a reassuring sign in a city where the *bain-marie* is a chef's best friend.

Out in the restaurant, waiters are double checking the table settings. Most waiters view working in the Middle East as a job that enables them to send money home, nothing more – and it shows. Roberto contends that if you encourage the staff to work hard and learn, they'll not only get a career out of it, they'll make far more money from tips. The problem, however, is not just unenthusiastic staff; in many restaurants the waiters have never tasted the food they serve or tried the wines – let alone learnt to match the two. Roberto, as most good restaurateurs do, insists that all the staff have sampled the menu, know the ingredients and can suggest a wine to match.

The long-standing problem of sourcing fresh ingredients in Dubai has, for the most part, been solved, but Roberto would still like more that the two deliveries he receives per week. Roberto says importers are conservative and not willing to risk having produce go unsold.

Another problem is that the good restaurants in Dubai are attached to hotels – and fall under the watchful eye of the hotels' food and beverage bean counters. Pressure is applied to restaurants to keep costs down, change the menu ('what if we put in a sushi bar, but with an Italian twist…') and push through too many customers. BiCE is so busy that there's little wastage and this, he says, keeps his food costs the same as other restaurants who don't use expensive ingredients like BiCE. In turn, this keeps cost-cutting measures and silly promotion ideas out of the restaurant.

There are many other restaurants in Dubai that aspire to the same kind of dining experience that BiCE offers and nearly all of these still don't manage to put it all together to make a satisfying dining experience. Roberto agrees and states in his characteristically Italian way, 'a beautiful body needs a good soul'. Far too many new restaurants in Dubai have a famous-name chef attached (who generally fax in their menus from faraway locations), beautiful décor and a friendly maître d', but just don't work as a satisfying dining experience. As Roberto so eloquently states, 'you can have some eggs, oil and lemon juice, but you don't have a beautiful mayonnaise unless you blend it properly'.

breadth and depth and the food is sublime. Ramsay's combination of French technique and light touch is an excellent fit in Dubai. Forget the 'celebrity chef' nonsense, Ramsay's a chef's chef and this outlet lives up to his demanding standards. For a real treat, give your taste buds and wallet a workout with the degustation menu.

YUM! Map pp210-11 *Noodle Bar*
☎ 222 7171; InterContinental Dubai, Baniyas Rd; mains Dh35; ☸ noon-1am

Similar in style to **Noodle House** (p81), Yum! has an open kitchen, a fashionable interior, honest, well-priced food and an alcohol licence – an all-too-rare combination in Dubai. Try the combination plate of spring rolls, seafood parcels and minced shrimp, and the *tom kha gai* (chicken and coconut soup). The wok specials, such as *char kway* (stir-fried noodles), are also excellent. There are only a few vegetarian dishes scattered through the menu, but they're tasty. The service is a tad slow for a restaurant whose tagline is 'Live Fast, Eat Fast', but the open kitchen's fun to watch while you wait.

CHEAP EATS
AL ASAIL RESTAURANT
Map pp208-9 *Russian/Arabic*
☎ 227 2002; Naif Rd, near Deira Gold Souq; mains Dh13; ☸ 11am-10pm

Keeping Dubai's Russian population from overt homesickness is this local restaurant. While it keeps busy dishing up Arabic favourites, you should try the traditional Russian dishes. The only problem – the menu's in Russian and you'll be lucky to find anyone who can interpret it – so follow our advice: order *pelmeni* (boiled meat dumplings, excellent with sour cream or tomato sauce), *vareniki* (potato dumplings) and *golubsti* (cabbage rolls stuffed with rice and meat and cooked in a spiced tomato sauce). It's hearty stuff – giant servings and plenty of extras and it's guaranteed to take the edge off a hangover.

AL BURJ CAFETERIA
Map pp208-9 *Shwarma*
near entrance to Deira Gold Souq; snacks Dh 5-15; ☸ 6pm-midnight

A nifty little stand-up near the entrance to the Deira Gold Souq, it offers delicious shwarma and fresh fruit juices. Perfect for recharging your batteries before another round of getting that gold price down.

CAFÉ HAVANA Map pp208-9 *Café*
☎ 295 5238; Deira City Centre, Level II; coffee Dh12; ☸ 8am-midnight

Winning coffee and prime people-watching opportunities make this café the best choice for resting up before tackling more of the centre's shopping possibilities. For many visitors it provides one of the only chances to hang with the local Emirati men who kick back for hours here.

CAFETERIA AL ABRA
Map pp208-9 *Shwarma*
intersection of Al-Sabkha & Baniyas Rds, next to abra station; snacks Dh5-10; ☸ 6pm-midnight

Right next to the *abra* (water taxi) station in Deira, it is an ideal spot for a snack while watching the activity on the Creek. It has top shwarma and samosas, along with fruit juices and sodas.

GULF RESTAURANT & CAFETERIA
Map pp208-9 *Indo-Pakistani*
cnr Al-Sabkha Rd & Deira St; snacks Dh8-20; ☸ noon-midnight

A decent Indo-Pakistani restaurant serving up generous portions of chicken, lamb or fried fish on a pile of rice with salad for only Dh12. The freshly squeezed juices (always a must when in Dubai) are only Dh5 – try the mango.

HATAM Map pp208-9 *Persian*
Baniyas Rd; meals Dh15-25

Hatam is highly recommended for its terrific Iranian food at very reasonable prices. A traditional *chelow kebab* (rice topped with a grilled kebab, which appears on the menu as 'sultan kebab') costs Dh17, including soup and salad. Most full dinners cost under Dh20.

BUR DUBAI
An eclectic mix of fine dining and workers cafés is just one of the wonderful contradictions of this area of Dubai. The great thing is that you can grab a local bite for lunch in Karama for next to nothing and indulge yourself for dinner at some great restaurants.

ANDIAMO! Map pp206-7 *Italian*
☎ 317 2222; Grand Hyatt Dubai, Al-Qataiyat Rd; mains Dh50; ☸ 12.30-3pm & 6-11.30pm

The newish Grand Hyatt is turning heads with its restaurants and the open-kitchened, colourful Andiamo! has attracted its fair share of

Elements Café (below)

diners – especially families. The food, while not veering far from the classics, is authentic and skilfully cooked. Great antipasto selections, fresh pasta and pizzas cooked in a fabulous-looking wood-fired oven make this a welcome addition to Dubai's ever-popular Italian dining scene.

ANTIQUE BAZAAR

Map pp212-13   *Indian*

☎ 397 7444; Four Points Sheraton, Khalid bin al-Waleed Rd; mains Dh50; ☯ 12.30-3.30pm & 7.30pm-3am

Somewhat predictably, this restaurant resembles a wonderful antique bazaar and depending on your taste will either have you cringing or looking for price tags (but, no the antiques are not for sale). While the food is enjoyable, it's only the large ensemble of musicians (starting at 9pm) that will divert your attention from the interior. It's very popular and the combination of attractions makes for a fun night out.

Top Five Bur Dubai Eats

- Asha's (above)
- Fatafeet (p79)
- Indochine (p77)
- Peppercrab (p77)
- Thai Chi (p78)

ASHA'S

Map pp214-15   *Contemporary Indian*

☎ 324 4100; Pyramids, Wafi City, Al-Qataiyat Rd; mains Dh50; ☯ 12.30-3.30pm & 7.30pm-2am

An admirable attempt by Asha Bhosle (of Bollywood singing fame and the object of affection of Cornershop's hit single *Brimful of Asha*) to update some Indian classics. Thankfully most dishes hit all the right notes, especially the chef's choices, but those who 'prefer the original' can still order the traditional Indian dishes. With knowledgeable service, funky décor, balanced wine list and a winter terrace, you might want an encore.

DÔME Map pp212-13   *Café*

☎ BurJurman Centre, Trade Centre Rd; mains Dh25; ☯ 7.30am-11.30pm

This Australian franchise, located on a busy corner of Bur Dubai, is always busy serving up pleasing coffee to local office and shop workers and tourists alike. It boasts a diverse menu from pizzas and gourmet sandwiches to scrumptious cakes and its outdoor seating – in the cooler months, of course – is a pleasant place for a break after checking out the fashions upstairs.

ELEMENTS CAFÉ Map pp214-15   *Café*

☎ 324 4252; Wafi City, Al-Qataiyat Rd; mains Dh30; ☯ 10-1am

One of the most stylish cafés in Dubai, it attracts an equally hip crowd keen for a break from designer-clothes shopping. While it is worth a visit to check out the interior alone, the eclectic menu now features some smashing Spanish tapas – the omelette (tortilla) is wonderful, as is the fried calamari. Because it's in the shopping centre (as opposed to the Pyramids complex) there's no alcohol served.

IL RUSTICO Map pp216-17 *Italian*
☎ 398 2222; Rydges Plaza Hotel, Al-Dhiyafah St, Satwa Roundabout; mains Dh50; ☷ noon-3pm & 6pm-midnight

A fittingly rustic interior, yummy pastas, wood-fired pizzas and value for money have earned this cosy restaurant a loyal following. The home-made bread, fresh produce (including some hit vegetarian options) and friendly service don't hurt either. As a result it's very popular so be sure to book ahead.

INDOCHINE Map pp206-7 *Vietnamese*
☎ 317 2222; Grand Hyatt Dubai, Al-Qataiyat Rd; mains Dh75; ☷ 7-11.30pm

Once the shock of the hotel's rainforest foyer (and the four dhow hulls embedded in the ceiling) has worn off, you'll find Indochine an attractive restaurant with well-spaced tables and an open kitchen equally ready to shock your tastebuds. While full of flavour, the menu is well balanced and if you're unfamiliar with dishes just ask the informed staff or order the set menu. The salads, *goi hoa chuoi ga* (chicken with banana flower) and *goi ngo sen tom* (shrimp and lotus leaf) are especially tasty. If you can't make it to dessert, just order one of the exquisite Asian teas.

LEMONGRASS Map pp214-15 *Thai*
☎ 334 2325; near Lamcy Plaza; mains Dh30; ☷ noon-midnight

This is a cute little independent restaurant serving traditional Thai cuisine (no alcohol). Sip a lemongrass juice while digging into the lemongrass set – a selection of starters for two. It does a decent *larb gai* (minced chicken salad), and the chicken and beef curries are all very edible. The vegetarian options, especially the green curry with eggplants, will have you wanting more. Home delivery is available.

MEDZO Map pp214-15 *Italian*
☎ 324 0000; Pyramids, Wafi City, Al-Qataiyat Rd; mains Dh60; ☷ 12.30-3pm & 7.30-11.30pm

Another stylish restaurant in the Pyramids complex, Medzo offers Italian fare with a twist. While the extensive and inventive menu might send purists running to the nearest trattoria, enough (but not all) of the experiments work to make this a worthwhile option. Starters such as Cigali lobster and chorizo tart seemed unlikely to work, but did. The quality of the produce is tops – just trust your instincts and if the weather's cool book a table outside.

PEPPERCRAB Map pp206-7 *Singaporean*
☎ 317 2222; Grand Hyatt Dubai, Al-Qataiyat Rd; mains Dh100; ☷ 7pm-midnight

Peppercrab is one of the best places to eat seafood in town and it's also the most fun. There's something slightly subversive about digging into the restaurant's signature dish with your fingers, while in the luxurious surroundings of

Indochine (above)

this hotel. Fish and seafood are the order of the day – much of which you can select as it swims past in the restaurant's tanks that front the open kitchen. But not all the dishes are this straightforward – starters include a wonderful oyster omelette and an unusual grilled fish mousse in palm leaves. It's all decadent stuff, and combined with the friendly staff and outdoor seating, it will have seafood lovers swooning – just remember to take off the silly oversized napkin when you're finished.

SEVILLE'S

Map pp214-15 *Spanish Tapas*
☎ 324 7300; Pyramids, Wafi City, Al-Qataiyat Rd; mains Dh50; ✆ noon-2am Sat-Wed, noon-3am Thu & Fri
Authentic tapas, live music, knockout sangria and an outdoor terrace make Seville's the most popular choice for Spanish food in Dubai. All of the usual tapas are on offer – the *gambas al ajillo* (prawns cooked in garlic and oil) and *chorizo a la sidra* (Spanish sausage cooked in cider) are particularly noteworthy. If you're still hungry after that there are main courses such as traditional paella with mixed seafood or chicken. There's a happy hour from 6pm to 9pm, making it a fine choice to meet up for some snacks before a night clubbing.

THAI CHI

Map pp214-15 *Contemporary Thai & Chinese*
☎ 324 4100; Pyramids, Wafi City, Al-Qataiyat Rd; mains Dh50; ✆ noon-3pm & 7.30-midnight
While it still feels like the too-cute name came before the dining concept, the food at Thai Chi stands up to allay any fears. While the room confirms its duality by consisting of a stylishly traditional Thai area and a less-formal Chinese one, you can order from both menus in both locations. The Thai menu is very extensive and thankfully there are set menus (including a decent vegetarian one) for those who can't decide. The Chinese menu is extensive as well (no set menu, though) and the Peking duck is a must if you go down the Chinese path.

TROYKA

Map pp212-13 *Russian*
☎ 359 5908; Ascot Hotel, Khalid bin al-Walid Rd; mains Dh50; ✆ noon-3pm & 7pm-3am
Troyka is a welcome taste of home for the Russian expat community, who love the fact that the caviar is reasonably priced, the borscht and beef stroganoff hearty, and the musicians and dancers authentic. To get into the spirit (and the spirits), book a table for 10pm and toast your way through to closing time.

Thai Chi (below)

YAKITORI
Map pp212-13 *Japanese*
☎ 352 0900; Ascot Hotel, Khalid bin al-Walid Rd; mains Dh50; ✆ 12.30-3pm & 6.30-11.30pm
A favourite haunt for those who know their *hashi* (chopsticks) etiquette, this is a restaurant where you should follow the Japanese edict that 'the best way to cook a fish is not to'. While the décor is fine and the staff friendly, the sashimi and sushi are the star attraction – along with the knowledgeable chef. Given the quality of the seafood on offer, it's also excellent value.

CHEAP EATS

AUTOMATIC
Map pp212-13 *Lebanese*
☎ 227 7824; Al-Rigga Rd; mezze Dh12-15, mains Dh25-45
A branch of this reliable chain of Lebanese restaurants, it offers great mezze and mains. Try the *shish tawooq* (marinated grilled chicken on skewers) or the mixed grill. There are branches in the Al-Khaleej Shopping Centre (☎ 355 0333) on Al-Mankhool Rd and in the Beach Centre (Map pp216-17; ☎ 349 4888) on Jumeirah Rd.

BASTA ART CAFÉ
Map pp212-13 *Café*
☎ 353 5071; Al-Fahidi St, Bastakia Quarter; mains Dh20; ✆ 10am-8pm
There's simply not enough of this style of place in Dubai. Set in a traditional house, the café

provides welcome relief from the traffic chaos in this area. The food is respectable café fare, but it's just great to sit in the courtyard of one of the original houses in the Bastakia area. Check out the local art before you leave.

CHHAPPAN BHOG

Map pp214-15 *Indian/Vegetarian*
☎ 396 8176; Sheikh Khalifa bin Zayed Rd, Karama; mains Dh8-12
This long-standing favourite, serving up mainly North Indian dishes, is very popular with the local Indian population. It has a fast-food counter and an excellent Indian sweets shop downstairs.

COCONUT GROVE Map pp216-17 *Goan*

☎ 398 3800; Rydges Plaza Hotel, Al-Dhiyafah St, Satwa Roundabout, Satwa; mains Dh30; ☾ noon-3pm & 7pm-12.30am
Great curries and biryani bring in regular customers looking for authentic dishes from Kerala and Goa. The pine-enhanced interior and costumed waiters add to the southern Indian experience. While the heat of some of the dishes may be a heart-stopping experience, the bill won't be – uncommon in a hotel restaurant in Dubai.

FATAFEET

Map pp212-13 *Egyptian/Lebanese*
☎ 397 9222; Dubai Creek, opposite UK embassy; mains Dh25; ☾ 10.30am-midnight
This very popular Creekside restaurant and café serves up tasty Egyptian and Lebanese fare. With its tentlike indoor seating and outdoor tables dotted forever along the Creek, it is also a great place to linger over *sheesha* after a filling feast. During the cooler months it's extremely popular and at night it's quite a scene.

FOOD CASTLE Map pp214-15 *Indian*

☎ 335 5717; Sheikh Mohammed Bldg, Karama; mains Dh13; ☾ 24hr
While it dishes up decent Indian and Chinese food, the real specialities of the house are the Keralan curries. Settle down in the outdoor garden (complete with a cooling little fountain) and sample the *beef olathiyathu* (spicy dry curry), the *kozhi varatharachathu* (chicken with coriander) or one of the excellent seafood curries. Wash them down with a fresh juice (there's no alcohol) and head into the Karama Shopping Centre for some bargains.

INDIA HOUSE

Map pp212-13 *Indian/Vegetarian*
☎ 352 6006; Al-Hisn St, Bur Dubai; meals Dh15-20
An admirable vegetarian choice, this restaurant has a great selection of North and South Indian vegetarian dishes and a more upmarket interior than most restaurants around here. It also serves Chinese dishes – Indian style.

KAN ZAMAN Map pp212-13 *Arabic*

☎ 393 9913; Heritage Village, Al-Shindaga Rd; mains Dh27; ☾ 11-3am
While staying in Dubai, a meal and *sheesha* down by the Creek is almost obligatory. Kan Zaman is fantastically situated for this and makes a great way to finish a visit to the Heritage Village. Outside the oppressive heat during the height of summer, the large outdoor area is the place to leisurely sample some mezze and grills and watch the passing parade of boats. While there is no alcohol, puffing on *sheesha* long enough will be enough to achieve a head-spinning state.

KARACHI DARBAR

Map pp214-15 *Pakistani*
☎ 334 7272; Karama Shopping Centre; mains Dh11; ☾ 4-2am
A firm favourite with 'guest workers', the Karachi Darbar keeps the real workers well-fed with a huge menu of Pakistani, Indian and Chinese specialities. You could try the chicken or mutton Kashmiri, but the vegetarian dishes, such as fried dhal or vegetable korma, are delicious with the obligatory biryani rice side dish.

Karachi Darbar (above)

KWALITY Map pp212-13 _Indian_
☎ 393 6563; opposite Ascot Hotel, Khalid bin al-Waleed Rd; mains Dh20; ⏱ 1-3pm & 8-11.45pm

A branch of this dependable Indian chain of restaurants, it's hard to go wrong with hearty portions of favourite dishes such as chicken _makhani_ (butter chicken) or _rogan josh_ (lamb curry). As with most Indian restaurants there's a large number of tasty vegetarian options.

MR CHOW Map pp212-13 _Chinese_
☎ 351 0099; near Imperial Suites Hotel; mains Dh40; ⏱ 11-2.30am

Eat in, takeaway or home delivery, Mr Chow has a long menu of the usual Chinese fare – as well as several Thai dishes. It's well cooked, the chicken and seafood dishes are the best and the portions are mammoth.

RAVI'S Map pp216-17 _Pakistani_
☎ 331 5353; Al-Satwa Rd, Satwa; mains Dh12; ⏱ 24hr

Well known for its honest, inexpensive fare and all-day opening hours, Ravi's consists of a 'bachelors' section and a family section – where the Westerners eat. Order a curry, a biryani and some bread and you can't go wrong.

SHEIKH ZAYED ROAD

The new hotels along the strip have breathed real life into the dining scene here. The phenomenal pace of growth in Dubai is amply demonstrated by our top five list (see the boxed text below) – not much more than a couple of years ago there wouldn't have been one.

AL TANNOUR Map p218 _Lebanese_
☎ 331 1111; Crowne Plaza Hotel, Sheikh Zayed Rd; mains Dh60; ⏱ 8pm-3am

While it doesn't have the most exciting décor – traditional village style – it has some of the best authentic Lebanese food in Dubai. Go for

Fruit and drink takeaway shop

a huge array of mezzes, a couple of grill dishes (try the chicken) and eat it with the wonderful fresh bread – made right in front of you. Book a table for late – 10.30ish – and watch the band and belly dancer.

BENJARONG Map p218 _Thai_
☎ 343 3333; Dusit Dubai, Sheikh Zayed Rd; mains Dh70; ⏱ 7.30pm-midnight

Benjarong is a quietly elegant Royal Thai restaurant with gorgeous décor, unobtrusive traditional Thai music and dance, refined service and food that will have you leaving the restaurant in a trancelike state of bliss. For starters try the _gung hom sabai_ (deep fried prawns wrapped in egg noodles) or the _tom yam goong_ (hot prawn soup with lime, lemongrass and chilli). The mains are just as delectable – the green curry is the pick of the bunch. Thai aficionados should make sure the waitresses understand that you can handle the heat – otherwise they'll tone it down.

EXCHANGE Map p218 _Steakhouse_
☎ 311 8000; Fairmont, Sheikh Zayed Rd; mains Dh75; ⏱ 7pm-1am

Modelled on New York's legendary Oak Room at the Plaza Hotel, the Exchange is one of several restaurants bringing steakhouse sophisti-

---

Top Five Sheikh Zayed Road Eats

- Benjarong (above)
- Hoi An (opposite)
- Noodle House (opposite)
- Spectrum on One (opposite)
- Trader Vic's (opposite)

cation to Dubai. With its understated beige and brown colour scheme, decent service and vintage wine list it discreetly whispers 'business dinner' – but it's a winning option for those with a craving for filet mignon and a glass or two of a big bold and old red.

HOI AN

Map p218   *Contemporary Vietnamese*

☎ 343 8888; Shangri-La, Sheikh Zayed Rd; mains Dh75; ☾ 7.30pm-1am

Named and decorated after the ancient city of Hoi An, the food and décor of this delightful French Vietnamese restaurant do justice to Hoi An's history as an East–West trading centre. The starters are superb – try the crispy crab rolls. The mains don't disappoint either, with the lemongrass duck breast a highlight. The service is a bit wobbly, so try one of the exotic teas at the end of the meal while waiting for your bill to materialise.

MARRAKECH Map p218   *Moroccan*

☎ 343 8888; Shangri-La, Sheikh Zayed Rd; mains Dh65; ☾ 1-3pm & 8pm-midnight

While **Tagine** (see p85) still has the edge in ambience, this relative newcomer is a worthy addition to the underdeveloped Moroccan dining scene in Dubai. All the Moroccan staples are sensational – the couscous royale and tagines are noteworthy. So book a table by the fountain, sip some mint tea, order the old favourites and relax listening to the best live Moroccan music in the UAE.

NOODLE HOUSE Map p218   *Asian*

☎ 319 8757; Emirates Towers, Sheikh Zayed Rd; mains Dh25; ☾ noon-11.30pm

One of the most affordable and fun hotel restaurants in Dubai, the Noodle House is a minimalist and stylish restaurant fronted by an open kitchen running the width of the restaurant. The concept is simple – everyone sits on long wooden communal benches and orders by ticking dishes on a tear-off menu pad. There's enough variety on the pan-Asian menu to please everyone – everything from

curry laksa to duck pancakes – and there are good wines by the glass as well as Asian beers (Tiger beer on tap, no less). The only problem is finding a spare spot on a bench – this place is always busy and buzzing.

SPECTRUM ON ONE

Map p218   *Modern Global*

☎ 311 8101; Fairmont, Sheikh Zayed Rd; mains Dh50; ☾ 7pm-1am

Everyone's familiar with the problem. You're a group of friends who can only agree on one thing when it comes to tonight's dinner – you're all hungry. Before sacrificing a perfectly good dining opportunity at a food court in a mall, book a table at Spectrum on One. The Fairmount's signature restaurant has eight individual open kitchens representing cuisine from around the world – stop off at Normandy for seafood, nip down to Thailand for a curry and perhaps over to Japan for yakitori. While it still might sound a little too 'food court' for some (and it did open with a very shaky start), the food and service is now good enough to allay those fears. Besides, who really wants to waste a Dubai meal at a mall?

TOKYO @ THE TOWERS

Map p218   *Japanese*

☎ 330 0000; Emirates Towers, Sheikh Zayed Rd; mains Dh75; ☾ 12.30-3pm & 7.30pm-midnight

Modern and minimalist, this slice of Tokyo offers first-rate sushi and teppanyaki while you watch the teppanyaki chefs show off their knife skills. The bento boxes are good value, the teriyaki is mouthwatering and the sushi and sashimi are both very fresh. Go easy on the sake though – there's a karaoke bar next door that might prove too tempting.

TRADER VIC'S Map p218   *Polynesian*

☎ 331 1111; Crowne Plaza Hotel, Sheikh Zayed Rd; mains Dh70; ☾ 12.30-3pm & 7.30-11.30pm

While certainly not the most attractive branch of this long-standing chain, this chaotically busy restaurant certainly has a loyal following in Dubai. While navigating your way to your table through the Polynesian-themed interior can be a challenge – especially after one of their lethal signature cocktails at the bar – the menu that awaits is consistently a hit. The 'island titbits' sampling of starters helps soak up that alcohol and the main courses emanating from the wood-fired clay oven are all recommended. Perfect for groups but you'll need to book a couple of days in advance.

> ### Did You Know?
>
> Most of Dubai's good restaurants have symbols on their menu indicating that a dish contains pork or has been prepared using alcohol. This is for Muslims who, as a rule, don't partake in either.

VU'S Map p218 *Fine Dining*
☎ 319 8771; Emirates Towers, Sheikh Zayed Rd; mains Dh100; ⏱ 12.30-3pm & 7.30pm-midnight
Atop Emirates Towers, Vu's has spectacular views, a chic interior and a well thought-out menu featuring a combination of French and Italian cuisine. It has all the makings of a wonderful special-occasion restaurant, but the food has been maddeningly inconsistent in the past – unforgivable when the prices are as lofty as the views. While things have thankfully improved in the kitchen, it's still the gorgeous room and views that command your attention.

JUMEIRAH

The ever-increasing number of resorts along Jumeirah Beach makes for countless dining possibilities. Nearly every hotel along the strip has at least one exceptional restaurant in breathtaking surroundings, and for most of the restaurants here (especially our top five – see the boxed text below), you need to make a reservation at least a day in advance. There are also some popular cafés here where you can catch local residents enjoying their downtime. For those not staying at one of the resorts, a trip down the beach is a must – combine it with some pre- and post-dinner drinks (see p90) and you'll have a brilliant night out.

AL QASR Map pp216-17 *Arabian/Lebanese*
☎ 346 1111; Dubai Marine Beach Resort & Spa; mains Dh55; ⏱ 12.30-3.30pm & 6.30pm-2.30am
Al Qasr offers all the ingredients for the classic Lebanese night out. Mezze. Mains. Band. Belly dancer. Al Qasr scores well on all counts, making it a hot spot for Lebanese expats – who take eating out very seriously. It's great for groups – book a table for 10pm and settle in for a long night.

APARTMENT
Map pp206-7 *French/Fine Dining*
☎ 406 8181; Jumeirah Beach Hotel; mains Dh100; ⏱ 7pm-11.30pm
A sophisticated yet cosy series of hideaways in a downstairs corner of this always-busy hotel, the Apartment brings the food of France's youngest two Michelin star–earning chef Patrick LeNôtre to the table. While the menu has some odd touches (but some surprisingly excellent vegetarian options), sticking to the

signature dishes – a wonderful fillet of beef with foie gras followed by *crème brûlée* with grapefruit sorbet – will keep Francophiles happy. There's a well-chosen (but not so well-priced) wine list and apart from one of the best maître d's in Dubai, the service is a little haphazard given the restaurant's positioning as a fine-dining experience.

BELLA DONNA Map pp216-17 *Italian*
☎ 344 7710; Mercato Mall, Jumeirah Rd; mains Dh35; ⏱ 11am-11pm
Kudos to these guys for taking a shopping space in a mall, that probably would have become a fast-food outlet, and creating a casual but stylish eatery. Of course it's Italian, given the shopping centre's 'theme', but the menu and décor thankfully take no part in the mall's design schizophrenia. The pizzas and pasta are honest, fresh and tasty, and the coffee's smooth and strong – just the ticket to get you out shopping again. If it's not too hot dine alfresco on the small balcony.

BICE Map pp206-7 *Italian*
☎ 399 1111; Hilton Dubai Jumeirah, Al-Mina al-Seyahi; mains Dh75; ⏱ noon-3pm & 7pm-midnight
In the fickle world of Dubai dining, where every hotel food-and-beverage manager is looking to open the next gimmick eatery, it is gratifying to recommend a restaurant because of its fresh produce – well cooked and simply presented – just as Italian fare should be. The restaurant is understated and smart, the service is attentive and knowledgeable and there's always someone on hand to assist with the well-selected wine list. Remember to book a table and arrive hungry – you'll want to try the excellent cheese selection or a classic tiramisu.

CELEBRITIES Map pp206-7 *Fine Dining*
☎ 399 9999; One&Only Royal Mirage, Al-Mina al-Seyahi; mains Dh90; ⏱ 7-11.30pm, closed Sat
With its elegant interior and tremendous views, Celebrities is just the place for a romantic

Top Five Jumeirah Eats
- **Apartment** (above)
- **BiCE** (above)
- **Eauzone** (opposite)
- **Tagine** (p85)
- **Zheng He's** (p85)

Bella Donna (opposite)

tête-à-tête. The food, which could be called modern European with a slight Arabic twist, is light, well executed and shows solid technique – something that couldn't be said when it first opened a couple of years ago. The service is knowledgeable and the ambience really can't be beaten. Try the chocolate mousse for dessert.

DER KELLER Map pp206-7 — German

☎ 406 8181; Jumeirah Beach Hotel, Jumeirah Rd; mains Dh50; 🕑 6-11.30pm

Happily serving up huge portions of traditional German fare to the hordes of Teutonic tourists on package tours, Der Keller actually manages to recreate that beer-cellar atmosphere – albeit with views of the Arabian Sea. All the usual dishes are here – the sausages and sauerkraut are notable and the bar stays open until 1am.

EAUZONE Map pp206-7 — Fine Dining

☎ 399 9999; One&Only Royal Mirage, Al-Mina al-Seyahi; mains Dh65; 🕑 7.30pm-midnight

By the time you've walked across the low-lit boardwalk to the tranquil poolside setting of this adventurous eatery, you're already relaxed. But have a quick scan of the menu and you'll soon realise that this is food that demands your attention. You'll be puzzling over how the flavours are going to combine and

the dishes work, but just relax, you're in very capable hands. Firm favourites are the *tian* (tower) of scampi and the lamb with green tea, salt and an awesome side of truffled mashed potato. If you're still hungry for a little more adventure, for dessert try the selection of sorbet – it's as delicious as it is diverse.

FUSION

Map pp206-7 — Malaysian-Indonesian-Thai

☎ 399 5555; Le Royal Meridien Beach Resort, Al-Mina al-Seyahi; mains Dh55; 🕑 7pm-midnight

Yet another stylish and understated Dubai eatery, this alluring space serves up this trinity of cuisines without turning it into a pan-Asian melange. The seafood dishes are the stars of the show, but there are prime vegetarian and meat dishes available on the extensive menu. The staff are well trained – a welcome and notable feature of this hotel – and there's a well-matched wine list as well as a nice little bar area serving outstanding cocktails.

LA BAIE Map pp206-7 — Fine Dining

☎ 399 4000; Ritz-Carlton, Al-Mina al-Seyahi; mains Dh70; 🕑 7-11pm

While it's an elegant space, the gentleman's club–style dining of this restaurant appears rather incongruous at a beach resort. The chef, however, seems to have settled into Dubai by offering cuisine that leaves you one dish away from a fabulous meal. There are some great flavours on offer, as well as solid technique – the foie gras is outstanding, the jasmine-smoked beef delightful – but some of the combinations of ingredients are a little unusual. There's an excellent wine list and the service is exemplary – just choose your dishes carefully.

LA PARILLA Map pp206-7 *Argentine*
☎ 406 8181; Jumeirah Beach Hotel; mains Dh100; ☯ 12.30-4pm & 7pm-2am

There's almost too much to take in at this high-altitude restaurant – the stupendous views, food being flambéed all around you, and sensuous tango dancers doing their thing. While there are vegetarian options and seafood on the menu, meat dishes take centre stage and you'd better be as hungry as a gaucho after a hard day's ride. Book early to get a table with a view of the Burj Al Arab.

MARINA SEAFOOD MARKET
Map pp206-7 *Seafood*
☎ 406 8181; Jumeirah Beach Hotel; mains Dh100; ☯ 12.30-4pm & 7pm-2am

Situated at the end of a long curving breakwater, much of this airy restaurant has commanding views of the Burj Al Arab (specify a table with a Burj view when you book). If you can take your eyes off Dubai's iconic structure long enough, the staff will talk you through the mind-boggling array of fresh seafood (both local and flown in from afar). Cooking methods are both Asian and European and there's a matching wine list. It's an excellent

lunch venue and has an outdoor bar upstairs. Take the golf buggy out here in the summer.

NINA'S
Map pp206-7 *Contemporary Indian*
☎ 399 9999; Arabian Court, One&Only Royal Mirage; mains Dh60; ☯ 7-11.30pm

The rich interior is very funky and the food takes Indian classics on an interesting European vacation. Try the tasting menus for a selection of starters and mains, and don't be concerned that you won't be able to get out of your chair – it's lighter than most Indian fare. Nina's, along with **Asha's** (p76), is pushing Indian cuisine to destinations uncharted.

OSSIGENO Map pp206-7 *Italian*
☎ 399 5555; Le Royal Meridien Beach Resort, Al-Mina al-Seyahi; mains Dh85; ☯ 7pm-midnight

Ossigeno is a smart and unfussy restaurant with an emphasis on quality ingredients and decent serving sizes. The food's not about to change the direction of Italian cuisine but is competently cooked. There's an extensive Italian wine list, but the wines by the glass are not much to get excited about. The service is attentive and the desserts are worth saving room for. A good beachside choice if you can't get a booking at **BiCE** (p82).

PRIME RIB Map pp206-7 *Steakhouse*
☎ 399 5555; Le Royal Meridien Beach Resort, Al-Mina al-Seyahi; mains Dh85; ☯ 7pm-midnight

This smart neo-Deco dining room specialises in Angus beef imported from the United

Kitsch Kitchen Korner

For every good dining idea in Dubai, there's usually several less than stellar ideas. Blame it on the Burj, blame it on Palm Island, but the gimmicky dining experiences in Dubai just keep coming.

- **Aeroplane** (Map pp208-9; Golden Tulip Aeroplane Hotel) Considering that most tourists coming to Dubai have endured a hellish flight that's longer than the *Lord of the Rings* trilogy, who really wants to sit in a mock-up of an aeroplane cabin – especially when it's a dry 'flight'?
- **Al Mahara** (Map pp206-7; Burj Al Arab) Sure, it's a seafood restaurant with a stunning aquarium, but do you really need to arrive by a 'fake' submarine complete with a 'captain' and a 'control deck'? Is this really a fitting way to arrive at one of Dubai's most expensive restaurants?
- **Bamboo Lagoon** (Map pp210-11; JW Marriott Hotel) There are plenty of other restaurants in Dubai guilty of bringing the world in – Polynesian huts, a rainforest and trickling fountains – but it's the performers in grass skirts that push this one over the edge.
- **Go West** (Map pp206-7; Jumeirah Beach Hotel) Sitting in your own wagon, served by cowgirls and cowboys – it's so surreal you'll find yourself humming the Village People's anthemic hit.
- **Venezia** (Map pp206-7; Metropolitan Hotel) Ah, Venice. A restaurant complete with a canal, gondola and gondolier, bridges, street lamps and faux buildings. It's all here. The only question remains is why, oh why?

States. In typical steakhouse fashion there's a fair smattering of seafood on the menu as well, but certainly here the cow is king. The music of early jazz greats pleasantly fills the room, the staff know their stuff and there's a comprehensive wine list. A sound choice for carnivorous diners.

RETRO Map pp206-7   *Modern European*
☎ 399 3333; Le Meridien Mina Seyahi Resort, Al-Mina al-Seyahi; mains Dh90; ⏰ 7-11pm

Retro is often (mistakenly) heralded as one of Dubai's best fine-dining establishments, but it's really just competent and sporadically imaginative bistro food served in a restaurant with retro-futuristic touches in the décor. Not that there's anything wrong with that. The menu changes often (but the lamb or duck dishes are usually good), the wine list is fine and the service excellent. The outdoor seating is pleasant when weather permits.

TAGINE Map pp206-7   *Moroccan*
☎ 399 9999; One&Only Royal Mirage, Al-Mina al-Seyahi; mains Dh75; ⏰ 7-11pm

Tagine offers one of those all-encompassing dining experiences. As soon as you walk in you feel as if you've wandered into a wonderful restaurant in a back street of Fez. A marvellous taste of Morocco is on offer here from the

harira (spicy chickpea soup) to the pigeon pastilla and to the rich tagine or couscous royale. If you like Moroccan music book a table near the live musicians.

THAI BISTRO Map pp216-17   *Thai*
☎ 346 1111; Dubai Marine Beach Resort & Spa; mains Dh50; ⏰ 7-11.30pm

In the increasingly crowded Thai restaurant scene in Dubai, Thai Bistro earns its place with its lovely alfresco terrace and competent Thai cuisine. The setting over the pool is tranquil, the soups are good and the service relaxed. The parade of partygoers heading to the bars and clubs opposite makes for an interesting sideshow, but Thai lovers will find it hard to ignore such incongruous dishes as profiteroles on the dessert menu.

ZHENG HE'S
Map pp216-17   *Contemporary Chinese*
☎ 366 8888; Mina A'Salam, Madinat Jumeirah; mains Dh70; ⏰ noon-3pm & 7-11.30pm

With its dazzlingly beautiful interior and an alfresco area featuring one of the most stunning views in Dubai, the Zheng He experience gets off to an excellent start. With surroundings like this the food doesn't need to be as good as it is to keep people coming back, but thankfully the kitchen doesn't disappoint. Try the dim sum for starters and move on to one of the meat or tank-fresh fish dishes for a memorable meal in superlative surroundings.

Peppercrab (p77)

CHEAP EATS

CAFÉ GERARD Map pp216-17 *Café*

☎ 344 3327; Magrudy's Shopping Centre, Jumeirah Rd; coffee Dh10

A great people-watching café in the atrium of this small shopping centre. Seating is occupied by an intriguing mix of customers: Emiratis juggling cigarettes and cell phones; ladies who lunch and a few sunburned tourists, all relaxing over coffees. There's another branch in **Al-Ghurair City** (Map pp208-9).

CHINESE KITCHEN Map pp206-7 *Chinese*

☎ 394 3864; Al-Wasl Rd; mains Dh25; ☽ noon-3pm & 6pm-midnight

An independent Chinese restaurant serving authentic home-made Chinese specialities from Szechwan and Canton. Try the wontons, the scrumptious seafood dishes or the duck. The décor can be filed under 'Chinese restaurant', the service friendly and it does takeaway.

JAPENGO CAFÉ Map pp216-17 *Café*

☎ 345 4979; Palm Strip, opposite Jumeirah Mosque; mains Dh35; ☽ noon-midnight

This eternally packed slice of Jumeirah Beach life attracts customers who like to watch each other and the world go by from the outdoor seating. The food is eclectic (to say the least) with strange bedfellows such as pizza and sushi sharing the one menu, but the café carries it off with its own casual charm.

LIME TREE CAFÉ Map pp216-17 *Café*

☎ 349 8498; near Jumeirah Mosque, Jumeirah Rd; mains Dh20; ☽ 7.30am-8pm

This pleasant green villa is very popular with Jumeirah expats missing those good local cafés back home. There's a daily menu often featuring frittatas, quiches and salads, and there's a range of delectable cakes worth saving room for. It's the kind of café that's all too rare in Dubai, so it's always busy.

Entertainment

Entertainment

Dubai is the most happening city in the Gulf, and if it wasn't for Beirut, it would be the hippest in the Middle East. With an enormous range of bars, pubs, clubs, cinemas and one-off events, there's no shortage of things to do. The problem will be deciding where to go on which night. The entertainment scene is constantly changing. The best way to keep up is to read *Mumtazz* or *What's On* magazines. Almost everything – rhythm and blues (R & B), funk, trip-hop, pop, rock, jazz or quiet piano music – is available somewhere.

How much will you spend? If you're drinking, plan on spending well over Dh150 and even nondrinkers could easily go through half that in cover charges and soft drinks. Dubai's licensing laws require venues serving alcohol to be attached to hotels or private clubs. As a result you may also pay a service charge.

As befits a port city, Dubai's nightlife has its seamy side. Plenty of hotels in Deira and near Bur Dubai have nightclubs and cabarets where women offer fee-based hospitality. They're often ethnically based (eg 'Dhaka by Night, the Bengali Disco Inferno') and are advertised with posters showing women in luridly spangled clothing and heavy make-up. Quite a few popular watering holes turn sleazy late at night, or have one night a week when working girls appear.

Bars and clubs don't stay hip for long as Dubai's party people are a fickle bunch. Creative media types are the first to adopt a new bar or club, which often reaches the peak of its popularity when airline crews follow their lead. Then, almost overnight, the focus shifts elsewhere. Several venues in Dubai have gone in and out and back into fashion depending on the promoter of the club.

Hindi movie posters, Strand cinema (p98)

Getting Out with the In Crowd

To stay in touch with what's happening, there's a range of options:

- Read the monthly glossy entertainment magazines, such as *What's On*, and the daily newspapers.
- Check out the info racks in record shops, such as the Virgin MegaStore and Ohm Records, where you can pick up promotional leaflets.
- Make sure you grab a copy of *Mumtazz*, a monthly guide to dance clubs, or log on to www.mumtazz.com.
- For tickets to concerts, club nights and other major events you can phone the Time Out ticket line on 800 4669 or buy online at www.itptickets.com.
- For details about acts at Dubai Tennis Stadium visit www.aviationclubonline.com.
- For details of those promoted by Motivate Publishing, email marketing@motivate.com.

SHEESHA CAFÉS

When in Dubai you have to try one of the city's most relaxing and traditional pastimes – *sheesha*. A *sheesha*, also known as a water pipe, hubble-bubble or nargileh, is a long-stemmed, glass-bottomed smoking implement standing about 50cm high. They are common in various forms across most of the Middle East. The ones used in Dubai are similar to those found in Lebanon and Egypt. *Sheesha* pipes are packed with flavoured tobacco, such as apple, anise, strawberry, vanilla, coffee or tropical – the range of flavours is endless and good *sheesha* cafés, like good wine bars, pride themselves on the variety on offer on their menus. The

going rate for a *sheesha* is Dh10 to Dh15. *Sheesha* cafés are open until well after midnight, much later during the cooler winter months when the city's population spends its evenings outdoors.

AL-AREESH RESTAURANT Map pp206-7

☎ 324 3000; Al-Boom Tourist Village, Bur Dubai; ☽ noon-4pm, 7pm-midnight

Smoke some *sheesha* in a peaceful setting on the lawn, under palm trees, overlooking the eastern end of the Creek.

COSMO CAFÉ Map p218

☎ 332 6569; the Tower, Sheikh Zayed Rd; ☽ 8.30-1am

This stylish café is where the beautiful people go to smoke *sheesha*. Popular with young Arabs, stay here for any length of time and you might think you're watching a fashion show.

FATAFEET CAFÉ Map pp212-13

☎ 397 9222; Al-Seef Rd, Bur Dubai; ☽ 10.30am-midnight

Fatafeet is one of the best places to enjoy a *sheesha* in Dubai. Offering tasty traditional Egyptian food on the menu, friendly service, Lebanese music videos and old black-and-white Egyptian movies on TV, you'll also admire great views across the water to Deira. The ideal time to go is at sunset for the reflections on the glass buildings and when the whole city takes on a golden glow.

KAN ZAMAN Map pp212-13

☎ 393 9914; Heritage & Diving Villages, Shindagha; ☽ 11-3am

Kan Zaman is more of a restaurant than a *sheesha* joint, but its sprawling size, buzzy atmosphere, popularity with Emiratis and Arab expats and wonderful waterfront location make it a must for a *sheesha*.

Dimitri Chami's Top Five Sheesha Cafés

If you want to know where the best *sheesha* in town is, it's best to consult an aficionado – and no-one enjoys their *sheesha* more than the Lebanese. Former Beirut boy Dimitri Chami has lived in Dubai for 13 years and like most Lebanese guys he loves life – he loves his family, his food and he sure loves his *sheesha*. Dimitri and friends catch up for *sheesha* several times a week and these are Dimitri's Dubai recommendations:

- Cosmo Café (above), Sheikh Zayed Rd
- Fatafeet Café (above), Bur Dubai
- Reem Al Bawadi (p90), Jumeirah Rd
- Shakespeare & Company (p90), Sheikh Zayed Rd
- Shisha Courtyard (p90), Jumeirah

Nights on the Town – Itineraries

As Dubai has become a bit of an urban sprawl (in a very short period of time) and traffic chaos reigns supreme on Wednesday and Thursday nights, it's wise to stick to one area of town for the evening. Here are some suggested itineraries for a night on the town.

Bur Dubai

There are two excellent options in Bur Dubai for an action-packed night out – Wafi City or the Grand Hyatt Dubai. If heading to Wafi, begin the evening with wine and cheese at **Vintage** (p94), followed by tapas and sangria at **Seville's** (p94), dinner at **Asha's** (p76) or **Medzo** (p77), cocktails at **Ginseng** (p92) and dance the rest of the hours away at **Planetarium** (p96). The Grand Hyatt offers an equally lively night, where you can enjoy dinner at **Indochine** (p77) or **Peppercrab** (p77). You could then have some sheesha upstairs at Awtar, while you watch a belly dancer or Lebanese singer, before joining the crowd at Dubai's biggest dance club, the **Mix** (p96).

Deira

Split a night in Deira between the InterContinental Dubai and Hilton Dubai Creek. Have a glass of champagne and watch the sun go down at **Up on the Tenth** (p94) at the InterContinental. Stroll up the road to the Hilton for a predinner drink at the **Carbon Lounge** (p92), before having the ultimate fine-dining experience at Gordon Ramsay's **Verre** (p74). Follow your meal with a cocktail at **Issimo Cocktail Bar** (p93) or a dance at **M-Level** (p96), depending on the night. If you feel like a quiet one take a stroll along the waterfront and watch the dhows being loaded in the cool of the evening. Still up for some more? Head back to the InterContinental and **Ku Bu** (p93) for a cocktail, or into **La Moda** (p72) to watch the band.

Sheikh Zayed Road

You can spend one night at the World Trade Centre end of Sheikh Zayed Rd. Start the evening off with a sunset drink at **Vu's Bar** (p94), then a glass of vino or two at the **Agency** (p91). If you're still keen on bar-hopping head over to **Bar** (p92) at Spectrum on One at Fairmont hotel. For a casual meal, return to Emirates Towers and the buzzy **Noodle House** (p81). If you want a more formal dinner you can head upstairs to **Vu's** (p82) restaurant or to fine Vietnamese fusion cuisine at **Hoi An** (p82) at the Shangri-La. After dinner, check out the Moroccan band at **Marrakech** (p93), or make your way back to the Fairmont for a dance at **Tangerine** (p96).

Jumeirah

Start your night at the far end of Jumeirah Beach Rd by enjoying a relaxed sunset drink on the veranda at **Bahri Bar** (p91) at the Mina A'Salam. If your views of the Burj Al Arab aren't close enough, head down to the bar by the beach. Still not satisfied? Take a taxi to the Burj and head up to the **Skyview Bar** (p94). Don't eat too many of those delicious hors d'oeuvre – save room for a magnificent meal at one of the One&Only Royal Mirage's fabulous restaurants, such as **Eauzone** (p83), **Nina's** (p84) or **Tagine** (p85). Chill out to some Arabic fusion with a postdinner drink on the **Rooftop Bar** (p93). If you want to mellow some more, head to the atmospheric **Shisha Courtyard** (p90). If you're up for some dancing wait in line to get into **Kasbar** (p95) – it's worth it. For a change of scenery take a cab up Jumeirah Beach Rd to **Sho Cho's** (p94) and **Boudoir** (p95), where you can boogie the night away.

REEM AL BAWADI Map pp206-7

☎ 394 7444; opposite Jumeirah Park; ✆ 8-3am

A hit with Arab expats, this café has authentic Arabic food and an oasislike atmosphere.

SHAKESPEARE & COMPANY

Map p218

☎ 331 1757; Kendah House, Sheikh Zayed Rd; ✆ 7-1.30am

This casual and comfy café will immediately make you feel at home. Frequented by women and families too, it serves sheesha on the shady terrace outside.

SHISHA COURTYARD Map pp206-7

☎ 399 9999; One&Only Royal Mirage, Jumeirah; ✆ 7pm-1am

If the chance to recline in a *majlis* (reception room) and smoke *sheesha* in the atmospheric Arabian courtyard of a magnificent Moroccan-style hotel aren't enough to tempt you in, the more than 20 different *sheesha* flavours may.

BARS & PUBS

Cosmopolitan Dubai has an ever-increasing range of bars and pubs to suit all tastes and moods – groove the night away at a funky Asian fusion or minimalist designer bar, drink sangria and salsa at a Spanish tavern, chill out and enjoy the balmy breeze at a beachside bar, unwind with a beer or two at a typical Irish pub, or sip cocktails as you admire the city lights and starry sky from above. The multicultural nature of the place means that you'll hear an amazing mix of music in any one night, from R & B to bhangra, experimental Arabic vibes to the latest Ibiza anthem.

You will also rub shoulders with a wild variety of people. Dubai isn't as segregated as some international cities. You may find yourself sharing space with slick Lebanese expats in suits, gorgeous long-legged Russians or French media types. Don't be surprised to see Gulf Arabs enjoying a good glass of white. Officially it's illegal for them to purchase alcohol, but nobody cares – after all, this is Dubai, probably the most tolerant and cosmopolitan city in the Middle East.

Pubs and bars in Dubai are open until 2am or 3am and are well stocked with a wide range of spirits, wines and beers from around the globe. You could pay anything from Dh15 to Dh30 for a pint of beer or Dh20 to Dh50 for a glass of wine, depending on the quality and vintage. Bars and pubs in five-star hotels also add a service charge although this is sometimes built into the cost. Drinks may seem expensive, but once you calculate the price in your own currency, you'll find they're very reasonably priced compared to most European countries and even compare favourably with those of the same standard in Australia and North America. Your drinks will often be accompanied by large bowls of nuts, finger food or hors d'oeuvre that are frequently replenished, making the prices seem all the more reasonable. Most bars and pubs also have a happy hour with half-price drinks, two-for-one deals or other promotions, such as ladies' nights, when those of the right gender get them for free (see the boxed text on p92). Happy hour times vary from place to place, as do ladies' nights. Check out *Mumtazz* (www.mumtazz.com) or the monthly entertainment mags for details.

AGENCY Map p218
☎ 330 0000; Emirates Towers Shopping Boulevard, Sheikh Zayed Rd; ☽ 12.30pm-1am Sat-Thu, 3pm-1am Fri

This smart wine bar is one of the most popular and a favourite after-work spot, for good reason. There's an extensive list of Old and New World wines, a good range of quality wines by the glass, themed tasting selections (Dh75 for four wines), and a variety of tasty snacks and 'wine teasers'. Try the chicken liver pâté with apricot chutney (Dh30), basil-marinated Gorgonzola and Roma tomatoes (Dh28), marinated Manchega cheese with garlic-cured olives (Dh28), fried squid and chips with alioli (Dh24) or the cheese selection (Dh58).

APARTMENT Map pp206-7
☎ 406 8181; Jumeirah Beach Hotel, Jumeirah; ☽ 7pm-1am

Although it's better known as a sophisticated fine-dining restaurant (see p82), the Apartment consists of several luxuriously furnished rooms, one of which resembles a comfortable living room while another is more like a cellar bar. If you have a dinner booking, go early for the complementary wine and cheese, otherwise enjoy a quiet glass of champagne before the beautiful people hit the bar around 1am.

BAHRI BAR Map pp206-7
☎ 366 8888; Mina A'Salam, Madinat Jumeirah; ☽ noon-2am

There's no better place to unwind than the vast veranda of this colonial Arabian-style bar, complete with comfy sofas, Persian carpets and candlelight. From the balcony of the Bahri Bar you can sip a chilled glass of white, eat Arabian tapas, enjoy the balmy breeze and take in breathtaking views of the harbour and sea. Or you can admire the best architecture Dubai has to offer with the magnificent Burj Al Arab in front of you and the magical Mina A'Salam all around you. The interior of the bar is equally atmospheric.

BALCONY BAR Map p218
☎ 343 8888; Shangri-La, Sheikh Zayed Rd; ☽ noon-2am

In one of the most elegant and tastefully styled hotels in the city, you can enjoy coffee, cigars and cognac in a dark-wood designer bar.

Top Wine Bars
- **Agency** (above), Emirates Towers
- **Apartment** (above), Jumeirah Beach Hotel
- **Bar** (p92), Spectrum on One, Fairmont hotel
- **Vintage** (p94), Wafi City

Ladies' Nights

Every night is ladies' night in Dubai. It's just a matter of choosing the right bar or club for cheap or free drinks... Here's a sampler.

- Saturday – at **Harry Ghatto's** (below) the girls get 40% off the bill
- Sunday – free cocktails at **Tangerine** (p96) or two free drinks at **Oxygen** (p96)
- Tuesday – a big night in Dubai – two-for-one cocktails before 10pm at **Ginseng** (p92), two free drinks at **Zinc** (p97) between 6pm and 11pm, or, better yet, free-flowing champagne at **Boudoir** (p95)
- Wednesday – women get two free drinks from 8.30pm to 11.30pm at **Long's** (p93) and two free drinks before 1am at **Planetarium** (p96)
- Friday – **Seville's** (p94) offers two free drinks between 6pm and 8pm, free paella at sundown

BAR Map p218

☎ 332 5555; Spectrum on One, Fairmont, Sheikh Zayed Rd; ☼ 7pm-1am

In addition to an array of dining areas and interactive kitchens, there's a stylish bar at the back of Spectrum on One, overlooking Sheikh Zayed Rd. With a long bar, moody wood, a few comfortable seating areas, an enormous glassed-in wine cellar and an innovative cocktail menu (try the Bikini Martini), this is a bar for people who take their drinking seriously.

THE BAR Map p218

☎ 330 0000; Emirates Towers, Sheikh Zayed Rd; ☼ 6.30pm-1am

This very dusky but fashionable bar, just off the hotel lobby, has changed its identity a few times. Adjoining the Rib Room, it's the perfect place for a pre- or postdinner drink. If the TV inside is too annoying, take up a position on the voguish white leather seats out front and enjoy the people-watching.

BARASTI BAR Map pp206-7

☎ 399 3333; Le Meridien Mina Seyahi Resort; ☼ 6pm-2am

This laid-back outdoor restaurant and seaside bar is the spot to sip a drink and watch the sun go down on a balmy afternoon. The big night here is Friday, when a DJ pulls in a funky young crowd for the Mina Moon Beach Party. On other nights of the week it's more of a peaceful place to watch the waves roll in.

BOLLYWOOD CAFÉ Map pp212-13

☎ 355 6633; Regal Plaza Hotel, Bur Dubai; ☼ 7pm-3am

The Bollywood Café is most definitely a bar and not a café, and can be rather sleazy at that. This is the place to go for the bizarre experience of seeing a live Bollywood performance with beautiful Indian women miming to the movie hits. You probably won't want to stay too long, especially if you're a single woman, as the late shows can get spicier than the curries.

CARBON LOUNGE Map pp208-9

☎ 227 1111; Hilton Dubai Creek, Deira; ☼ 6pm-1am

A sleek setting, superb cocktails and slight views of Dubai Creek make this a perfect spot for a Bellini before dining at **Glasshouse** (p72) or **Verre** (p74).

EL MALECON Map pp216-17

☎ 304 8281; Dubai Marine Beach Resort & Spa, Jumeirah; ☼ 7.30pm-3am

While flavourful Cuban-inspired food is served in this graffiti-walled interior – inspired by Havana's favourite bar the Bodeguita del Medio – El Malecon is better known for its live Cuban and Latino music, cocktails and salsa dancing. The place hots up around midnight when you'd think you were at Carnivale. Pens are available so you can add your autograph to the walls and salsa lessons are offered some nights.

GINSENG Map pp214-15

☎ 324 4777; Wafi City, Bur Dubai; ☼ 7pm-2am Fri-Wed, 7pm-3am Thu

Sip the best *caiparinhas* (drinks made with traditional Brazilian sugar cane cachaça) in town at this funky East-meets-West bar while admiring the contemporary orange, red and beige interior and giant wall mirrors. Spicy Asian tapas are on the menu while DJ Stickyfingers serves up very cool grooves. Saturday's special is a dozen dim sum and bottle of wine for Dh99.

HARRY GHATTO'S Map p218

☎ 330 0000; Tokyo @ the Towers, Emirates Towers Shopping Boulevard, Sheikh Zayed Rd; ☼ 7.30pm-3am

At the back of Tokyo @ the Towers, this intimate karaoke bar is popular with the afterwork crowd and gets packed on a Wednesday night after the sake has taken effect.

ISSIMO COCKTAIL BAR Map pp208-9

☎ 227 1111; Hilton Dubai Creek, Deira; 🕓 9pm-3am

Café by day, cocktail bar by night, late Wednesday night is the best time to go to Issimo, when it transforms into Jazz Clinic. Sink into the black leather sofas and unwind to the smooth sounds of jazz and trip-hop, or sit yourself on a stool and mingle with the mellow yet sociable crowd.

JULES Map pp210-11

☎ 282 4040; Le Meridien Dubai, Al-Garhoud; 🕓 11-3am

This American-themed bar has a resident Filipino band and a menu featuring Cajun, Tex-Mex and Filipino food. It attracts a mixed crowd, gay and straight – Filipino expats, Gulf Arabs and businesswomen from the former Soviet Union – Dubai nightlife in a nutshell.

KU BU Map pp208-9

☎ 222 7171; InterContinental Hotel, Deira; 🕓 6pm-3am

If this dark groovy bar with contemporary Afro-cool interiors isn't intimate enough, there are tiny secluded corners made all the more cosy by velvet curtains. Get comfy with some cocktails and your friends, and the slick music will ensure you stay settled for the night.

MAI TAI LOUNGE Map p218

☎ 331 1111; Trader Vic's, Crowne Plaza Hotel; 🕓 7pm-1.30am

Even if you don't want to eat at this delicious Polynesian restaurant, you can still enjoy the exotic oversized cocktails, stylish island atmosphere and tasty seafood snacks as you bop away to the Cuban band.

MARRAKECH Map p218

☎ 343 8888; Shangri-La, Sheikh Zayed Rd; 🕓 1-3pm, 7.30pm-1am

More of a restaurant than a bar, but the staff will let you stick to drinks and mezzes and watch the lively performance by the magnificent three-piece traditional Moroccan band. In between sets sit back and enjoy the authentic Moroccan surroundings to the trickle of the fountain.

ROOFTOP BAR Map pp208-9

☎ 399 9999; One&Only Royal Mirage, Jumeirah; 🕓 5pm-12.45am

Chill out for a while on the cushion-covered banquettes of this exotic *The Thousand and One Nights*–styled bar and you'll be heading to the souq the next day to recreate this oriental fantasy palace back home. From the moment you climb the candle-lit stairs, to your first

Top Ye Old Pubs

The old English-style pubs in Dubai were the lifeblood of the expat, an informal social club where one could meet others who shared a love of bad food and warm beer. Given the expat scene today where no-one talks to people outside their clique unless they've been sampling a two-for-one vodka promotion, the pubs are still a good place to meet for conversation and a few ales.

So, for your drinking and socialising pleasure, here are some of the better ones. But don't blame us if you get stuck talking to an oil engineer who's been in the Gulf on and off since the '70s and is reminiscing through his beer goggles...

- **Aussie Legends Bar** (Map pp216-17; ☎ 398 2222; Rydges Plaza Hotel, Satwa; 🕓 3pm-3am Fri-Wed, noon-3am Thu) The pride and joy of Dubai's first Aussie bar is the telly pumping out footy and cricket.
- **Carters** (Map pp212-13; ☎ 324 0000; Pyramids, Wafi City; 🕓 noon-2am) This kitsch pub and restaurant is a Dubai institution. Overlook, or find humour in, the colonial Egyptian theme, or head to the outdoor terrace instead.
- **Dubliners** (Map pp210-11; ☎ 282 4040; behind Le Meridien Dubai, Al-Garhoud; 🕓 11-3am) This smoky, boozy Irish bar serves pub grub and stays open late.
- **Irish Village** (Map pp210-11; ☎ 282 4750; Aviation Club, Dubai Tennis Stadium, off Al-Garhoud Rd, Deira; 🕓 11-1.15am) Popular with British expats, this casual watering hole, with its large outdoor area, is the best of the Irish pubs.
- **Long's Bar** (Map p218; ☎ 312 2202; Tower Rotana Hotel, Sheikh Zayed Rd; 🕓 noon-3am) This American-style pub is renowned for having the longest bar, live bands and staying open late. On Friday happy hour lasts all day with drinks costing Dh12.
- **Rock Bottom Café** (Map pp212-13; ☎ 396 3888; Regent Palace Hotel, Sheikh Khalifa bin Zayed Rd, Bur Dubai; 🕓 10-3am) Another Dubai institution, this is the pub/pick-up joint people end up at when common sense should tell them to go home. Eat free fish and chips from 3pm to 7pm on Sunday.

glimpse of the rooftop decked out with Persian carpets and Moroccan lanterns, you won't want to leave. Just wait till you get settled in with a glass of wine to watch the sun set over the sea. During the hot summer months, the inside bar is equally atmospheric.

SEVILLE'S Map pp214-15

☎ 324 7300; Wafi City, Bur Dubai; ☾ noon-2am Sat-Wed, noon-3am Thu-Fri

This popular Spanish bar-cum-restaurant has the best sangria and tastiest tapas in town. During the cooler months you can settle on the outdoor terrace overlooking an amazing swimming pool and allow the Spanish guitarists to entertain you.

SHO CHO'S Map pp216-17

☎ 346 1111; Dubai Marine Beach Resort & Spa, Jumeirah Rd; ☾ 7.30pm-12.30am Sat-Wed, 7.30pm-2.30am Thu-Fri

The interior of this glossy sushi bar (with in-house DJ) is way sharp – futuristic white leather chairs, neon-blue light and fish tanks in the walls. During the winter months, the bar swells to an outdoor deck where you can enjoy the balmy beach breezes and music – from 10pm to 2am kick back to deep house on Wednesday and Thursday, tribal and progressive house on Friday.

SKYVIEW BAR Map pp208-9

☎ 301 7438; Burj Al Arab, Jumeirah; ☾ 11-2am

The boldly coloured ceilings and carpets and over-the-top décor may make your stomach churn, but the head-turning views of Dubai make it all worthwhile. Phone ahead to make sure the hotel isn't at full capacity, then pay Dh200 at the security entrance, which can be redeemed at any of the outlets inside. Unfortunately for most, who can only afford to stay for the one quick drink, saying you've been to the world's first seven-star hotel is what it's

all about. The wines are superb, the complementary snacks are continually replenished, and the hors d'oeuvre are rather delicious, so ask for a window seat and settle in for some time.

UP ON THE TENTH Map pp208-9

☎ 205 7333; InterContinental Dubai; ☾ noon-3am

Not as sophisticated as we all once thought when it was one of the few upmarket bars in the city, the floor to ceiling windows of this five-star piano bar still provide superb views of Dubai Creek. There's good champagne and live jazz some nights.

UPTOWN Map pp206-7

☎ 348 0000; 24th fl, Jumeirah Beach Hotel, Jumeirah Rd; ☾ 7pm-2am

Sit inside in this elegant bar or outside on the terrace – from either position you'll savour spectacular views of the turquoise sea, the magnificent Burj Al Arab and the sublime sandy coast towards the centre of Dubai.

VINTAGE Map pp214-15

☎ 324 0000; Wafi City, Bur Dubai; ☾ 6pm-1.30am

Wine aficionados not only love the awesome wine list, sophisticated atmosphere and wide range of grape by the glass, the delicious cheese selections also tempt the tasters in. Particularly popular is the Monday and Friday promotion – cheese fondue for two with a bottle of wine for Dh100.

VU'S BAR Map p218

☎ 330 0000; 51st fl, Emirates Towers, Sheikh Zayed Rd; ☾ 6pm-2am

At 220m above Dubai, Vu's has amazing views over the city. Most of the drinks also have equally amazing prices, although there are some delicious and more reasonably priced wines by the glass. The super stylish décor, starry sky and views down Sheikh Zayed Rd will compensate.

DANCE CLUBS

In the past Dubai's bars and restaurants often turned into nightclubs, until a whole spate of purpose-driven spaces started to appear, including Dubai's first superclub, Mix. Dance events have taken off, with visits by everyone from influential club-culture king Norman Jay to Café del Mar's Jose Cassias; and hotels such as Le Meridien Mina Seyahi Resort host regular Moon Parties and fly in Ibiza DJs. At these wild, heaving events you can expect to see fire-eaters, jugglers, trapeze artists, stilt walkers, bongo players and podium dancers. Dubai's club scene is not as segregated as it once was, although there are still Arabic, Filipino and Indian clubs, with their own types of music and atmosphere. These days the crowds are much more mixed and the fun can happen anywhere, anytime. Motion Beach, with its Café del Mar ambience, happens every Friday afternoon at the Hilton Dubai Jumeirah, although Wednesday, Thursday and Friday nights are the big ones. Most people don't go out until midnight and dance floors don't heat up until 2am or 3am.

Like any city in the world, you'll find that established clubs may be physically or spiritually transformed for a particular night of the week or month. Global Funk takes over Tangerine (www.globalfunkdxb.com), Fluid Productions turns Tangerine into Peppermint Lounge (www.peppermintclub.com) and DJ Dany brings Beirut's megaclub Crystal to Tangerine. With the help of DJ Stephane Pompougnac from Paris, Boudoir becomes Hotel Costes (www.glamourdubai.com), Lady DJ Fizzi turns Planetarium into Club Persia (www.clubpersia.net) and Ohm Records turns Mix into DV8. One of the hottest places at the moment is Terminal, recently opened at the Millennium Airport Hotel by the 9714 guys. Formerly known

as MIS, this creative bunch is behind the success of **Issimo Cocktail Bar's** (p93) Jazz Clinic, Secret Garden, various one-off events and the funky lifestyle store **Five Green** (p128).

Log on to www.mumtazz.com to stay in touch with what's going on.

BOUDOIR Map pp216-17

☎ 345 5995; Dubai Marine Beach Resort & Spa, Jumeirah Beach Rd; ☽ 7.30pm-4.30am

An opulent Parisian-style restaurant-cum-cocktail bar-cum-nightclub draped with rich red velvet booths, hanging glass beads, gilt-edged frames and crystal chandeliers – think Baz Luhrmann's *Moulin Rouge* – trés chic. This is the place where international supermodels come when they're in town.

KASBAR Map pp206-7

☎ 399 9999; One&Only Royal Mirage, Al-Sufouh Rd; admission Dh50; ☽ 9.30pm-3am Mon-Sat

The admission fee to this Moroccan-themed nightclub, set in a lavish hotel complex, entitles you to one free drink. The décor alone is worth the fee. The club is built on three levels overlooking the dance floor; the uppermost is the most exclusive. The music is a mix of popular dance hits and techno-Arabic. If you want to meet a wealthy young sheikh, this would be the place.

MAHARLIKA Map pp214-15

☎ 334 6565; President Hotel, Sheikh Khalifa bin Zayed Rd, Karama; admission Dh25; ☽ 6pm-3am

The main attractions of this popular Filipino nightclub are the vibrant changing floorshow and live bands, which have included Hot City, Hot Stuff and Elvis Presley Asia. Filipinos get in for free. Everyone else pays Dh25 but that gets you one free drink.

M-LEVEL Map pp208-9

☎ 227 1111; Hilton Dubai Creek, Deira; ☺ 9pm-3am

This super hip space on the Hilton's mezzanine level hosts one-off events, launches, private parties and nights such as Pulse. The venue is beautifully designed with a casual but sleek ambience and there's an outdoor deck where you can take a break from the dance floor and freshen up during the winter months.

OXYGEN Map pp210-11

☎ 282 0000; Al-Bustan Rotana Hotel, Deira; ☺ 6pm-3am

It's a small club, but the mainstay of clubbing on this side of the Creek. Oxygen attracts regular touring DJs and the crowds that follow them. It's a superlative weekend choice regardless of who's playing.

PLANETARIUM Map pp214-15

☎ 324 4777; Wafi City, Bur Dubai; ☺ 10pm-3am

Planetarium has reached legendary status in Dubai and it hosts special appearances by international disc jockeys and club acts. DJ Charlie C mans the decks for the always popular Real Flava R&B nights (on Wednesday and Friday), but rumours do exist that the clubs is closing for renovation. Check it out while you can.

TANGERINE Map p218

☎ 332 5555; Fairmont, Sheikh Zayed Rd; ☺ 8pm-3am

A mellow bar early on during the evening, Tangerine hots up around 11pm with a stylishly dressed crowd taking over the VIP area. When it's not too busy you can check out the rich oriental interior. When it is, expect the power-crazed door staff to be selective about who gets in.

The Fairmont (p145), home of several entertainment venues

MIX Map pp206-7

☎ Grand Hyatt Dubai, Bur Dubai; ☺ 9pm-3am, closed Sat

Dubai's first superclub comes complete with a big bar, swanky VIP area, bongo players and podium dancers, and plays host to a number of themed nights. Because it holds so many people, even with a couple of hundred punters inside it still looks empty, so check out the vibe first before settling in.

DJ Stickyfingers' Top Five Nights

Former Londoner Noel Miller, AKA DJ Stickyfingers, is still one of the hottest DJs in Dubai after seven years in the city. Noel was on a Dubai stopover when he decided to stay. A short time later he was manning the decks at Carters – after telling management the music sucked. These days you can listen to him on Arabian Radio Network or hear him at one of his many DJ residencies. Here are some of his favourite Dubai nights.

- **Boudoir** (p95) on Tuesday
- **Issimo Cocktail Bar** (p93) on Wednesday
- **Mix** (above) on Thursday
- **Sho Cho's** (p94) on Wednesday
- **Tangerine** (above) on Wednesday

TERMINAL Map pp210-11

☎ 398 2206; Millennium Airport Hotel; ☾ 10pm-3am

This brand new bar has been given a back-to-basics dark and dingy look. Expect some of the most innovative nights around. Oriental fusion sounds, bhangra nights and abstract jazz.

ZINC Map p218

☎ 331 1111; Crowne Plaza Hotel, Sheikh Zayed Rd; ☾ 7pm-3am

A bar, restaurant and club in one, Zinc has three bars and a large dance floor. It's busy most nights but on Saturday it's full of Dubai workers getting in some last-minute partying before returning to work on Sunday. You'll hear R & B and MTV standards, but it's fun.

CONCERTS, LIVE MUSIC & EVENTS

While some older expatriates like to reminisce to the hits of the '70s and '80s, there is an ever-increasing proportion of young professionals who are in touch with what's happening around the globe. This market segment is enticing the major players in the music world to add Dubai to their tours. As a result, the choice is far greater than it was a few years ago, when the most exciting performers to hit town were Elton John, Billy Joel, Sting, Enrique Iglesias or Geri Halliwell. While Blondie, Bryan Adams, Mariah Carey and Whitney Huston recently performed in Dubai, now the city also sees some massive cutting-edge, DJ-driven dance nights and franchised global club events such as Ministry of Sound.

If you want to experience something different, take the opportunity to catch some Arabian, Middle Eastern, Persian or subcontinental stars. The legendary Fairouz, Cheb Mami, the 4 Cats and Ehab Toufic, Nawal al-Zoghbi, Homaira and Mansour, Iranian heart-throbs Daryush and Ebi, Persian pop stars Arian and Shadmeher, Lebanese megastars Haifa and Nancy Ajram, and Pakistani Hadiqa Kani (the highest selling female artist on the subcontinent), have all performed in Dubai. Other types of music performed live in Dubai include jazz, classical, sitar and flamenco guitar. You can easily find good Moroccan bands, Indian sitar players and Spanish flamenco guitarists in five-star hotel restaurants. Classical music concerts and performances are also organised by embassies and cultural organisations including Alliance Française and the British Council.

Dubai attracts the bizarre big events – the *Shaolin Show*, *Spirit of the Horse*, Michael Flatley's *Lord of the Dance* and *Cirque Surreal*. Bollywood superstar AR Rahman, who worked with Andrew Lloyd Webber on *Bombay Dreams*, recently brought his *Unity of Light* show here – a three-hour spectacle supported by a troupe of 100 performers playing to huge audiences.

Live music is on offer at the large hotels, while concerts and big events are usually held at the Aviation Club, Dubai Tennis Stadium, Nad al-Sheba Club, Dubai International Convention Centre, Dubai Country Club, the Dubai Creek Golf & Yacht Club, Al-Wasl Football Stadium, and Dubai Media City Amphitheatre. One-off DJ-powered dance nights take place at some of these venues, but more often at Mix, on the beach at Le Meridien Mina Seyahi Beach Resort & Spa or at out-of-town venues.

Tickets for concerts vary from Dh120 to Dh400 for VIP seats. Dance party prices depend on which DJs are playing, but expect to pay at least Dh80 for a special event.

THEATRE & COMEDY

The live theatre scene is becoming more interesting. The British Airways Playhouse visits often, usually to perform a rollicking comedy at the Crowne Plaza Hotel. British Touring Shakespeare Company also tours frequently. The local Dubai Drama Group performs Tom Stoppard plays such as *Arcadia* and *Rosencrantz and Guildenstern are Dead*, often at the Dubai Country Club. Tickets range from Dh60 to Dh160.

If you want to see something different, try to catch a Punjabi musical – perhaps *Kitchen Katha* – or a Hindi play such as *Amar Akbar Ann-Toni*. You don't need to understand the language – the action speaks louder than the words. As part of the Hindi Theatre Festival of Laughter, held in January, you can see a family comedy such as *Hadh Kar-Di Aapne* or a social comedy such as *Abhi To Main Jawan Hoon*.

The Laughter Factory offers the best alternative comedy in town, with two or three comedians on the one bill. Recent visitors included Tom Rhodes, Steve Royle and Gavin Webster from London's Comedy Store, and Australian comedians Adam Hills, Steve Hughes and Trevor Cook. There are occasional one-off comedy shows, generally staged at the Crown Plaza Hotel. There is always plenty of publicity so watch the papers. Tickets cost around Dh80.

CINEMA/FILM

The latest films are generally released a few weeks after their American release and are widely screened around town. Although Hollywood blockbusters dominate, the odd independent or art-house film is shown. French films get the most screen time as there is a large French-speaking audience in Dubai from Europe and the Levant. **Alliance Française** (Map pp214-15; ☎ 335 8712; next to Mövenpick Hotel Bur Dubai, diagonally opposite the American Hospital) hosts week-long French film festivals. The Dubai International Film Festival (p11) takes place in December. A few small film societies have also emerged in recent years, screening movies for discussion, sometimes in members' own homes.

A number of cinemas cater to the Asian population, showing films in Hindi, Tagalog, Malayalam and Tamil. Women and families sit in the balcony seats, while the men occupy the cheaper floor seats. If you've never seen a Bollywood movie, check one out – they're great fun, often well over two hours long, and packed with songs, dance routines, melodrama, romance and perhaps violence. The plots are rarely so complicated that you can't understand the film if you don't know the language.

Films are subject to censorship and, as sex and romance are prime ingredients of most Hollywood recipes, some films may be cut to shreds. Dubai has high-tech cinemas, offering comfy seating and nachos-to-your-seat service. Movie times are published in the tabloid section of the *Gulf News*, in the entertainment section of the *Khaleej Times* and in the monthly entertainment mags.

AL-NASR Map pp214-15
☎ 337 4353; Al-Nasr Leisureland, off Oud Metha Rd, near Rashid Hospital; admission Dh15-20
This cinema shows mostly South Indian movies (Hindi, Tamil, Malayalam, Tagalog) and some

Hindi (Bollywood style) movies. South Indian movies are much the same as Hindi movies, except the lead actors tend to be podgy little guys with moustaches and the scripts tend to be more serious.

CINESTAR Map pp210-11
☎ 294 9000; Deira City Centre, Deira; admission before 6pm Dh20, after 6pm Dh30
This 11-screen complex shows a range of Hollywood hits and independent American, British and European films.

DEIRA Map pp208-9
☎ 222 3551; Omar ibn al-Khattab Rd, Deira; admission Dh15-20
This is an old-fashioned movie house screening South Indian films.

GRAND CINEPLEX Map pp206-7
☎ 324 2000; Al-Qataiyat Rd, Grand Hyatt Dubai, Bur Dubai; admission Dh25-30
This 10-screen complex shows English-language movies, mostly from Hollywood.

HYATT GALLERIA Map pp208-9
☎ 209 6469; Al-Khaleej Rd, Deira; admission Dh20
In the Hyatt Galleria shopping centre, attached to the Hyatt Regency Dubai, this smallish, two-screen cinema shows English-language films

LAMCY Map pp214-15
☎ 336 8808; Lamcy Plaza, Al-Qataiyat Rd, Bur Dubai; admission Dh20
A two-screen cinema showing Bollywood movies; it's more comfortable than most of the cinemas that show Indian movies.

MOVIES UNDER THE STARS
Map pp214-15
☎ 324 0000; Wafi City Rooftop; ☽ 8pm-late
Settle into a beanbag with some popcorn on Sunday/Monday nights during the cooler autumn, winter and spring months for themed film nights under the sky. You may see anything from *Lock Stock and Two Smoking Barrels* to *The Matrix*.

STRAND Map pp214-15
☎ 396 1644; Khalid bin al-Waleed Rd, Bur Dubai; admission Dh15-20
An ageing landmark cinema, the Strand screens Indian and other Asian films.

1 Local man 2 Musician, Jimmy Dix restaurant, Mövenpick Hotel Bur Dubai (p143) 3 Fishmonger, Karama Shopping Centre (p129), Bur Dubai 4 Belly dancer, Mövenpick Hotel Bur Dubai (p143)

1 Minarets pierce the skyline, Dubai Creek 2 Carpets on display 3 Woman in traditional dress drinking Arabic coffee 4 Camel farmer

1 Souvenir and seller, Bur Dubai
Souq (p120), Bur Dubai *2* Deira
City Centre (p126), Deira *3* Bur
Dubai Souq (p120), Bur Dubai
4 Perfume Souq (p124), Deira

1 *Lamborghinis, Wafi City Mall (p131), Bur Dubai* 2 *Deira Gold Souq (p120), Deira* 3 *Shoes, Bur Dubai Souq (p120), Bur Dubai* 4 *Deira Spice Souq (p120), Deira*

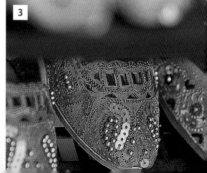

1 Golf pro James Shippey, Emirates Golf Club (p112), Sheikh Zayed Rd 2 Abra carrying passengers, Dubai Creek 3 Man in traditional attire outside modern clothing store 4 Lime Tree Café (p86), Jumeirah Rd, Jumeirah

1 *Traditional wind tower (p28)*
2 *Emirates Towers (p145), Sheikh Zayed Rd* 3 *Grand Cineplex (p98), Bur Dubai* 4 *Iranian Mosque (p57), Jumeirah*

1 Cinestar (p98), Deira City Centre 2 Dusit Dubai (p144), Sheikh Zayed Rd 3 Model of The Palm residential project (p137) 4 Expat workers, Dubai Creek

1 *Fatafeet (p79), Dubai Creek*
2 *Jumeirah Beach Park (p58), Jumeirah* 3 *Boat captain, Dubai Creek* 4 *Le Meridien Mina Seyahi Resort (p147), Jumeirah*

2624

496

HOBIE CAT

HOBIE CAT

Sports, Health & Fitness

Sports, Health & Fitness

Dubai has a full calendar of spectator sports over the winter months, with the Dubai Desert Classic golf event and the Dubai World Cup horse races attracting huge crowds. Winter (December to February) is also the best time of year for the other outdoor activities listed in this chapter – in summer months (May to September) these activities are relegated to early mornings and late afternoons because of the relentless heat. Dubai's health clubs and spas are busy year round keeping residents' bodies in beach-ready shape.

WATCHING SPORT

BOAT RACING

DUBAI INTERNATIONAL MARINE CLUB Map pp206-7
DIMC; ☎ 399 4111; www.dimc-uae.com; Al-Sufouh Rd, Le Meridien Mina Seyahi Resort

If fast boats give you a bit of a thrill you should come to Dubai in late October or early November when the city hosts the Class One World Offshore Championship powerboat races. Admission is free and entertainment is provided for kids.

Wooden powerboat racing is gaining popularity and the races, open only to UAE nationals, use standard outboard engines. Wooden boats of a slightly older vintage – large dhows similar in size to the ones you see on the Creek – race under sail. Up to 50 of them take part in a race and when they're lined up with their sails hoisted it's a spectacular sight. Races take place every weekend from October to May at the DIMC. Admission to the event is free, but you won't really see much from the club as the races take place 8km off the coast.

The President's Cup Dubai–Muscat Sailing Regatta is held every year in March. It begins in Dubai at the DIMC and finishes in Muscat at the Marina Bandar al-Rowdha. Call the Race Department of the DIMC for more information and the exact dates of any of these events.

CAMEL RACING

DUBAI CAMEL RACECOURSE
Map pp206-7
☎ 338 2324; off Oud Metha Rd, near Nad al-Sheba Club

Racing of the much beloved camel is a major spectator sport across the UAE and a visit to the camel races is worth the early wake-up call. The astonishing sight of pint-size

At the camel farm

The Ubiquitous Camel

While driving just outside the city of Dubai there are road signs stating 'Beware of Road Surprises' and indeed one surprise is occasionally finding camels ambling along the median strip or by the side of the road. The camel is of great symbolic importance to the Bedouin and depictions of camels have been found in the UAE dating back beyond 2000 BC. As the Bedouin were – and some still are – nomadic, the camel was used to transport belongings as they moved camp. The camel has enormous stamina and can go without water for up to two weeks, quite an asset given the huge distances between wells in the Empty Quarter.

These days the camel is still a source of milk and you will see fresh camel milk in some of Dubai's supermarkets. The wool is still used, as is the meat – a calf is often slaughtered for a celebratory feast such as a wedding. One of the reasons that camel racing is so popular is that it helps maintain that link with the not-so-distant past when a good camel was the difference between making that next well or perishing in the unforgiving desert. For a wonderful account of the importance of the camel, read Wilfred Thesiger's *The Arabian Sands* (p40).

jockeys atop these ships of the desert travelling at speeds of up to 60kph is equalled by the madness of the local camel owners in their 4WDs driving around the inside of the track urging on their prides and joy. The downside, however, is that if you're expecting local jockeys with their *gutras* (headcloths) flowing in the breeze you'll be disappointed. Most of the jockeys are boys from India and Bangladesh. While a decree was issued in 1993 prohibiting children from racing camels, there's evidence that the practice still exists.

Races take place early on Thursday and Friday mornings and on public holidays during winter and spring. The races usually start around 7am and continue until about 9am. If you miss out on a race meeting you can usually catch training sessions each morning at about the same time or at around 5.30pm.

CRICKET

SHARJAH CRICKET STADIUM
Map p150

☎ 06 532 2991; 2nd Industrial Rd, Industrial Area 5, Sharjah; admission Dh20-150

International cricket is held in nearby **Sharjah** (p153), which hosts matches in October, November, March and April. The Sharjah Cup

The Second Religion

When walking around the streets of Dubai you may come across large groups of Indian or Pakistani men gathered outside small eateries. It's not the food that has their attention – there must be a cricket match being shown live on TV. Many of these workers can't afford cable TV and don't have access to the matches so the local eateries are a popular place to watch.

is held in March or April. Participating teams change every year, but there are three competing nations each time, one of which is India or Pakistan. These are usually day-night matches, starting at 2.30pm and finishing at around 10.15pm. Sharjah Cricket Stadium has held more one-day matches than any other venue in the world. A match between India and Pakistan held here has to be seen to be believed.

DESERT RALLIES

Motor sports are very popular with Emiratis and the Emirates Motor Sports Federation has a calendar of events throughout the year, with the important events being held in the cooler months. A round of the FIA Cross-Country Rally World Cup, the UAE Desert Challenge, attracts top rally drivers from all over the world and is held in October, starting in Abu Dhabi and finishing in Dubai. There are a number of smaller rally events during February and March, including the 1000 Dunes Rally and the Spring Desert Rally, which are both 4WD events. Visit the Emirates Motor Sports Federation website (www.emsf.ae) for more details.

HORSE RACING & POLO

NAD AL-SHEBA CLUB Map pp206-7

☎ 336 3666; www.nadalshebaclub.com; Nad al-Sheba district, 5km southeast of Dubai centre; general admission free, admission to members stand from Dh60

A love of horses runs deep in Arab blood and a number of sheikhs run stables with some of the finest horses in the world. Sheikh Mohammed, Dubai's crown prince, is a racing celebrity and well known in the international racing community. The Dubai International Racing Carnival, running from February through to the end of March, culminates in the Dubai World Cup (www.dubaiworldcup.com), the richest horse race in the world. Horse-lovers should have the morning stable tour (p56) pencilled into their Dubai calendar.

The racing season lasts from November to March. Races are held at night from about 7pm (9pm during Ramadan). The members stand is licensed and there are different food and beverage packages available. Check the Emirates Racing Association website (www.emirateracing.com) for the exact dates of race meetings throughout the year. Even if you don't like horse racing the meets provide a great people-watching experience.

During winter there are dozens of desert endurance races. Members of the royal families riding stunning Arabian horses compete in these events and usually win with a combination of beautifully prepared horses and skilful riding. The race length is generally at least 100km and horses (and riders) are checked frequently over the course of the event for signs of distress. Visit the UAE Equestrian and Racing Federation website (www.uaeequafed.ae) for more information.

GOLF

EMIRATES GOLF CLUB Map pp206-7
☎ 347 3222; Interchange No 5, Sheikh Zayed Rd; admission Dh145

It's no surprise that the Dubai Desert Classic (www.dubaidesertclassic.com) attracts some of the world's biggest golfers. It's one of the world's richest golf tournaments, with prize money of US$2 million in 2004. The four-day

tournament takes place annually in late February or March. Tickets can be purchased from the website. Many golf-crazy expats take the week off to watch the world's best play their local course – especially if celebrity-mad Dubai has paid Tiger Woods enough appearance money to turn up.

TENNIS

DUBAI TENNIS STADIUM Map pp210-11
☎ 316 0101; www.dubaitennischampionships.com; Al-Garhoud; admission Dh30-100

There's usually a good turnout of top names for the women's event of the Dubai Tennis Championships, but the men's event still lacks the kudos to attract the big names. Tickets range from Dh30 for the main days to Dh100 for the finals and can also be purchased for the fortnight. The event is held in late February.

RUGBY

DUBAI EXILES RUGBY CLUB Map pp206-7
☎ 333 1198; www.dubaiexiles.com; Ras al-Khor Rd, near the Dubai Country Club

The Dubai Rugby 7s tournament (www.dubairugby7s.com) is one of Dubai's most fierce contests. Besides the boozing, the rugby competition attracts teams from rugby powerhouses such as New Zealand, France, South Africa and Fiji, as well a team of expats banded together as the Arabian Gulf team. This popular event usually falls in the first weekend of December and attracts around 20,000 enthusiastic spectators for the final. A 'season' ticket costs Dh150, which includes entry to the rock concert after the final – but don't get excited, Dubai's reputation for lining the pockets of pensionable performers saw Suzi Quatro perform in 2003.

OUTDOOR ACTIVITIES

Dubai offers a wide range of activities and sports clubs – far too many to list here. *Dubai Explorer* is the best source for this sort of information. It has alphabetical listings of all the activities available in Dubai, where to do them and how much it will cost you. *What's On* also has information on clubs and leisure activities in Dubai.

DESERT SAFARIS

Desert safaris are popular activities for tourists and expats alike and a great way to experience the rugged terrain of the UAE. Driving over the dunes is exhilarating and sometimes quite frightening – it's best done with an experienced driver so you encounter more of the former and less of the latter. There are dozens of off-road 4WD journeys from Dubai that take in amazing desert and mountain scenery, wadis (seasonal watercourses), ruins, archaeological sites and remote villages. Having said this you should keep in mind that 'bashing' around the place in a 4WD is potentially damaging to the environment.

The best way to enjoy a desert or wadi drive is to book a trip with one of the many tour operators (p151). Generally speaking, a half-day desert safari or wadi drive with lunch/dinner costs around Dh250 per person. They usually leave Dubai in the early afternoon so that you can watch the sunset over the desert. Overnight desert trips cost Dh350 to Dh450, which will get you some dune driving, a camel ride, a barbecue dinner (sometimes with a belly dancer for entertainment) and a night at a Bedouin-style camp site where you can sleep under the stars.

You can also rent a 4WD for around Dh900 per day. But, unless you are an experienced desert driver, it's not a good idea to take to the sands on your own, although desert driving courses are available. If you do know what you're doing and want to do some off-road driving, the *UAE Off-Road Explorer* is the best and most useful guide available.

The most popular event is the Gulf News Overnight Fun Drive, held annually in December. In 2003 there were over 3,000 participants doing the two-day drive over the dunes from Dubai to Fujairah. If you are interested in the fun drive, details are posted on the *Gulf News* website (www .gulfnews.com); you'll need to get your tickets well in advance.

GO-KARTING
DUBAI KART CLUB Map p150
☎ 050 651 5945; Jebel Ali, just beyond the main entrance to the Jebel Ali Hotel & Golf resort

This club offers membership at Dh850 per annum and competition days are held 14 times a year, culminating in the UAE championship. If you are catching public transport, minibuses only go as far as Jebel Ali Port so you will have to catch a taxi the rest of the way.

Desert safari

Did You Know?

To play on 'brown' or sand golf courses, golfers are given a patch of artificial grass to slide under the ball on the fairways. The sand on the putting 'greens' is brushed smooth to approximate the rolling effect of grass.

Alternatively it costs around Dh65 one-way in a metered taxi from the centre of Dubai.

FORMULA ONE Map pp206-7

☎ 338 8828; www.nadalshebaclub.com; Nad al-Sheba district, 5km southeast of Dubai centre; per 10 min adult/child (8-12 years) Dh50/40; 🕑 4-11pm Sat-Wed, 2-11pm Thu-Fri

Based at the Nad al-Sheba Club, it offers 'endurance races' and 'grand prix' races as well as racing under lights.

GO-KARTING Map p150

☎ 349 7393; Jebel Ali, just beyond the main entrance to the Jebel Ali Hotel & Golf Resort; per 15 min Dh75; 🕑 2pm-dusk Mon, noon-dusk Tue-Sun

While it's a good three-quarters of an hour's drive from Dubai centre, this track is an FIA-licensed circuit offering the best facilities in the Dubai Emirate. It's based at the same location as Dubai Kart Club.

GOLF

Dubai is the best golf destination in the Gulf. There are several great grass courses of international-standard on offer as well as driving ranges, tuition and superb '19th hole' facilities. It costs a fortune to maintain the courses in this harsh climate, however, and this is reflected in the green fees.

There is a discount on some courses if you have United Arab Emirates Golfers' Association (UGA) membership. Golfers are expected to wear golf attire. Jeans and beach wear are not allowed. For more information about the Emirates and Dubai Creek courses, go to www.dubaigolf.com.

ARABIAN RANCHES DESERT COURSE

☎ 884 6777; cnr Umm Suqeim St & Emirates Ring Rd, Arabian Ranches; per 18 holes Thu-Sat Dh340, Sun-Wed (cart incl) Dh280

Designed by former golf champion Ian Baker-Finch, Arabian Ranches 18-hole course takes advantage of the area's natural geographical features. Five different tee boxes cater for levels of proficiency up to championship standard. At the time of research the course had just opened and other facilities were still being developed.

DUBAI COUNTRY CLUB Map pp206-7

☎ 333 1155; Ras al-Khor Rd; per round Dh65

There's a reason the green fees are so much lower than at the other clubs – there are no greens, only browns! The all-sand 18- and 9-hole courses are worth a round, or have a swing on the floodlit driving range.

DUBAI CREEK GOLF & YACHT CLUB Map pp210-11

☎ 295 6000; Deira, near the Al-Garhoud Bridge

Host of the Dubai Desert Classic in 1999 and 2000, the club was closed for redevelopment at the time of research. The golf courses are due to reopen in 2005, but some of the facilities are open.

EMIRATES GOLF CLUB Map pp206-7

☎ 347 3222; Interchange No 5, Sheikh Zayed Rd; 18-hole Majlis course Dh370 (Thu-Sat Dh425), 18-hole Wadi course Dh330 (Thu-Sat Dh365), plus compulsory cart rental Dh50

The current site of the Dubai Desert Classic, Emirates Golf Club features two courses of

Exterior of the Dubai Creek Golf & Yacht Club (above)

championship standard. The clubhouses, designed to resemble Bedouin tents, are striking. Men must have proof of a handicap under 28 and for women the maximum handicap is 45.

MONTGOMERIE Map pp206-7
☎ 390 5600; www.themontgomerie.com; Emirates Hills Residential Estate; 18-holes Thu-Sat Dh550, Sun-Wed Dh425

Set on 81 hectares of unique landscaping, this 18-hole Colin Montgomerie–designed course has lived up to the hype that preceded its launch. As well as the main course, extensive practice facilities include a swing studio to get that hook or slice under control. Given the price of the green fees though, you'd almost expect 'Monty' to be teeing off with your group.

NAD AL-SHEBA CLUB Map pp206-7
☎ 336 3666; www.nadalshebaclub.com; Nad al-Sheba district, 5km southeast of Dubai centre; peak fees 9-hole/18-hole Dh150/295, off-peak fees (7.30am-3.20pm all day Sat, Sun, Wed & 4-10pm Thu-Fri) 9-hole/18-hole Dh110/220

With a floodlit 18-hole course and the back nine situated within the racecourse, it's a unique setting to play golf. The course is usually closed during horse races, so call to see what time you can tee off on race days. The club also offers 'Learn Golf in a Week' and other packages to get that handicap down.

HORSE RIDING

CLUB JOUMANA Map p150
☎ 804 8058; Jebel Ali Hotel & Golf Course; private 30-min lesson Dh60, 1hr desert ride Dh115; ⏲ 7am-noon Tue-Sun

The resort has new stables and tuition is available for all levels. Note that it may be closed during the heat of summer.

DUBAI EQUESTRIAN CENTRE
Map pp206-7
☎ 336 1394; near the Nad al-Sheba Club; 5 1hr lessons adult/child Dh525/475, 5 30-min lessons child only Dh150; ⏲ lessons from 6.30-9.30am & 4.30-7pm

Given the deep interest of the Al-Maktoum family in all things equestrian, it's perhaps no surprise that Dubai hosts this world-class riding school. It boasts dressage arenas, a floodlit main arena, training facilities and stables for 150 horses.

ICE SKATING

AL-NASR LEISURELAND Map pp214-15
☎ 337 1234; off Oud Metha Rd, Oud Metha; admission incl boot hire Dh10; ⏲ 2hr sessions starting at 10am, 1pm, 4pm & 7.30pm

It's certainly bigger than the Hyatt rink – big enough for ice hockey. The centre has a bowling alley and fast-food outlet.

HYATT GALLERIA Map pp208-9
☎ 209 6550; Hyatt Regency Dubai, off Al-Khaleej Rd; without/with skate hire Dh15/25; ⏲ 10am-1.30pm, 2-5.30pm & 6-9pm Sat-Thu, closes 8pm Fri & holidays

Despite being in a shopping mall and quite small, it's a great way to 'chill' when it's 40 plus degrees outside.

RUNNING

In the cooler months it's not as crazy as it sounds, especially when undertaken at 6am or 6pm. Groups and clubs meet regularly and there's even a marathon that takes place in January (see p9). There are also 'hashing' clubs, where the emphasis is more on the social aspects of running. See www .deserthash.net or www.creekhash.net.

DUBAI CREEK STRIDERS Map p218
☎ 321 1999; meet at World Trade Centre Hotel car park, Sheikh Zayed Rd; ⏲ 6.15am

A long-established club that runs weekly on Friday morning with shorter runs during summer (around 10km) and longer runs during the cooler months. There's no joining fee, but contact the club first before turning up.

DUBAI ROAD RUNNERS Map pp206-7
☎ 050 624 3213; www.dubai-road-runners.com; north entrance to Safa Park, Al-Wasl Rd; per adult Dh5; ⏲ 6.30pm Sat

The club welcomes runners of any age or ability to run one or two laps of the park (3.4km per lap). Each runner predicts the time in which they will run the course – the closest time wins a prize and funds raised are used to support events held during the year.

SANDBOARDING

This sport starts with taking a snowboard-like board up the highest dune you can find. It usually ends about a month later when you've finally removed the last traces of sand from every orifice. It's best to try it on a desert safari (p151) first, before booking a specific trip.

ARABIAN ADVENTURES Map pp206-7

☎ 343 9966; Emirates Holidays Bldg, Interchange No 2, Sheikh Zayed Rd

For a half-day of sandboarding and camel riding (you ride up the dune and board down) it costs Dh195 per person.

DESERT RANGERS

☎ 340 2408; www.desertrangers.com

Starting in the morning, this half-day trip costs Dh195 per person and requires a minimum of four people. The company also offers other adventure sports.

ORIENT TOURS Map pp210-11

☎ 282 8238; Al-Garhoud Rd, Al-Garhoud; adult/child Dh180/125

Orient Tours offers a similar deal of sandboarding and camel riding. The company will pick you up and drop you back at your hotel.

SKATING, IN-LINE SKATING & BMX BIKING

DUBAI DESERT EXTREME Map pp206-7

☎ 324 3222; off Al-Garhoud bridge, Al-Garhoud; per hr Dh10; ⏱ 5-11pm Sat-Wed, 4pm-midnight Thu-Fri

Dubai finally has a skate park, located in the Wonderland Theme and Waterpark. There's enough to entertain most street enthusiasts for a couple of hours and you can rent equipment on site, but there's no vertical ramp yet. Helmets (available for hire) are compulsory.

WATER SPORTS

Water sports are big business in Dubai, as the tourism industry increasingly promotes the city as a year-round destination. Most water-sports facilities are based either at big hotels or at private clubs, and are priced accordingly. If you intend to spend a lot of time in the water or working on that tan, stay at one of the beach hotels (p146).

Diving

Although the waters around Dubai are home to some coral reefs, marine life and a few modern shipwrecks, visibility is not great. Most dive companies take you up to the East Coast to dive in the waters between Khor Fakkan and Dibba, and off the east coast of the Musandam Peninsula, Oman. For more information on diving in these areas, see p158. Not including equipment hire, a day's diving (with two dives) costs between Dh200 and Dh500. Dives are offered to people at all levels. If you are uncertified you might want to take a diving course (see the boxed text on p160).

The Emirates Diving Association is the official diving body for the UAE and takes a strong interest in environmental matters. The association has a useful and detailed website (www.emiratesdiving.com). The 180-page *UAE Underwater Explorer* (Dh65), which has information on 30 dive sites, is another handy resource,

AL-BOOM DIVING Map pp216-17

☎ 342 2993; www.alboommarine.com; Al-Wasl Rd, Jumeirah, just south of the Iranian Mosque

The knowledgeable staff (PADI certified) offer courses as well as dive trips, air fills and maintenance for experienced divers.

SCUBA INTERNATIONAL Map pp212-13

☎ 393 7557; www.scubainternational.net; Diving Village, Shindagha

Dives off Dibba (East Coast) cost Dh300, including equipment. Diving on wrecks off the coast costs from Dh200 per day (includes two dives).

SCUBATEC DIVING CENTRE Map pp214-15

☎ 334 8988; www.scubatec.net; Sana Bldg, cnr Sheikh Khalifa bin Zayed & Al-Adhid Rds, Karama

Scubatec offers a two-dive trip off Khor Fakkan for Dh525 (including equipment), as well as dives on wrecks in the Gulf from Dh250. With a few days notice they can also arrange a dive on the pearling beds in the Gulf.

Fishing

While fishing in the Creek is not allowed (and not advisable), there's good fishing along Jumeirah Beach. For more serious angling, a deep-sea fishing trip is your best bet. If luck is on your side and the weather conditions are right, you're likely to catch flying fish, tuna, barracuda, kingfish and sailfish. The best time to fish off the coast of Dubai is from September to April when the water is cooler. You should try to book at least a week ahead as boats are often chartered well in advance.

BOUNTY CHARTERS Map pp206-7

☎ 348 3042; Dubai International Marine Club, Al-Sufouh Rd, 22km south of Dubai centre

Charges Dh1500 for four hours and Dh1800 for six, and the type of fishing can be tailored to suit. You can also charter the boat for longer periods but need to book well in advance.

CREEK CRUISES Map pp208-9

☎ 393 7123; Quay 2/3, Dhow Wharfage, Deira

This well-equipped 12m yacht can hold up to 10 passengers. It leaves from the docks just east of the Sheraton Dubai Creek. Expect to pay around Dh2500 for a four-hour trip.

DUBAI CREEK GOLF & YACHT CLUB
Map pp210-11

☎ 205 4646; near the Deira side of Al-Garhoud Bridge

The club rents out a 10m boat, including skipper, for up to six passengers. It costs Dh1500 for four hours or Dh2200 for eight hours, which includes fishing tackle, bait, lunch and drinks.

Jet-Skiing

There are jet skis based at the Oasis Beach Hotel, the Ritz-Carlton, the Hilton Dubai Jumeirah, the Metropolitan Resort & Beach Club and the One&Only Royal Mirage. If you're not staying at one of these hotels, you'll need to pay for the use of the hotel beach club for the day, plus around Dh100 for 20 minutes of jet-skiing, making it an expensive way to annoy the other guests.

You can go jet-skiing on Dubai Creek, just south of Al-Garhoud Bridge on the Bur Dubai side, although we don't recommend water activities in the Creek as it is not clean. No bus run close to here so if you don't have your own transport, you'll need to take a taxi. This area is undergoing development, so it's not clear how much longer the jet skis will operate from this spot.

There are jet skis for hire on the calmer waters of the Khor al-Mamzar, south of Al-Mamzar Park, which is slightly cleaner.

Kite Surfing

This relatively new sport has gained quite a following in Dubai and kite surfers generally congregate at Wollongong Beach, near the **Wollongong University** (Map pp206-7). Because of safety concerns on Wollongong Beach there is now a licensing system of kite surfers. For information contact **Fatima**

Sports (Map pp206-7; ☎ 050 455 5216; www .fatimasport.com; Wollongong Beach, near Wollongong University).

Surfing

It's not exactly the North Shore of Oahu but rideable waves are found during winter along the Jumeirah Beach stretch. Swell size rarely gets above a couple of feet but there's a small and dedicated band of locals who frequently surf the mushy conditions. The only problem as a visitor is there's nowhere to hire a surfboard. Regardless, if you have access to equipment your best bet is to check out what's commonly known as Wollongong Beach, near the **Wollongong University** (Map pp206-7), where the kite surfers hang out, or check out the Surfers of Dubai website (www.surfersofdubai.com) for details of swell conditions.

Water Parks

Wild Wadi Waterpark (p60) is a Dubai landmark and an attraction in itself, so we've included it in the Neighbourhoods section.

Water-Skiing & Wakeboarding

If you are staying at a five-star hotel with a beach club, it costs Dh100 for half an hour of water-skiing. If you are not a guest you will have to pay the daily admission fee to the beach club (about Dh60 to Dh200). For the best conditions and equipment try the Dubai Water Sports Association.

DUBAI WATER SPORTS ASSOCIATION
Map pp206-7

☎ 324 0131; Bur Dubai side of the Creek; per 15 min water-skiing/wakeboarding Dh45/60 plus admission Dh15; ☼ 8am-6pm

Good equipment and staff make this the best option to get behind a boat. The admission cost allows you entry into the club and use of the pool, deck chairs or spa, or to hang out at the bar and restaurant.

To get here from the Deira side of the Creek, go along Al-Qataiyat Rd towards Al-Garhoud Bridge. Take the first exit on the right after the Dubai Police Club. Continue past the nursery and turn right just before the Dubai Docking Yard. The bitumen road ends here, but continue along a sand track for 1.4km as it skirts around a large fenced-in compound. You'll see the club ahead and to your right.

Treated like a Pharaoh

Pharaohs Club (Map pp214-15; ☎ 324 0000; Wafi City, Al-Qataiyat Rd) For gym junkies looking for something exclusive, this place fits the bill. From the sphinxes and hieroglyphic columns at the entrance to the artificial beach and lazy river (pool with mild current) on the rooftop, it's truly awesome. A week's membership costs Dh250, which is cheaper than paying Dh50 per day at the hotels or Dh200 per day to use the facilities at the beach clubs. Massages, spas and beauty treatments are available for men and women in luxurious surroundings. It even has a climbing wall. If you are in the area, it's worth dropping in just to look at the facilities or to have lunch at one of the restaurants in the complex.

HEALTH & FITNESS
HEALTH CLUBS

All five-star and most mid-range hotels have health clubs, which are free for guests. The facilities of the larger places include a gym, sauna, swimming pool, squash courts and tennis courts. Generally if you are not a guest you must be a member or a member's guest to use the facilities. A few do accept day visitors. If you decide to use one of the hotel beach clubs for the day you will enjoy access to their gym facilities as well. Average day fees are Dh60 to Dh200. All clubs listed here have treadmills, bikes, step and rowing machines, free weights and resistance machines as well as massage, sauna and steam room. Some good clubs to try are **Fitness Planet** (Map p218; ☎ 398 9030; Al-Hana Centre, Satwa; admission Dh40), **Griffins Health Club** (Map pp210-11; ☎ 607 7755; JW Marriott Hotel; admission Sat-Wed Dh83, Thu-Fri Dh88), **Inter-Fitness** (Map pp208-9; ☎ 222 7171; InterContinental Dubai; admission Sat-Wed Dh50, Thu-Fri Dh75) and **Nautilus Academy** (Map pp212-13; ☎ 397 4117; Al-Mussalla Towers, Bur Dubai; admission Dh40).

MASSAGE & DAY SPAS

While you can book a massage at all of the health clubs listed earlier, for the luxurious full day-spa treatment visit one of the

Nip 'n Tuck

Rhinoplasty, liposuction, brow lifts – Dubai does a roaring trade in plastic surgery. These same people looking for aesthetic perfection also spend a lot of time at the gym doing weights and yoga, and at the spa getting facials and massages, as well as back waxing. Back waxing? Yes, that's because we're talking about the *men* in Dubai.

spas listed below. Most Dubaians like to look good and it's no surprise that regular trips to the spa are circled on many a Dubaian's calendar.

CLEOPATRA'S SPA Map pp214-15
☎ 324 7700; Wafi City, Al-Qataiyat Rd
The heavenly Cleopatra's Spa was Dubai's first health spa and with its luxurious surroundings is still considered the best around. There's a laundry list of services from facials and body wraps to Ayurveda therapies that originated in India thousands of years ago. The opulent spa is open to men as well as women and it's a great place to recharge your batteries.

GIVENCHY SPA Map pp214-15
☎ 399 9999; www.oneandonlyresorts.com; One&Only Royal Mirage, Al-Sufouh Rd
This gorgeous complex offers Givenchy signature treatments such as body scrubs and wraps as well as facials and massages. Combine this with the amazing surroundings, including a *hammam* (bathhouse), and you'll be checking the room rates (p148) because you won't want to leave. Men are welcome too.

YOGA & PILATES
GEMS OF YOGA Map p218
☎ 331 5161; White Crown Bldg, Junction 1, Sheikh Zayed Rd
Several different types of yoga classes, including group classes.

HOUSE OF CHI & HOUSE OF HEALING Map pp214-15
☎ 397 4446; www.hofchi.com; 6th fl, Al-Musalla Towers, Khalid bin al-Waleed Rd, Bur Dubai
Offers Pilates, yoga and massage therapy.

PILATES STUDIO Map pp206-7
☎ 343 8252; near Thunder Bowl, Sheikh Zayed Rd
Offers all levels of Pilates.

Shopping

Shopping

Believe the hype – Dubai is a shopper's paradise. In one city you can shop the globe. You can trawl the souqs for Arabian products – frankincense and oud, spicy Oriental perfumes, characterful old *khanjars* (traditional curved daggers) and Omani silver – or exotic goods from the surrounding region – Iranian caviar, Persian carpets, Palestinian embroidery, or curly toed Aladdin slippers from Afghanistan and Pakistan. Visit a store next door and you're likely to find the latest releases of every conceivable international product – digital cameras, MP3 players and miniscule photo-taking mobile phones. On another level of the mall you'll find Jimmy Choo shoes, a Tiffany & Co bracelet or Stella McCartney's latest collection.

Shopping the souqs is what the Dubai experience is all about for most people, whether visitor, expat or Emirati. For locals, the souqs are as much a part of their everyday shopping as the morning market is for Europeans, or the supermarket is for North Americans. There's the fish souq for fresh seafood, a fruit and vegetable souq nearby, the spice souq for herbs, spices and plastic goods, the textile souq for fabrics, the Deira Covered Souq for a wide range of household items, shoes, clothes, kids toys… Then there's the perfume souq, gold souq and even a camel souq! For the expats who work in banking, oil, education, the media, health or hospitality, the souq is a reminder that they live in the Gulf, and that there's a whole other exotic, atmospheric and exciting world out there that they take for granted.

For the lucky traveller, who will have days or weeks to fill with shopping, nothing compares to the chaos and vibrancy of the souq – the textures, colours and lights, the pungent aromas, the cacophony of sound and music, the call to prayer echoing off the walls of the narrow lanes, the street hawkers fiercely competing for customers. But the shopping malls are also worth some of your time. Not only is the best shopping located in malls, but you'll

Electronic goods on display

Shopping and eating on these busy streets continues until midnight most nights, even later on weekends (Thursday and Friday).

- **Al-Dhiyafah Rd** (btwn Al-Satwa & Al-Mina Rds, Satwa) A giant Book Corner, *sheesha* shops, Lebanese Sweet Palace, and the same sort of restaurants, cafés, fast-food outlets and Internet cafés that you'll find on Al-Rigga Rd.
- **Al-Rigga Rd** (Rigga) When you tire of shopping at Al-Gurhair City head here to refuel – there's a wide range of tasty Middle Eastern restaurants featuring outdoor seating, such as **Automatic** (p78), Al-Safadi and Al-Najani, Iranian sweet shops, Damascus Sweets and Ice Cream, and several Internet cafés.
- **Al-Satwa Rd** (btwn Al-Dhiyafah & Al-Hudheiba Rds) This street contains lots of electronics and sweet shops. It's the place to buy shoes, textiles, bags and suitcases. If you're in the area it's worth a wander for the buzz.
- **Sheikh Zayed Rd** Upmarket shopping at Emirates Towers Shopping Boulevard, stylish cafés and *sheesha* spots, and some super restaurants in the many five-star hotels.

also experience as much local colour in Deira City Centre as you would in Deira Covered Souq. Megasupermarkets, such as Carrefour, are not only for European expats but are where the locals go to buy bulk groceries to feed their families of 10 and more. The exclusive designer stores, think Dolce & Gabbana, fashion outlets (Zara and Mango are popular examples), and perfume and cosmetics emporiums, such as Paris Gallery, are where elegant young Emirati women like to shop. The young national men hang out and talk on their mobile phones, chat on their laptops in wireless cafés, or scour the shelves at Plug-ins for cutting-edge digital gadgets.

Much maligned in other parts of the world, the mall makes sense in Dubai. With soaring temperatures for much of the year it's an oasis for city dwellers. The central area with its dancing fountains, cafés or entertainment stage is akin to a town square. Couples and older people stop and settle in on a seat to watch the world go by, while the youngsters do the passagietta, writing text messages to each other or using Bluetooth to send their numbers.

The lack of duty and taxes and relatively cheap shipping costs mean that travelling here for the shopping alone makes a visit worthwhile. Malls are scattered around the city, located on main roads and easy to reach by taxi or by foot during the winter months. Shining marble floors, fountains and bracing air-conditioning are the norm in the many shopping malls. These palaces of retail altogether contain tens of thousands of shops. All have food halls and restaurants, ATMs and exchange offices. And the shopping is only going to get better, with the opening of a new souq at Madinat Jumeirah Arabian Resort and the construction of the world's largest shopping mall.

Opening Hours

Work your shopping around your other activities – while museums and tourist

Clothing Sizes

Measurements approximate only, try before you buy

Women's Clothing

Aus/UK	8	10	12	14	16	18
Europe	36	38	40	42	44	46
Japan	5	7	9	11	13	15
USA	6	8	10	12	14	16

Women's Shoes

Aus/USA	5	6	7	8	9	10
Europe	35	36	37	38	39	40
France only	35	36	38	39	40	42
Japan	22	23	24	25	26	27
UK	3½	4½	5½	6½	7½	8½

Men's Clothing

Aus	92	96	100	104	108	112
Europe	46	48	50	52	54	56
Japan	S		M	M		L
UK/USA	35	36	37	38	39	40

Men's Shirts (Collar Sizes)

Aus/Japan	38	39	40	41	42	43
Europe	38	39	40	41	42	43
UK/USA	15	15½	16	16½	17	17½

Men's Shoes

Aus/UK	7	8	9	10	11	12
Europe	41	42	43	44½	46	47
Japan	26	27	27½	28	29	30
USA	7½	8½	9½	10½	11½	12½

Shopping

Souq to Souq

The souqs have no set opening hours. Most open before 10am and while some close between 1pm and 4pm, many are open right through to 9pm or 10pm. For most people, especially in the hotter months, visiting the souqs is done in the late afternoon or early evening.

Bur Dubai Souq (Map pp212-13) On the waterfront of the Bur Dubai side of the Creek is this traditional souq. Under a wooden arcade, you'll find a few Arabian handicrafts and 'antique' stores, a number of textile shops selling fabrics from India, Thailand, Indonesia and Korea, clothes and shoe stores, some selling cheap Dubai T-shirts, and several stalls selling cute souvenirs and toys. This is the place to get your mosque alarm clock and dancing Daler Mehndi (an Indian pop star) doll. Wander along narrow lanes between wind-tower buildings to the bustling backstreets surrounding the souq and you can get a sari or suit made, haggle for digital cameras and electronics, buy cheap luggage and stock up on the latest Bollywood tapes.

Deira Covered Souq (Map pp212-13) Enclosed in the area between Al-Sabkha Rd and 67 St, and Naif Rd and Al-Maktoum Hospital Rd, the most interesting area is right in the middle, just west of the Al-Sabkha Rd bus station. Here you'll find textiles, spices, kitchenware, walking sticks, *sheeshas*, clothes and a lifetime's supply of henna. Attractively patterned muslin headscarves and shawls cost about Dh10 with bargaining. Pretty wooden bead bracelets are Dh1 each. A small box of henna costs Dh5. The prices of textiles here are the same as in the Bur Dubai Souq.

Deira Gold Souq (Map pp208-9) Even if you don't plan on buying anything, it's worth a visit to the souq to take in the atmosphere and ogle at the jewellery on offer. The main drag of the Gold Souq runs along Sikkat al-Khail St, between Suq Deira and Old Baladiya Sts. The other part of the souq runs along 45 St, which comes off Sikkat al-Khail St to form a T-shape. Wooden lattice archways and roofs cover the entire area.

Deira Spice Souq (Deira Old Souq; Map pp208-9) This is the place to wander around for an authentic taste of traditional Dubai. The spices are mainly found at the souq's eastern end, closest to the Creek. Sacks overflow with frankincense, oud, dried lemons, ginger root, cardamom, dried fruit, nuts, pulses and saffron. For a few dirhams you can take home a bag of whatever exotic ingredients you want. Other shops in this souq sell tacky trinkets, kitchenwares, rugs, glassware and textiles, all at very low prices. The alleyways here are atmospheric and narrow, and are wonderful to explore.

Palm Lane Market (Map pp206-7; Safa Park) To expats and locals this market is something of a novelty in Dubai, but this is what most visitors would be used to back home – arts and crafts, bric-a-brac, ethnic products, and original jewellery and fashion. Opened by a couple of South African women who pitched the concept to Dubai Municipality, the 70-stall market is held from 10am to 3pm on the first and last Thursday of each month during winter. Unique items on sale include Stanley Van Breda's jewelled lingerie straps, which have proven to be a real hit. Decorated with pearls, beads and crystals, the straps range from Dh45 to Dh300.

Souq al-Arsah (p154) If you have the time take a trip to Sharjah, which is the best place to shop for old Arabian souvenirs. In this beautifully restored atmospheric souq, you may actually come across genuine Arabian *khanjars*, trays, coffeepots, Bedouin jewellery and canes. You'll also find Kashmiri pashminas, Syrian tablecloths, Iranian bedspreads, Indian cushion covers, wooden inlaid boxes, carved tables and hanging lamps.

attractions may be open for only a short time or specific hours each day, shops and malls are open from 10am to 10pm most days, even later during the Dubai Shopping Festival (see the boxed text on p121). The souqs keep roughly the same hours, except for a few hours in the afternoon (approximately 1pm to 4pm), when the shopkeepers close their stores for a siesta. Giant malls such as Deira City Centre are buzzing on a Friday night when everyone goes out to shop for the busy week ahead.

Bargaining

Bargaining can be exhausting. Hang in there, be firm and be prepared to spend some time at it. Prices can drop by 20% to 50%. Once the shopkeeper agrees to your offer, you are expected to pay. Going on to offer a lower sum is impolite. Even in shopping centres in Dubai you can ask for a discount or for their 'best price'. Saying you are a resident gets you even better prices.

Best Buys
ARABIAN SOUVENIRS & BEDOUIN JEWELLERY

Most 'Arabian' souvenirs are made in India or Oman, although more and more are being produced locally. Browse the souvenir and handicraft stores at **Deira City Centre** (p126) and **BurJurman Centre** (p127) for the highest quality. **Karama Shopping Centre** (p129), Bur Dubai and Deira souqs are the places to go for low prices. The **Sharjah** (p155) souqs have the greatest range. You can also check out the stalls in the **Heritage Village** (p54), while most five-star hotels also have stores selling quality souvenirs, jewellery and carpets, although prices are higher.

A memorable souvenir is a *dalla* (copper coffeepot), which cost from Dh15 for small ones (about 8cm high) to Dh500 for large ones (about 50cm high). Antique *dallas* cost from Dh300 to Dh1000, depending on their condition. Decorated metal food platters, used for special occasions such as wedding banquets, can cost Dh150. Add some foldable wooden legs and you have a lovely coffee table.

Carved wooden or leather stuffed camels make a cute souvenir and cost anything from Dh10 to Dh250. Woollen camel bags, which are normally slung over a camel's back and have large pockets either side, can be used to make cushions. They mainly come from Afghanistan and cost anything from Dh150 to Dh500, depending on their size and quality. You can buy these and camel rugs at a market attached to the **Dubai Camel Racecourse** (p108). The camel rugs and cloths are made of heavy cotton in a wide range of designs and colours, and cost between Dh20 and Dh50.

Sheeshas (also known as water pipes, hubble-bubbles and nargilehs) make great souvenirs. Most come in cases, making them easy to transport, and cost from Dh120 to Dh150. If you intend to use it for more than decoration, check that air flows through well. There are a number of accessories you'll need; you can buy these separately for a few dirhams each, or in a complete kit. *Sheeshas* are available from souqs, specialised stores, tobacconists, supermarkets and souvenir shops.

Much of the Bedouin jewellery on sale in Dubai originates from Oman. If you are travelling on to Oman or Saudi Arabia you may find a better selection at cheaper prices. Silver Bedouin bracelets, necklaces and earrings are sold by weight, but often the shopkeeper has a fixed price for such items. You'll also pay more for intricate workmanship and quality. For a plain studded bracelet you may pay Dh100, while larger and more ornate items, such as a bride's chest and headpiece, will probably cost around Dh1500. Larger silver prayer holders, gunpowder horns, and *khanjars* (see the boxed text on p123) make unique gifts. A gunpowder horn can cost as little as Dh100 or as much as Dh500 for well-crafted items in good condition. Quality prayer holders made of white metal are not as valuable as the silver ones, but they still make an affordable souvenir for around Dh25. Any *khanjar* under Dh500 will be worn and well-used, and may be attached to a frayed belt. This kind of authenticity may be what you're looking for. Alternatively you can buy shiny *khanjars* and jewellery in velvet display boxes or glass-covered picture frames.

Shopping

Khanjars

Khanjars (traditional curved daggers) are worn mainly by Emirati men in the rural east and north of the country. Traditionally the handles of these daggers were made from rhino horn, although today they are almost always made from wood. *Khanjars* come in two basic designs: regular *khanjars* are identified by two rings where a belt is attached; Sayidi *khanjars* have five rings. Regular *khanjars* are decorated entirely, or almost entirely, with thin silver wire. The intricacy of the thread pattern, and the skill with which it is executed, are among the main determinants of value. Sayidi *khanjars* are often covered entirely in silver sheet and little or no wire is used.

The most important things to look for in assessing a *khanjar's* quality are weight and the workmanship on the scabbard. A *khanjar* is a substantial item and ought to feel like one when you pick it up. Some *khanjars* have a second knife inserted in a small scabbard attached to the back of the main scabbard. Don't pay too much of a premium for one of these – the knives in question are often cheap steak knives that have a bit of silver wrapped around the handle. Be wary of information regarding the age of individual pieces; few *khanjars* will be more than 20 to 40 years old, and quality of workmanship, not age, should be the prime criterion.

CARPETS

Persian carpets, Turkish and Kurdish kilims, Turkmen, Bukhara, Kashmiri and Afghan rugs are widely available. Whenever you buy a carpet you will be given a certificate of authentication guaranteed by the Dubai Chamber of Commerce & Industry, so you can be sure that the Turkmen rug you're about to spend Dh4000 on is actually a Turkmen rug. For more information on the history of Persian carpets, how they are made and what to look for when buying one, see the boxed texts the Art of Carpet Buying (below) and Top Five Carpet-Buying Books (p123).

For the best range of carpets, go to the **Central Market** (p155), in the neighbouring emirate of Sharjah, a 20-minute drive from Dubai, or to the shops listed in this chapter. The only problem is that each year the prices creep up as more tourists come here to shop. There is room to bargain, so if you're having trouble getting the price you want, just go to the next shop – there are dozens of them. Be aware that the carpet sellers here are not exclusively retailers; there are a few wholesalers as well. If you seek out these shops you'll get much better prices. In Dubai, **Deira City Centre** (p126) has the greatest number of carpet shops, as do the streets around Baniyas Sq.

DESIGNER FAKES

The shopping areas in Karama and Al-Satwa Rd sell imitation brand-name goods such as watches, sunglasses and handbags, along with copy CDs, DVDs and software. Although it is said that the authorities have cracked down on sales of these goods, shops in these areas openly sell this merchandise. Those that don't are likely to keep the imitation stuff under the counter, while others will whisper 'fake Rolex, fake Gucci' from a darkened lane. If you follow the sound you'll more than likely be lead up some stairs to a fake brand heaven.

ELECTRONICS

The UAE is the cheapest place in the region to buy electronics. If it plugs into a wall you can buy it here and the selection is huge. Shop attendants are not very knowledgeable about their stock so it helps to have done your research before setting off. If you're after the no-name stuff, it is also a good idea, and accepted practice in the UAE, to plug your new gadget in at the shop to make sure that it works properly. If you are looking for cheap electronics and digital technology, try Al-Fahidi St in Bur Dubai. Another place to look is the **Electronics Souq** (Map pp208-9), which covers an area around the corner of Al-Sabkha and Al-Maktoum Hospital Rds, near Baniyas Sq. A portable CD player may cost anything from

Shopping

The Art of Carpet Buying

Buying carpets requires great skill and patience and an understanding of the intricacies of the trade. These tips might help you navigate your way through the rigours of the purchasing process.

- Do not feel embarrassed or obliged to buy just because the shop attendant has unrolled 40 carpets for you; this is part of the ritual.
- Ask many questions and bargain hard over a long period of time (preferably two to three visits) to get the very best price.
- Remember that rugs from Iran or Turkmenistan are generally more valuable than those from Kashmir or Turkey. Silk rugs are more valuable than wool ones.
- The more knots there are per square inch, the more valuable the rug (flip the corner of a rug over and have a look at the back).
- Look closely at the detail in the design of the carpet and compare it with others. The more intricate the patterns the more expensive it will be. The value of a carpet is also raised by the name of the family who made it.
- Natural dyes are more expensive than artificial dyes. Antique rugs are always naturally dyed. A naturally dyed rug will appear to be slightly faded, but this is not considered a flaw. The settling down of natural dyes creates a carpet that is well balanced in colour and tone.
- If you are buying an artificially coloured carpet check that the colours have not bled. Artificial dyes are used widely now and can be just as attractive as the natural dyes. Unless you are a real purist it really doesn't matter.

Dubai Shopping Festival

The month-long Dubai Shopping Festival, held every year from January to February, is promoted aggressively and brings in hordes of tourists from around the world. This is the best time to visit Dubai. Aside from the massively reduced stock on sale in all the shopping malls, the weather is glorious and the city is abuzz with activity. There is nightly family entertainment, Arabian horse parades, traditional performances and heritage displays, art exhibitions, concerts, theatre, comedy, sports events and *abra* (small flat-deck motorboat) races. Outdoor souqs and amusement rides are set up in most neighbourhoods, with the best being by the waterside across from the UK embassy on the Bur Dubai side of the Creek. Here you can shop, watch the nightly fireworks and eat at **Fatafeet** (p79) or a range of other stalls selling food from around the world. The main attraction of the festival, however, is the giant funfair and kitsch Global Village. Scores of countries set up giant pavilions to sell their national products and host cultural performances. You can buy Bavarian food from the German pavilion, colourful embroidery from the Palestinian pavilion, Oriental perfumes from the Saudis, pottery from the Tunisian stand and so on. And in between shopping you can enjoy Chinese opera, whirling dervishes, Yemeni folk dancers and more. Arrive at the 4pm opening time to avoid the traffic and crowds, although it bustles around midnight.

Dh200 to Dh500. Multiregion DVD players, personal organisers and digital cameras can vary enormously in cost, but will probably be far cheaper than back home. For software, go to Khalid bin al-Waleed Rd in Bur Dubai between Al-Mankhool Rd and the Al-Fahidi Roundabout. Most people call this Computer St.

If all that sounds like too much trouble go to **Deira City Centre** (p126), check out the displays in Plug-Ins, get the prices for what you want and shop around. There are a few electronic shops around the centre that you can try. Before you buy, take a quick trip into the centre's Carrefour supermarket, which stocks electronics. What you're looking for may be there at a better price.

EXOTIC DELICACIES

Dubai is probably the cheapest place outside Iran to buy Iranian caviar. It's sold at supermarket delicatessens, five-star hotels, at the airport and at Burj Al Arab. Saffron, from Iran and Spain, is also available. You'll be offered saffron in the spice souq, but can also find it in most supermarkets. Delicious honey from Oman and Saudi Arabia is another special product sold in Dubai. You'll find it in the Deira Spice Souq, shops around the souq areas of Bur Dubai and Deira, and at good supermarkets. It ranges in colour from light golden to almost black, and can sell for anything between Dh10 and Dh500 a bottle. The high-priced honey is collected by hand from remote areas in the mountains and deserts of Oman.

FABRICS

The best place to buy fabrics is the **Bur Dubai Souq** (p120) and along Al-Fahidi St, Bur Dubai. In fact, that's mostly what you'll find there. All kinds and qualities of textiles from India, Indonesia, Thailand, Japan and Korea are available. Cotton fabrics, depending on the weave, cost anywhere from 30 fils to Dh5 per metre, silk costs around Dh8 per metre and linen about Dh7 per metre. There are also plenty of tailors, all of whom are good at what they do. They work very quickly so if you only have a few days in Dubai you'll still have time to have something made. A simple woman's skirt may cost about Dh30, while a more complex skirt, blouse or trousers will cost from Dh40 to Dh50. A man's shirt costs about Dh25, while you can get a suit made for about Dh150.

GOLD

Dubai has a well-deserved reputation as the City of Gold – even veterans of Middle Eastern gold markets will be blown away by the sheer scale of the **Deira Gold Souq** (see the

Top Five Carpet-Buying Books

- *The Carpets, Rugs and Kilims of the World* by Enza Milanesi
- *Kilims, a Buyer's Guide* by Lee Allane
- *Oriental Carpets: a Buyer's Guide* by Essie Sakhai
- *Oriental Rugs, a Complete Guide* by Murray L Eiland Jr and Murray Eiland III
- *Tribal Rugs* by James Opie

boxed text on p120) and the **Gold & Diamond Park** (p131). Every conceivable kind of jewellery and precious product is on offer: rings, necklaces, earrings, pendants, bracelets, coins and ingots. Designs are traditional and modern, futuristic and conservative. Artisans can alter the composition of alloys to create pink, white, yellow or green hues in the one piece of jewellery.

In most Gulf countries, a bride is laden with gold jewellery on her wedding day. Gold given to a bride must be new, so tradition alone keeps a constant flow of customers coming to Dubai. Strict laws involving authenticity can quickly put gold traders out of business if they try to dupe a customer, so if a shop attendant tells you that a piece of jewellery is 22 carat (meaning that 22 of the 24 parts of the alloy are gold, the rest being zinc, copper and silver) you can be confident it is.

Gold is sold by weight and prices fluctuate almost daily. There is room to bargain so don't accept the first price and shop around. Prices vary, depending on whether the piece was made by a machine or an artisan. A 22-carat machine-made gold bracelet could cost around Dh300, while an intricately handcrafted one may cost Dh500. An elaborate necklace can cost Dh1500. Small items, such as simple earrings or a pendant, can be purchased for under Dh150 in lower grades of gold and can go up to Dh500 or more for 21- or 22-carat gold.

KITSCH SOUVENIRS

If you're looking for the ultimate chichi souvenir from the UAE, it has to be a colourful mosque clock, which belts out the azan (call to prayer). With a little bargaining you can get these for Dh10 in the Deira and Dubai souqs. Then there's the camel lighter – press its hump and it spits fire – which is available from some of the trinket shops on 67 St, near Deira Covered Souq. Or a soft fluffy camel toy that sings in Arabic when you squeeze it (costing from Dh10 to Dh50 depending on the size and quality). See the boxed text Top Five Kitsch Souvenirs on this page for more suggestions.

PERFUME & INCENSE

When you pass Emirati women you are sure to catch a whiff of exotic perfume and incense. For centuries Arab women have smothered themselves in both. When there was no air-conditioning, and precious little water in the deserts to wash bodies and clothes, people needed something to cover the smell of perspiration. This is why *attar* (Arabic perfume) is very strong and spicy, unlike Western perfumes, which tend to be flowery and light.

You'll find perfume shops in all the shopping centres in Dubai, but the best place to look is the **Perfume Souq** (Map pp208-9), an area on Sikkat al-Khail St in Deira, just east of the Deira Gold Souq. Shopkeepers will want to daub you senseless with various perfumes, but a word of warning, the Arabic perfumes are oil-based and once on your clothes they can leave a stain. You can buy perfumes in bottles ranging from 12mL to 36mL. It is sold by the *tolah* (a unit of measure equalling 12mL or 12g) and prices vary, depending on the perfume. The cheapest costs about Dh10 per *tolah* while the most expensive is about Dh1500 per *tolah*. This expensive stuff, made from agar wood from Malaysia, is extremely concentrated. In fact, it's so concentrated that you will probably find it rancid and quite disgusting when you smell it in the perfume shop. When it settles down, though, it has a lovely, spicy fragrance and one drop is enough to last the whole day.

The perfume shops also sell an enormous range of incense. It can be in the form of compressed powder, crystals, rock or wood (oud). *Luban* (frankincense) is probably the most common form of incense. The quality varies. Frankincense from Japan is not as valuable as that from Iran or the Dhofar region of southern Oman. The cheaper frankincense costs about Dh20 per kilogram and the more expensive stuff is about Dh50. The *somok* (wooden incense) is the nicest and most valuable of all incenses and is produced from Malaysian agar wood. When burnt it emits a sweet, rich log-fire smell. Agar incense ranges in price, depending on quality, from Dh10 to Dh30. To burn incense you can either buy an electric incense burner, which has a metal plate that heats up, or you can buy a box of Magic Coal charcoal (it's Japanese, comes in a black box and is the longest-lasting coal) or heat beads. Set them alight over a gas burner or hotplate until they glow, then put a piece of incense on top. The colourful burners themselves make great souvenirs.

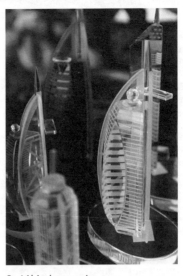

Burj Al Arab souvenirs

DEIRA

AJMAL Map pp210-11   *Perfumes*
☎ 295 1010; Deira City Centre, Al-Garhoud Rd, near Dubai Creek Golf & Yacht Club, Deira; ⏱ 10am-11pm

This is the best chain of makers of exotic *attars* (Arabian oils and perfumes) in the region and is generally crowded with local women buying up. Part of the fun is trying, but if you're stuck ask for 'Fakhrul Arab' *attar*, a heavenly scent in a jewel-encrusted coffeepot-shaped bottle.

AL-GHURAIR CITY
Map pp208-9   *Shopping Centre*
☎ 223 2333; cnr Al-Rigga & Omar ibn al-Khattab Rds, Deira; ⏱ 9am-1pm & 5-10pm Sat-Thu, 5-10pm Fri

Dubai's first shopping centre has expanded to include more than 400 shops, some terrific textile and jewellery stores, elegant shops selling upmarket *abeyyas* (women's full-length

Top Five Shopping Malls

- BurJuman Centre (p127)
- Deira City Centre (p126)
- Emirates Towers Shopping Boulevard (p131)
- Mercato Mall (p133)
- Wafi City Mall (p131)

robes) and *shaylas* (headscarves), *gutras* (men's white headcloths) and *agals* (headropes used to hold the *gutra* in place), a cinema complex, cafés and Book Corner, the largest bookstore in Dubai.

AMINIAN PERSIAN CARPETS
Map pp210-11   *Carpets*
☎ 295 1010; Deira City Centre, Al-Garhoud Rd, near Dubai Creek Golf & Yacht Club, Deira; ⏱ 10am-11pm

An excellent source of fine handmade Persian carpets and Oriental rugs.

ART & CULTURE
Map pp208-9   *Handicrafts & Souvenirs*
☎ 222 7171; InterContinental Dubai, Deira; ⏱ 10am-10pm

This crowded shop in the hotel lobby has high-quality souvenirs and Bedouin jewellery. It also has some fine *kandouras* (the Gulf version of the kaftan) and robes.

BOOK CORNER Map pp208-9   *Books*
☎ 223 2333; Al-Ghurair City, cnr Al-Rigga & Omar ibn al-Khattab Rds, Deira; ⏱ 9am-1pm & 5-10pm Sat-Thu, 5-10pm Fri

This is the largest bookstore in Dubai and it sells an enormous selection of books in Arabic and English. The travel section stocks a wide range of Lonely Planet guides, and every other brand out there on the market, along with phrase books, maps and atlases. There is also an excellent selection of glossy coffee-table books on Dubai and the UAE, and other local-interest books.

CARREFOUR Map pp210-11 *Supermarket*

☎ 295 1010; Deira City Centre, Al-Garhoud Rd, near Dubai Creek Golf & Yacht Club, Deira; ☺ 10am-11pm

Popular with expats and national families, Carrefour is perpetually crowded – it has the best selection of everything. Highlights include a fabulous fresh seafood market, the best bread you'll find in Dubai, and an awesome deli counter with barrels of olives from all the Middle East, cheeses from around the globe, and freshly packed hummus, *muttabal* (purée of aubergine mixed with tahini, yogurt and olive oil) and vine leaves for that waterside picnic.

Did You Know?

Oud is Arabic for wood and when discussing incense it refers to small chips of wood that have been soaked in perfume. Oud is also a stringed musical instrument that's common throughout the Middle East.

DEIRA CITY CENTRE

Map pp210-11 *Shopping Centre*

☎ 295 1010; Al-Garhoud Rd, near Dubai Creek Golf & Yacht Club, Deira; ☺ 10am-11pm

Dubai's largest and most popular shopping centre has a cinema complex, restaurants and food court, and the greatest range of shops, including department stores, boutiques, electronics shops (including Plug-ins), a Virgin Megastore, Magrudy's bookstore, the biggest supermarket in the city (Carrefour), a whole promenade of specialist gold and jewellery stores, and a section specialising in high-quality handicrafts and carpet shops.

MAGRUDY'S Map pp210-11 *Books*

☎ 295 1010; Deira City Centre, Al-Garhoud Rd, near Dubai Creek Golf & Yacht Club, Deira; ☺ 10am-11pm

Magrudy's has the best range of English-language books in Dubai, particularly in the areas of travel, cooking, interiors, fiction, classics and bestsellers. You'll find all the glossy coffee-table books on Dubai, along with a good selection of texts on Middle Eastern history and politics. The magazine section is reasonable.

PRIDE OF KASHMIR

Map pp210-11 *Carpets & Handicrafts*

☎ 295 1010; Deira City Centre, Al-Garhoud Rd, near Dubai Creek Golf & Yacht Club, Deira; ☺ 10am-11pm

If the Kashmiri, Afghan, Persian or Pakistani carpets don't entice you, the home furnishings and handicrafts will. You'll find bedspreads, throws, wall hangings and cushion covers made from rich silks and velvets, patchwork and appliqué, and embroidered and sequinned fabrics.

RITUALS

Map pp210-11 *Home & Body Cosmetics*

☎ 294 1432; Deira City Centre, Al-Garhoud Rd, near Dubai Creek Golf & Yacht Club, Deira; ☺ 10am-11pm

Rituals' sensual range of products are all about re-establishing a balance in life that is centred on personal rituals – home, tea, laundry and cleaning, purifying, energising and relaxing rituals. Try the mandarin and basil incense, the Jasmine Dream candles, the Samurai Secret travel-sized hydrating cream, or lotus stones for the laundry.

VIRGIN MEGASTORE

Map pp210-11 *Music & DVDs*

☎ 295 1010; Deira City Centre, Al-Garhoud Rd, near Dubai Creek Golf & Yacht Club, Deira; ☺ 10am-11pm

Until you check out Virgin's selection of Arabic music, you won't realise the variety available – popular Emirati singers, traditional oud (stringed) instrumentals, Oriental lounge and chill-out music, and cool fusion experiments. Then there are favourites Umm Kolthum and Fairouz, Haifa and Nancy, the 4 Cats and more. Virgin has a café, a classical music room, a DJ booth and an enormous selection of DVDs, including some Egyptian musicals and a few independent films, such as Palestinian director Elia Suleiman's *Divine Intervention*.

Carbonated Consciousness

'Shake your conscience' is the credo of Mecca-Cola (www.mecca-cola.com), a Muslim-owned alternative to the popular carbonated water and sugar drink, Coca Cola. Created in France by a French Muslim, Mecca-Cola donates 10% of profits to charities. Surprisingly, it hasn't taken the Middle East by storm – but you can find it at **Spinneys** (p69) for Dh1 per can. While it doesn't provide the same sugar rush as 'the real thing', what other soft drink can stir your conscience?

Top 10 Exotic Supermarket Buys

- Al-Ain fresh camel milk – just to say you've tried it...
- Al-Jazeera Arabic coffee – look for the veiled lady on the tin.
- Al-Rawabi mango juice from Al-Ain – fresh is best, but this is pretty close.
- Al-Shifa honey – straw-coloured 'acacia' is scrumptious.
- Cardamom-flavoured condensed milk – delicious, and you can take it home.
- Iranian Caviar – take advantage of the low price, but despite the ice and packaging it won't last, so savour it on the balcony with a glass of bubbly and watch the sun go down.
- Mecca-Cola – it tastes good and a percentage of sales goes to charity (see the boxed text on p126).
- Nada strawberry juice from Saudi Arabia – ditto.
- Natco Rose Syrup – delicious with milk or on ice cream.
- *Zaatar* and sumach – the herb and spice most used by locals.

WOMEN'S SECRET

Map pp210-11 *Lingerie & Swimwear*

☎ 295 9665; Deira City Centre, Al-Garhoud Rd, near Dubai Creek Golf & Yacht Club, Deira; ☼ 10am-11pm

Japanese pyjamas, Hawaiian-print bikinis, embroidered hipsters, batik bathing suits, Brazilian string briefs, henna-patterned nightdresses – ethnic-inspired underwear, swimwear and nightwear from another successful Spanish franchise.

ZARA

Map pp210-11 *Clothing & Accessories*

☎ 294 0839; Deira City Centre, Al-Garhoud Rd, near Dubai Creek Golf & Yacht Club, Deira; ☼ 10am-11pm

Europeans will be very familiar with this stylish Spanish label. The clothes are not only fashionable they are highly affordable. The Dubai flagship store has a large women's, men's and kids' section. In addition to collections of casual, evening and work wear, you'll find funky shoes, handbags, belts, bikinis and lingerie.

BUR DUBAI

2000 HORIZON ANTIQUE

Map pp210-11 *Handicrafts & Souvenirs*

☎ 335 3544; Block T, Karama Shopping Centre, Karama; ☼ 9am-10.30pm Sat-Thu, 9-11am & 4-10.30pm Fri

You won't discover any authentic antiques here, but you will find enough exotic objects to recreate an Arabian palace back home. Choose from a wide selection of beautiful Moroccan and Syrian hanging lights, lamps and lanterns, wooden inlaid tables and painted screens. Beautiful beaded coasters and candle holders, and colourful Rajasthani puppets will complete the Oriental look.

AL OROOBA ORIENTAL

Map pp212-13 *Carpets*

☎ 351 0919; BurJurman Centre, Bur Dubai; ☼ 10am-10pm Sat-Thu, 2-10pm Fri

This excellent carpet, antique and handicrafts store stocks a wide range of the highest quality Oriental objects you'll find anywhere. In addition to their magnificent carpets it has a very fine selection of interesting Bedouin jewellery, intricately crafted coffeepots, *khanjars*, trays and some colourful kilims and Bedouin costumes.

Top Five Music Stores

- **Al Mansoor** (p131), Wafi City Mall
- **Diamond Palace** (below), BurJurman Centre
- **Music Master** (p133), Palm Strip
- **Ohm Records** (p130), Bur Dubai
- **Virgin Megastore** (p126 and p134), Deira City Centre and Mercato Mall

BURJURMAN CENTRE

Map pp212-13 *Shopping Centre*

☎ 352 0222; cnr Khalid bin al-Waleed & Trade Centre Rds, Bur Dubai; ☼ 10am-10pm Sat-Thu, 2-10pm Fri

BurJurman is popular with locals and tourists alike because of its central location and wide range of shops, including exclusive men's and women's designer labels, such as Kenzo, Donna Karan, Calvin Klein, Christian Lacroix, Alain Manoukian, La Perla, Salvatore Ferragamo and more. There is also a range of quality jewellery stores, including Damas Jewellery, Tiffany & Co, Rivoli and Cartier. You can top up your purchases at cosmetics and perfume emporium Paris Gallery, a Virgin Megastore and many more. Yet at the time of writing it was undergoing a massive expansion, which will double its size.

CITY SHOES Map pp214-15 *Shoes*
Karama Shopping Centre, Karama; 🕐 9am-10.30pm Sat-Thu, 9-11am, 4-10.30pm Fri
This large bustling shoe store sells Sketchers, Dr Martens, Timberland, Lumberjack and Birkenstocks at great prices. It stocks a range of Travelplus accessories, including adaptors, money belts and padlocks.

DAMAS JEWELLERY
Map pp214-15 *Jewellery*
Wafi City Mall; 🕐 10am-10pm Sat-Thu, 2-10pm Fri
Damas started in 1907 in the UAE and has its own range of innovative in-house brands as well as stocking a range of international jewellery heavyweights.

FIVE GREEN
Map pp214-15 *Clothing & Accessories*
☎ 398 2206; Garden Home, Oud Metha
This new urban lifestyle store, established by 9714 entrepreneur Shehab Hamad and his sister Shuhi, stocks cool clothes, music, art, photography, books and magazines by independent publishers and distributors. Labels include XLarge, BoxFresh, Paul Frank, Upper Playground and Fidel. Designed by Khalid al-Najar, the store is part retail, part performance space, hosting everything from spoken word (poetry reading) to live bands and DJ sets.

FLAMINGO GIFTS
Map pp214-15 *Handicrafts & Souvenirs*
☎ 337 3285; Block S, Karama Shopping Centre, Karama; 🕐 9am-10.30pm Sat-Thu, 9-11am & 4-10.30pm Fri
This small store stocks a wide range of colourful pashminas, including the increasingly

---

Top Five Handicraft & Souvenir Shops

- Al Jaber Gallery (p126), Deira City Centre
- Art & Culture (p125), InterContinental Dubai
- Arts & Crafts (p127), BurJurman Centre
- Asala Antiques & Handicrafts (p126), Deira City Centre
- Gifts & Souvenirs (p128), Karama Shopping Centre

---

popular embroidered, pompom, leather-fringed and beaded styles. Pay as little as Dh10 for the synthetic ones. The 100% authentic pashminas start at Dh100 for those made by machine and up to Dh250 for those that are handmade. Friendly staff will show you the selection of Iranian bedspreads, Syrian tablecloths, Indian tapestries, Kashmiri shawls, Benares 'silk' tablecloths and Oriental cushion covers. Prices range from Dh5 to Dh120.

GIFT LAND Map pp214-15 *Kitsch Souvenirs*
☎ 353 8849; Karama Shopping Centre, Bur Dubai; 🕐 9am-11.30pm Sat-Thu, 9am-noon & 3-11.30pm Fri
Head past the tacky toys, toiletries and stationery to the back of the store where, amid the plastic fruit and religious trinkets, are the cheapest souvenirs around – leather camels, intricately patterned tin jewellery boxes with camels, carved wooden boxes and ashtrays inlaid with brass palm trees, stars and – you guessed it – camels. On your way out, grab one of those fluffy toy camels that play Arabic music when you cuddle them.

GIFTS & SOUVENIRS
Map pp214-15 *Handicrafts & Souvenirs*
☎ 337 7884; Karama Shopping Centre, Karama; 🕐 9am-10.30pm Sat-Thu, 9-11am & 4-10.30pm Fri
Here you'll find the widest range and highest quality handicrafts and souvenirs in Karama – camels in every shape and size, wooden inlaid boxes, brass Arabian coffeepots and coffee sets, Aladdin-style lamps, intricately patterned plates and bowls, and brass candle holders. Good deals include colourful *kandouras* (Dh100), *gutra* and *agal* sets (Dh25), incense sets, which include frankincense, clay burner and coal (Dh10), and Arabian perfume oils (Dh10). Delicate wooden carvings of miniature Arabian doors in picture frames make original gifts for as little as Dh40.

Top Five Camel Gifts

- cuddly camels that play music when you squeeze them
- *Camelspotting* CD – new music from the Middle East
- colourful camel mobiles for the baby's room
- camel-crossing road sign kitchen magnet
- oud-playing camel-jockey pen

GOODIES Map pp214-15   *Delicatessen*
☎ 324 4555; Wafi City Mall, Al-Qataiyat Rd; near Al-Garhoud Bridge on the Bur Dubai side of the Creek; ⌚ 10am-10pm Sat-Thu, 2-10pm Fri

If you're in Dubai during the milder winter months or Ramadan, stock up on some Arabian delicacies at Goodies (a popular Lebanese food hall) and join the many families having picnic suppers at one of the Creek-side parks. Goodies stocks barrels of olives, spicy peppers, pickles, white cheeses, vine leaves, hummus, tabbouleh, *baba ghanooj* (purée of grilled aubergine, tahini and olive oil), *muttabal*, fried *kibbeh* (meat-filled cracked wheat croquettes), Lebanese pastries and much more.

GULF GREETINGS
Map pp212-13   *Gifts & Cards*
☎ 351 9613; BurJurman Centre, cnr Khalid bin al-Waleed & Trade Centre Rds, Bur Dubai; ⌚ 10am-10pm Sat-Thu, 2-10pm Fri

Among the enormous range of gifts, wrapping paper, greeting cards and quality postcards, you won't be able to resist the pretty Arabian-themed greeting cards. They are so beautiful you'll take a stack back home but won't want to give them away.

Toy camels

IBN AL SAADA
Map pp214-15   *Handicrafts & Souvenirs*
☎ 336 7309; Block R, Karama Shopping Centre, Karama; ⌚ 9am-10.30pm Sat-Thu, 9-11am & 4-10.30pm Fri

Tell the salesman you're looking for a unique souvenir and he'll bring a Saddam Hussein Ace of Spades Shocker Lighter out from under the counter. The Dh15 zapper comes with a health warning. Pay attention or you'll get the shock of your life. Go for the Sheikh Mohammed baseball cap instead, although the store boasts it has the largest range of pashmina shawls – 275 different colours and styles.

KARAMA CENTRE
Map pp214-15   *Shopping Centre*
Kuwait St, Karama, btwn Sheikh Khalifa bin Zayed & Za'abeel Rds; ⌚ 9am-1pm & 4-9pm

As this shopping centre caters mainly to an Indian clientele, you'll find lots of terrific shops selling saris, embroidered Indian hippy tops and beautiful Indian children's clothes and toys, along with the usual copies of label jeans, watches and jewellery that Karama has become synonymous with.

KARAMA SHOPPING CENTRE
Map pp214-15   *Shopping Centre*
Karama, Bur Dubai; ⌚ 9am-10.30pm Sat-Thu, 9-11am & 4-10.30pm Fri

Also known as Karama Souq, this bustling area is the heart of Karama district. The many handicrafts and souvenir stores, and shops selling fake designer goods, are the main reason to visit. You'll also find cheap clothing, shoes and accessories, kids' clothes and toys, and a few grocery shops. There are some tasty Indo-Pakistani, Filipino and Lebanese restaurants nearby. The prices are already low, but a little bargaining will reduce them even more.

LOS ANGELES IN DUBAI
Map pp214-15   *Handicrafts & Souvenirs*
☎ 334 8148; Block P, Karama Shopping Centre, Karama; ⌚ 9am-10.30pm Sat-Thu, 9-11am & 4-10.30pm Fri

Ask and the friendly staff will leave you alone to select from the widest range of brass and wooden camels, shiny Aladdin-style lamps, glass Burj Al Arab paper weights, delicate tinted-glass perfume bottles and silver jewellery. Bright, colourfully painted pencil holders and boxes featuring Emirati scenes in a naive style make great gifts for kids.

NO NAME SHOE SHOP

Map pp212-13   *Shoes*

Dubai Old Souq abra station, Bur Dubai Souq

Live out *The Thousand and One Nights*–style fantasies at this small outdoor stall opposite the *abra* dock when you buy your very own pair of coiling Aladdin-style shoes from Pakistan and Afghanistan. Go for a pair of gold-threaded embroidered slippers for him and delicately coloured sequined slippers for her.

OHM RECORDS Map pp214-15   *Music*

☎ 397 3728; Trade Centre Rd, Bur Dubai; 5-10pm

The first store in the Middle East to carry vinyl, Ohm Records is one of the best things to happen to Dubai's music scene. It stocks a good selection, including house, trance, progressive, drum and bass and trip hop, as well as DJ equipment and accessories. Ohm is an active promoter of the Dubai DJ scene and holds workshops for aspiring DJs.

RAFI FRAME STORE

Map pp214-15   *Prints & Pictures*

☎ 337 3969; Karama Shopping Centre, Karama; 9am-10.30pm Sat-Thu, 9-11am & 4-10.30pm Fri

Unframed prints of oils, watercolours and drawings featuring typical Arabian and Emirati scenes – souqs, coffeehouses, oases, dhows – sell for as little as Dh20 for a small size to Dh100 for a large print. Small-framed prints cost Dh15 to Dh25.

SAYED MOHAMMED ALI AL-HASHEMI

Map pp214-15   *Handicrafts & Souvenirs*

☎ 337 7601; Block U, Karama Shopping Centre, Karama; 9am-10.30pm Sat-Thu, 9-11am & 4-10.30pm Fri

Although you'll find the usual selection of *sheesha* kits, mosque alarm clocks and Arabian trinkets, the highlights are the quirky key rings. Our favourite is a shiny gold Dubai key ring dangling with miniatures of the city's architectural highlights – Burj Al Arab, Jumeirah Mosque and the Dubai Creek Golf & Yacht Club.

SEVEN ART FASHION

Map pp214-15   *Handicrafts & Souvenirs*

☎ 336 6887; Block T & U, Karama Shopping Centre, Karama; 9am-10.30pm Sat-Thu, 9-11am & 4-10.30pm Fri

Among this wide selection of pashminas (Dh10 to Dh400), you'll find shawls with intricate patterns of embroidery, leather trimming

and less tasteful tassels. The imitation Christian Dior and Louis Vuitton prints are a popular choice. A more original souvenir is the Sheikh Zayed coffee mug (Dh10).

SPLASH BOUTIQUE

Map pp214-15   *Clothing & Souvenirs*

☎ 337 6449; Block R, Karama Shopping Centre, Karama; 9am-10.30pm Sat-Thu, 9-11am & 4-10.30pm Fri

The Karama branch of this popular discount clothing store has the standard fake Burberry bags, but prettier are the beaded handbags for Dh15. Another highlight is the Emirati dolls: She looks elegant in *abeyya*, burka and *shayla*, while he looks most dignified in his *dishdasha* (shirt-dress) – a bargain at Dh25 each or Dh35 for the set.

TETSA TRADING

Map pp214-15   *Handicrafts & Souvenirs*

Karama Shopping Centre, Karama; 9am-10.30pm Sat-Thu, 9-11am & 4-10.30pm Fri

This tiny crowded store is stocked with Indian tapestries, gold-threaded tablecloths, wall hangings textured with tiny mirrors and coloured beads, cute colourful camel mobiles and *sheesha* kits. More unusual are the wooden 'Russian dolls' painted as Emirati nationals, and the framed glass cases of butterflies, scorpions and spiders.

Skullcaps on display

TIFFANY & CO Map pp212-13 *Jewellery*

☎ 359 0101; BurJuman Centre, Bur Dubai; 🕙 10am-10pm Sat-Thu & 4-10pm Fri

Pretend you're Audrey Hepburn – Tiffany is affordable in Dubai. Although the brand is internationally renowned for diamonds, the sterling silver accessories won't blow the budget. The most popular Tiffany designs are the 'X's with a kick', the 'loving hearts', created by Paloma Picasso, and the key rings, necklaces and bracelets engraved with the 'return to Tiffany' legend.

WAFI CITY MALL
Map pp214-15 *Shopping Centre*

☎ 324 4555; Al-Qataiyat Rd; near Al-Garhoud Bridge on Bur Dubai side of the Creek; 🕙 10am-10pm Sat-Thu, 2-10pm Fri

This enormous Egyptian-themed shopping centre has a wide range of exclusive designer boutiques, shoe, accessory, cosmetic and jewellery shops, homeware and interior stores, including the One. It is also home to a number of wonderful restaurants and bars, fitness centres and spas, and attractions such as the Encounter Zone playground, which will keep the kids amused for ages.

SHEIKH ZAYED ROAD

AZZA FAHMY JEWELLERY
Map p218 *Jewellery*

☎ 330 0000; Emirates Towers Shopping Boulevard, Sheikh Zayed Rd; 🕙 10am-10pm Sat-Thu, 4-10pm Fri

Egyptian Azza Fahmy is one of the world's leading designers of fine jewellery in the Islamic and Arab traditions. Her unique pieces incorporate colourful gemstones and precious beads, classical Arabic poetry and Islamic wisdom in fine calligraphic inscriptions, and motifs and elements from different ages and civilisations. While her style has been labelled universal because it assimilates global influences, Azza claims her work expresses profound spiritual values lost to much of the Arab world.

EMIRATES TOWERS SHOPPING BOULEVARD
Map p218 *Shopping Centre*

☎ 330 0000/319 8999; Sheikh Zayed Rd; 🕙 10am-10pm Sat-Thu, 4-10pm Fri

This exclusive designer shopping mall is home to more than 40 luxury brands, including Cartier, Bvlgari, Damas Jewellery, Ermenegildo

Mannequins

Zegna, Galerie Hamadan, Giorgio Armani, Gucci, Jimmy Choo, Rivoli and Yves Saint Laurent. You can also stock up on your Romeo Y Julieta cigars at La Casa del Habano, buy a designer *shayla* at My Fair Lady Abaya Shop, or pick up a Prada bag at Villa Moda, in which to carry home all those purchases.

GOLD & DIAMOND PARK
Map pp206-7 *Gold & Jewellery*

☎ 347 7788; Sheikh Zayed Rd, near Interchange No 4; 🕙 10am-10pm Sat-Thu, 4-10pm Fri

Some shoppers prefer the air-conditioned Gold & Diamond Park to the Deira Gold Souq – here you'll find 30 retailers and about 120 manufacturers in a purpose-built building designed in traditional Arabian souq style. There's a lovely café and traditional jewellery displays, along with shops selling oddities such as purple, gold and black pearls. We prefer the souq, but this is certainly worth a look.

GUCCI Map p218 *Clothing & Accessories*

☎ 330 0000; Emirates Towers Shopping Boulevard, Sheikh Zayed Rd; 🕙 10am-10pm Sat-Thu, 4-10pm Fri

Conceived by Gucci director Tom Ford and interior architect William Sofield, this Gucci store is worth visiting just to admire the late-20th-century modernist design – a long, external cream limestone wall welcomes you into a slick, polished steel and rosewood interior. Inside

Villa Moda (below)

you'll find a wide range of Gucci fashion, accessories, jewellery, handbags and luggage.

JIMMY CHOO Map p218 *Shoes*
☎ 330 0404; Emirates Towers Shopping Boulevard, Sheikh Zayed Rd; ⏰ 10am-10pm Sat-Thu, 4-10pm Fri
Jimmy Choo, a master craftsman when it comes to designing glamorous, feminine footwear, became a household name after his shoes began making regular cameo appearances on *Sex and the City* and adorning stars' feet. Italian architects Vudafieri Partners and Lena Pessoa created the luxurious look of the Dubai flagship store, which features mirrored tables and suede fittings. Expect to pay anywhere from Dh1500 to Dh3000 a pair, although trying (and dreaming) is free.

VILLA MODA
Map p218 *Clothing & Accessories*
☎ 330 0000; Emirates Towers Shopping Boulevard, Sheikh Zayed Rd; ⏰ 10am-10pm Sat-Thu, 4-10pm Fri
First established in Kuwait by Majed al-Sabah, otherwise known as the Sheikh of Chic, this designer concept store stocks 50 of the hottest brands in fashion under one roof, including Prada, Stella McCartney, Alexander McQueen, Missoni, Easton Pearson, Miu Miu, Marni and Chloe, to name a few. If that isn't enough to satisfy, there's a cosmetics department specialising in hard-to-find brands, such as Three Custom Colour, which can customise face cosmetics for you. Even if you have no intention of buying, drop in to check out the funky *2001 – A Space Odyssey*–looking interiors, the time-capsule stores, and super cool, curvy white lacquer café. The store offers gift wrapping and valet parking.

JUMEIRAH
AL AREEJ
Map pp216-17 *Perfume & Cosmetics*
☎ 344 4161; Mercato Mall, Jumeirah Rd, Jumeirah; ⏰ 10am-10pm Sat-Thu, 2-10pm Fri
This perfume, cosmetics and accessories department store stocks every international brand imaginable: Gucci, Chanel, Dolce & Gabbana, Armani, Issey Miyake, Kenzo, Jean-Paul Gaultier, Christian Dior, Lancôme, Guerlain, La Prairie, Yves Saint Laurent and more.

BEACH CENTRE

Map pp216-17   *Shopping Centre*

☎ 344 9045; near Dubai Zoo, Jumeirah Rd, Jumeirah; ❂ 9.30am-1pm & 4.30-9.30pm

This blue glass shopping mall has a number of restaurants lining Jumeirah Rd. Inside you'll find a variety of businesses including Cyber Café (per hour Dh7.50), Kids to Teens clothes store, the Music Room, Photo Magic, the World of Art, a decent branch of Yateem Opticals, Baskin Robbins, Hobby Land, Crystal Gallery and Red Sea Exhibitions.

JUMEIRAH CENTRE

Map pp216-17   *Shopping Centre*

☎ 349 9702; near Jumeirah Mosque, Jumeirah Rd, Jumeirah; ❂ 9am-9pm Sat-Thu, 4-9pm Fri

The highlight of this centre is the Caviar Classic shop, although Al Liali Jewellery isn't bad either. There's also Essensuals, for aromatherapy and natural healing, a Body Shop, Baskin Robbins, Benetton, Sun & Sands Sports, Thomas Cook, Coffee Bean & Tea Leaf, the Nutrition Centre, Mother Care, Photo Magic and a good camera repair store.

JUMEIRAH PLAZA

Map pp216-17   *Shopping Centre*

☎ 349 7111; near Jumeirah Mosque, Jumeirah Rd, Jumeirah; ❂ 9.30-1pm & 4.30-9.30pm Sat-Thu, 4.30-9.30pm Fri

Here you'll find the super second-hand bookshop House of Prose, the Dubai International Arts Centre, and several stores including Kashmir Craft, Perfect Selection Stationery and Girls Talk Beauty Centre, all set amid a lush space of tropical vegetations and cascading fountains under a glass-roofed atrium.

MERCATO MALL

Map pp216-17   *Shopping Centre*

☎ 344 4161; Jumeirah Rd, Jumeirah; ❂ 10am-10pm Sat-Thu, 2-10pm Fri

This Italian Renaissance–style shopping centre has to be seen to be believed. As bizarre as it is, it's a lovely shopping mall to stroll around – bright and light with various courtyard cafés where you can relax and enjoy watching all the people pass by. Alongside a vast range of funky young clothes boutiques, including Bershka, Mango and Promod, are home interior stores, cosmetics outlets, such as MAC, a super Virgin Megastore, several good carpet shops and a Mini Cooper store.

MUSIC MASTER Map pp216-17   *Music*

☎ 346 1462; Palm Strip, opposite Jumeirah Mosque, Jumeirah Rd, Jumeirah; ❂ 10am-10pm Sat-Thu, 1.30-10pm Fri

Although it doesn't have as wide a range of CDs as Virgin, Music Master has a decent selection of classical music and lots of Arabic pop. Whereas you'll find more of the Oriental lounge and DJ mixes at Virgin, you'll get your Haifa and Nancy Ajram here.

ONE Map pp216-17   *Interiors*

☎ 345 6687; next to Jumeirah Mosque, Jumeirah Rd, Jumeirah; ❂ 9am-10pm Sat-Thu, 2-10pm Fri

This interiors and lifestyle store stocks very stylish contemporary furniture and cool accessories. Take a look just to see how Dubai expats furnish their homes. While you're there check out the excellent range of art, interiors and architecture books, such as *Islamic Art*, *Modern Moroccan* and *Global Style*, and the luxurious French bath products, candles and aromatherapy products. The One's own brand of South African soaps, massage bars and bath foams are wonderful. Cleopatra's Desire and the Mystical soak are our favourites, and cost Dh15 for a large tub.

PALM STRIP Map pp216-17   *Shopping Centre*

☎ 346 1462; opposite Jumeirah Mosque, Jumeirah Rd, Jumeirah; ❂ 10am-10pm Sat-Thu, 1.30-10pm Fri

This pleasant breezy mall has a range of stores in a compact space: you'll find Mango, the Young Designers Emporium, Beyond the Beach, the Bollywood-style MTV Fashions boutique, Music Master, N-Bar and a couple of thriving cafés.

PERSIAN CARPET HOUSE & ANTIQUES Map pp216-17   *Carpets*

☎ 345 6687; Mercato Mall, Jumeirah Rd, Jumeirah; ❂ 10am-10pm Sat-Thu, 2-10pm Fri

Many consider the Persian Carpet House to be the best source of fine handmade Persian

---

Top Five Carpet Shops

- **Al Orooba Oriental** (p127), BurJuman Centre
- **Aminian Persian Carpets** (p125), Deira City Centre
- **Persian Carpet House & Antiques** (above), Mercato Mall
- **Pride of Kashmir** (p126), Deira City Centre
- **Red Sea Exhibitions** (p134), Beach Centre

carpets and Oriental rugs. They stock a wide variety of carpets and rugs from Iran, India, Kashmir, Pakistan and Afghanistan, as well as a small range from Turkey, China and Russia. Their 'antiques' include old gramophones, radios, telephones, wooden chess and backgammon sets, coffeepots, wrought-iron chairs, *khanjars*, pistols and swords.

RED SEA EXHIBITIONS

Map pp216-17   *Carpets*

☎ 344 9045; Beach Centre, Jumeirah Rd, Jumeirah; ☯ 9.30am-1pm & 4.30-9.30pm

One of the best carpet shops in Dubai, Red Sea has an excellent selection of Oriental carpets, including many antique rugs, at very reasonable prices.

TOWN CENTRE

Map pp216-17   *Shopping Centre*

☎ 344 0111; Jumeirah Rd, Jumeirah; ☯ 10am-10pm Sat-Thu, 5-10pm Fri

This communitylike mall has a branch of Café Ceramique (where you can paint a piece of pottery while you have a cup of coffee), Al-Jaber Optical, Bang & Olufsen, Books Plus, Café Moka, Damas Jewellery, DKNY Fashion, Oasis, Nine West, Paris Gallery, Papermoon and the Kaya Beauty Centre.

Top Five Last-Minute Gifts from the Airport

- Authentic pashminas – exquisite quality guaranteed from Dubai Duty Free.
- *Blue Bedouin* CD – chilled-out beats from the Dubai desert.
- Choco-dates – delicious chocolate-covered almond-centred dates.
- *Gutra* and *agal* sets – slightly more expensive than the souq, but worth the extra dirhams to see your dad dressed as Sheikh Dave/Jim/Bob when you get back home.
- Veiled Arabian women fridge magnets – a playful reminder of your exotic sojourn.

VIRGIN MEGASTORE

Map pp216-17   *Music/DVDs/Books*

☎ 344 6971; Mercato Mall, Jumeirah Rd, Jumeirah; ☯ 10am-10pm Sat-Thu, 2-10pm Fri

Like its sister store at Deira City Centre, Virgin stocks the best range of CDs, including a wide selection of the latest Arabic music, pop, dance and fusion, along with DVDs and books. This is where you'll find a good selection of coffee-table books, Arabic-language books and CD-ROMs, and novels.

Sleeping

Sleeping

With hundreds of hotels and many more on drawing boards all over the city, Dubai certainly doesn't lack accommodation. The bad news, for those looking for something like a hostel or budget accommodation, is that Dubai increasingly caters for four- and five-star guests, although if you're travelling in the hotter months you can get amazing discounts. The good news, for those wielding platinum credit cards, is that there are plenty of superb places that can really give your credit limit a workout.

Accommodation Styles

There are basically two types of hotel accommodation in Dubai, the city hotels and the beach resorts. The city hotels, found in Deira, Bur Dubai and Sheikh Zayed Rd range from one star to five, while the beach resorts, found along Jumeirah Beach heading south, generally are five star (and above). The star rating versus facilities is generally in line with other parts of the world. For longer-term accommodation, there are furnished apartments, mainly found in Bur Dubai. While there are no official camping sites in Dubai, many residents spend weekends camping on beaches or in the desert, but given the temperatures and lack of facilities, camping is not really a feasible option for a Dubai holiday.

The type of hotel you should choose very much depends on what type of holiday you're after. The city hotels are great for access to the shopping malls, souqs and historic areas, but when it's really hot you might be jealous of those staying at a beach resort. Those looking for a more relaxing holiday should opt for one of the luxurious beach resorts, but keep in mind you're around 30 minutes away from Dubai centre – when the traffic's good – and a taxi will cost around Dh40 to Dh50 each way. But a couple of the resorts are so well appointed, you might not bother leaving!

Nonsmoking floors are becoming more common in Dubai's hotels – make sure you ask for one when you book as they are quickly snapped up.

Le Meridien Mina Seyahi Resort (p147)

On the Drawing Board...

The pace of resort development in Dubai is staggering and showing no sign of easing up, nor is the daring nature of the projects. Here's a selection of some of the latest.

Dubailand (www.dubailand.ae) Many projects in Dubai have been described as Disneyesque, so it was only a matter of time before a genuine Middle Eastern answer to Disneyland was announced. Dubailand will have the world's biggest mall, several hotels, an indoor ski complex and sports stadiums, as well as a variety of other high-impact attractions.

Hydropolis (www.hydropolis.com) Just when you thought it couldn't get any weirder along comes something even more anomalous – an underwater hotel. The marketing material talks a lot about water, 'regeneration of this basic substance', 'unaccustomed sensual impressions', and the resort being 'ideally suited for guests from top management seeking to regenerate their inner strength'. Sounds oddly like outtakes from *Dr Strangelove*.

Madinat Jumeirah (www.madinatjumeirah.com) While Mina A'Salam has already opened, it's only the first of three hotels to open in the Madinat Jumeirah resort. The other two, Al Qasr (300 rooms) and Dar Al Masyaf Villas (340 rooms), were scheduled to open in late summer 2004.

The Palm (www.thepalm.co.ae) The world's two largest artificial islands in the shape of palms will increase the coastline of Dubai by 120km and will be home to over 60 hotels. The Palm at Jumeirah is scheduled to welcome its first residents in early 2006.

The World (www.thepalm.co.ae) A project consisting of 300 islands designed in the shape of – you guessed it – the world. Measuring 5.5km in width and length, completion of the project is expected in 2008 and it will, of course, be an exclusive residence and tourist resort.

Check-in & Checkout Times

One of the most contentious issues in the hotel scene today is the ever shrinking time that you're actually able to use the room you've paid for. It's now become standard in most places that check-in is at 3pm and checkout at midday. Dubai follows suit, but generally if you arrive early staff will try to get you a room as soon as possible. Perhaps as a result, it doesn't stop them from ringing the night before you leave to find out exactly what time you're checking out.

Price Ranges

The hotel prices we've quoted are inclusive of municipal tax (10%) and service charge (10%). Keep in mind that these are the hotels' rack rates – the standard, published, high-season rates. You are only likely to pay this rate when occupancy peaks during the high season. Discounts are almost always offered on the rack rates so make sure you ask. Having business cards to show means you can qualify as a corporate client, which earns a substantial discount.

During summer the tourist traffic drops off, so from mid-May to mid-September hotels drop their rates, often up to 50% off the published rack rate. Always ask for the best price or whether there are any deals on; generally the hotels won't tell you unless you ask.

All mid-range and top-end hotels require you to leave your passport in their safe for the duration of your stay. They also require you to leave a credit-card authorisation of about Dh500 per night. If you don't have a credit card you will have to leave a cash deposit. This can make things difficult if

Don't Believe the Price...

We know we just wrote about not paying rack rates, but it's so important we're going to say it again – don't pay rack rates. Shop around – you can nearly always move up a star or simply to a better hotel with a little research. Get on the Internet and visit the hotel websites, where sometimes you can get a discount of as much as half the rack rate. Check with your airline and see what hotels they offer package deals for and do the maths, it can work out cheaper – this is especially true for the resort hotels.

you don't have a lot of cash with you, or if your credit card is nearly at its limit. The cheap sleeps included in this book generally cost from Dh100 to Dh150 per night – before you book one check out the boxed text on p137.

Reservations

Most reputable hotel chains have online booking facilities. Note that some of the less-expensive hotels offer online bookings but not through a secured server – meaning that you run a much greater risk of having your credit card details stolen while booking. Check out the published specials on their websites (if there are none currently available that generally means occupancy is high), or you can try Expedia (www.expedia.com) or Lastminute.com (www.lastminute.com).

For the peak periods Dubai can actually run out of hotel rooms, so you'll need to book well in advance.

DEIRA

Deira has Dubai's only real budget hotel district. Handy because of its central location, it can be a bit noisy if you're staying in the cheaper hotels that don't have double-glazed windows. There are a few good hotels with views of the Creek and some quality hotels near the airport – not a bad prospect if you like shopping as it's close to the many souqs and malls. Some of the less expensive hotels featured can easily slip into the 'Cheap Sleeps' category with a little negotiation.

AL-BUSTAN ROTANA HOTEL
Map pp210-11 *Hotel*
☎ 282 0000; www.rotana.com; Casablanca Rd, Al-Garhoud; s/d Dh1080/1320
Located near the airport, this hotel has an impressive lobby with rooms rising up around it. The facilities (great for families) and service are first class and the restaurants are fine (especially the **Blue Elephant** – p71), although the rooms, while a decent size, lack character. If you can score one of the frequent deals, it's one of the best on this side of the Creek.

AVARI DUBAI HOTEL Map pp210-11 *Hotel*
☎ 295 6666; www.avari.com; 45C St; s/d Dh847/957
This well-positioned hotel caters mainly for Asian business travellers. It is set back off the west side of Abu Baker al-Siddiq Rd, near the Clock Tower Roundabout. The standard rooms are quite decent and there's a rooftop pool and a gym.

CARLTON TOWER HOTEL
Map pp208-9 *Hotel*
☎ 222 2131; Baniyas Rd; s/d Dh400/450
A favourite with the Russian tour-group market, this old hotel has a great outlook right on the Creek. The hotel and rooms are showing their age, despite being tarted up. With a decent discount and an obligatory Creek view room it's fine as long as you've exhausted the possibility of the name-brand hotels first.

HILTON DUBAI CREEK
Map pp208-9 *Hotel*
☎ 227 1111; www.hilton.com; Baniyas Rd, Rigga; r from Dh1440
This Hilton is the best of Deira's hotels. Its ultra-modern design and cool atmosphere offer relief from the in-your-face opulence of Dubai's other five-star hotels, with the added bonus of Gordon Ramsay's restaurant **Verre** (p74) keeping tummies happy. The rooms are spacious, the huge beds are the most comfortable in Dubai and there's all the usual business facilities including wireless Internet. The rooftop pool provides an awesome view of the dhow wharf, but the gym's small for a hotel of this standard. Book a room with a view of the Creek and you won't be disappointed – especially at sunset.

HOLIDAY INN DOWNTOWN
Map pp210-11 *Hotel*
☎ 228 8889; www.ichotelsgroup.com; 37 St, near Al-Rigga Rd; s/d/ste Dh550/650/1260
Just north of Al-Rigga Rd, this hotel is a fairly subdued business-oriented affair. The rooms

are spacious and well-appointed and non-smoking rooms are available. It's close to some great shopping.

HOTEL DELHI DARBAR
Map pp208-9   *Hotel*

☎ 273 3555; Naif Rd; s/d Dh175/250

This Indian-oriented establishment is better than most of the hotels in this area, featuring spacious, clean rooms with decent bathroom, minifridge and TV. There's a popular Indian restaurant on the ground floor.

HYATT REGENCY DUBAI
Map pp208-9   *Hotel*

☎ 209 1234; www.dubai.regency.hyatt.com; off Al-Khaleej Rd; s/d/ste Dh1164/1254/2100

This behemoth on the Corniche was one of the first Dubai hotels to offer a vast range of facilities. Shops, restaurants, cinemas, massive conference facilities – even an ice-skating rink and mini golf course – are just some of the services on offer. Rooms are comfortable and have great views over the Gulf, Dubai and Sharjah; and it's where journalists gathered to watch the first Gulf War being played out. A pleasant choice for families and its close proximity to the souqs makes it a practical choice for ardent shoppers.

Hilton Dubai Creek (opposite)

INTERCONTINENTAL DUBAI
Map pp208-9   *Hotel*

☎ 222 7171; www.intercontinental.com; Baniyas Rd; s/d Dh1400/1540

This huge hotel is starting to show it's age, but it's well-established, well-run and well-situated on a busy part of the Creek. Now host to several excellent restaurants and good business facilities, it's enduringly popular with business travellers. All rooms have Creek views but the standard rooms are a tight fit – especially if you're as tall as the doorman who cuts a striking figure as you enter the hotel.

JW MARRIOTT HOTEL
Map pp210-11   *Hotel*

☎ 262 4444; www.marriott.com; Abu Baker al-Siddiq Rd; r from Dh1260, executive ste Dh3000

One of the more impressive city five stars, the Marriott has a stunning foyer as well as a relaxing 'town square' under a colossal skylight. The standard rooms are luxurious and spacious; and there are enough bars and restaurants to keep you busy for a few days – try the poolside Awafi if visiting in the cooler months. The only downside is the location: outside winter you'll be catching taxis everywhere.

LANDMARK HOTEL Map pp208-9   *Hotel*
☎ 228 6666; land1@emirates.net.ae; Baniyas Sq; s/d Dh500/600

Located on the north side of Baniyas Sq, Landmark is the best of the less expensive hotels in the area. Rated as a three star, there are fine facilities and friendly staff, and if you wrangle a discount it's a worthwhile choice as the Deira sights are all in walking distance.

LE MERIDIEN DUBAI Map pp210-11   *Hotel*
☎ 282 4040; www.lemeridien.com; Airport Rd; s/d/ste from Dh1200/1320/1600

A low-rise near the airport, the smallish rooms are built around a grassy courtyard. The main attraction is the myriad bars and restaurants, but while it has all of the usual Le Meridien amenities on paper, it's less exciting in the flesh – especially when compared to the other Le Meridien hotels near the beach. Worth considering if you can get a special deal.

LORDS HOTEL Map pp208-9   *Hotel*
☎ 228 9977; lords@emirates.net.ae; Al-Jazeira St; s/d Dh495/605

A well-positioned hotel that has spacious rooms and bathrooms.

Sleeping – Deira

NIHAL HOTEL Map pp210-11 *Hotel*
☎ 295 7666; nihalhtl@emirates.net.ae; 40C St;
s/d Dh390/540

Located near the Orchid Hotel, the Nihal Hotel's suites each have a small sitting room, enormous bathroom, bedroom and a kitchen with all the trimmings. It's a perfect choice in this price bracket for a longer stay.

ORCHID HOTEL Map pp210-11 *Hotel*
☎ 295 6999; orchidsl@emirates.net.ae; near the Clock Tower; s/d/tr Dh420/480/550

Off 37 St near the Clock Tower, this hotel is popular with Russian and Arab travellers, and offers some colourful bars and nightclubs. The rooms are not big, but it's clean and close enough to the action.

PHOENICIA HOTEL Map pp208-9 *Hotel*
☎ 222 7191; hotphone@emirates.net.ae; Baniyas Sq;
s/d Dh220/330

This large establishment is in a very central location overlooking Baniyas Sq. Standards seemed to have dropped over the last couple of years, but the rooms are fine for the money. Give the hotel bars a wide berth.

Sheraton Dubai Creek (opposite)

QUALITY INN HORIZON
Map pp208-9 *Hotel*
☎ 227 1919; www.qualityinn.com; Al-Rigga Rd;
s/d Dh540/660

This comfortable seven-storey, three-star hotel has decent-sized rooms and a practical location. There's an executive floor and nonsmoking rooms are available. On warm days cool down in the small rooftop swimming pool.

RAMEE INTERNATIONAL HOTEL
Map pp208-9 *Hotel*
☎ 224 0222; rameedxb@emirates.net.ae; 9C St;
s/d Dh250/350

This busy hotel is off Baniyas Sq and all of Deira's attractions are within walking distance. It's clean and fairly priced given the standard of the rooms.

RENAISSANCE DUBAI HOTEL
Map pp208-9 *Hotel*
☎ 262 5555; www.marriott.com; Salahuddin Rd;
r from Dh1050, executive ste Dh2400

A plush business hotel run by the Marriott chain, it's situated in one of the less picturesque areas in Rigga. It makes up for it by offering substantial discounts off the rack rates quoted. The rooms were refurbished a few years ago and it has a couple of popular restaurants as well as all the expected five-star amenities.

RIVIERA HOTEL Map pp208-9 *Hotel*
☎ 222 2131; www.rivierahotel-dubai.com; Baniyas Rd; s/d Dh400/450

The Riviera has refurbished its rooms and installed Internet access, but it's still a little overpriced for the facilities available and the overall standard of the hotel. However, it's in a great position, close to the souqs and right on the Creek, so if you get a good discount (and a Creek-view room) you could do a lot worse.

SHERATON DEIRA Map pp208-9 *Hotel*
☎ 268 8888; www.starwood.com; Al-Mateena St;
s/d Dh462/500

Positioned a little away from Dubai's leisure activities, this Sheraton is very much geared towards business guests. You will frequently be catching taxis as the dining facilities aren't up to much. In its favour, the rooms are fine and it has excellent rates for a five-star hotel – especially if you score a prime Internet rate – so it's good value. The hotel has a business

Call to Prayer

If you haven't visited a Muslim country before, be prepared to be woken at about 4.30am each morning by an inimitable wailing. This is the azan, the call to prayer. At the first sign of dawn, you'll hear a cacophony of droning sounds as muezzins chant the call to prayer through speakers positioned on the minaret of each mosque. Before speakers were used to summon people from their beds, the muezzins used to climb a ladder up to the minarets and call out from the top.

There are five prayers each day: at dawn; when the sun is directly overhead; when the sun is in the position that makes the shadow of an object the same length as that object; at the beginning of sunset; and at twilight when the last light of the day disappears over the horizon. Of course, things are worked out a little more technically than this and exact times are printed in the daily newspapers.

Once the call has been made, Muslims have half an hour in which to pray. There is an exception for the dawn prayer; after the call they have about an hour and 20 minutes in which to wake up and pray, before the sun has risen. The sixth time printed in newspapers indicates this sunrise deadline.

If Muslims aren't near a mosque, they can pray anywhere, so long as they face Mecca. You'll find a qibla (an arrow that indicates the direction of Mecca) in every hotel room in Dubai, usually on the ceiling, desk or bedside table.

If someone cannot get to a mosque, they will stop wherever they are to pray – by the side of the road, in hotel lobbies, in shops – so you may have to step around people occasionally. This is OK, just be as unobtrusive as you can, and if possible don't walk in front of them. All public buildings, such as government departments, libraries, shopping centres and airports, have prayer rooms or designated areas where people can pray.

The phrase that you will be able to make out most often during the call to prayer is *Allah-u-akbar*, which means God is Great. This is repeated four times at the start of the azan. Next comes *ashhadu an la illallah ha-illaah* (I testify there is no god but God). This is repeated twice. So is the next line *ashhadu anna Muhammadan rasuulu-ilaah* (I testify that Mohammed is His messenger). Then come two shorter lines, also sung twice; *hayya ala as-salaah* (come to prayer) and *hayya ala al-falaah* (come to salvation). *Allah-u-akbar* is repeated two more times, and then comes the last line *laa ilaah illa Allah* (there is no god but God).

The only prayer call with a difference is the one at dawn. In this azan, after the exhortation to come to salvation, comes the gently nudging extra line *as-salaatu khayrun min al nawn* (it is better to pray than to sleep), which is also repeated.

---

and conference centre, and is fairly close to the airport.

SHERATON DUBAI CREEK

Map pp208-9 *Hotel*
☎ 228 1111; www.starwood.com; Baniyas Rd; r Dh1200

After recently undergoing an extensive renovation, the hotel now takes full advantage of it's super position, smack bang on the Creek. There are plenty of room options, some with superb floor-to-ceiling windows providing an excellent Creek vista. There are also Japanese-themed rooms, which, while beautifully realised, are obviously not the choice if you're after that Arabesque experience. Facilities are of a high standard and rooms with Creek views are worth the premium paid.

SUN & SAND HOTEL Map pp210-11 *Hotel*
☎ 223 9000; www.sunsandhotel.com; 37 St; s/d Dh450/550

Happily situated near the Clock Tower, the Sun & Sand Hotel is somewhat boldly decorated. The amenities are decent for the price. There's

a rooftop swimming pool, gym and shuttle services to the beach and shopping malls.

TAJ PALACE HOTEL Map pp208-9 *Hotel*
☎ 223 2222; www.tajpalacedubai.com; 23D St, Rigga; s/d/ste Dh1100/1200/2300

Run by the India-based Taj group, the Taj Palace is a vast luxury hotel in the heart of the Rigga area. It has all of the hallmarks of a Taj property – elegant rooms and attentive service, as well as an Ayurvedic spa. The hotel offers another form of cleansing besides the spa – it has a no alcohol policy. If that's of no concern to you, the hotel is also home to a couple of first-rate restaurants, Handi (Indian) and Topkapi (Turkish).

CHEAP SLEEPS

AL-KHAYAM HOTEL Map pp208-9 *Hotel*
☎ 226 4211; khayamh@emirates.net.ae; Suq Deira St; s/d Dh150/180

This respectable family hotel – so no 'night visitors' – has only 26 rooms, which are modestly sized but clean.

DEIRA PALACE HOTEL

Map pp208-9   *Hotel*

☎ 229 0120; 67 St; s/d Dh130/150

This large family hotel has decent clean rooms but somewhat uncomfortable beds.

DUBAI YOUTH HOSTEL

Map pp206-7   *Hostel*

☎ 298 8161; uaeyha@emirates.net.ae; Al-Nahda Rd; dm Dh35-50, s Dh60-80, d Dh120-145

By far the cheapest (acceptable) accommodation in town, the hostel consists of an old wing with two- and three-bed dorms, and a new wing with very comfortable single and double rooms. Rooms in the new wing have air-con, TVs, minifridge and bathrooms and are equal to a three-star hotel. Breakfast is available for Dh10 and lunch and dinner for Dh15. Women, as well as men, can be accommodated and there are separate rooms for families.

If you don't have a Hostelling International (HI) card, the dorm beds and rooms cost an extra Dh15 per night. Membership cards are available from the hostel and from Dubai National Air Travel Agency (DNATA) outlets, and at the **DNATA Airline Centre** (Map pp210-11) on Al-Maktoum Rd. There is no age limit on staying at the hostel or obtaining a card.

To get here from central Deira take Salahuddin Rd to Al-Giyada Intersection, turn left into Al-Ittihad Rd, and then right onto Al-Nahda (Qusais) Rd. The place on the left with a stadium is the Al-Ahli Club. The hostel is another 100m along on the same side of the road. Bus No 13 runs from the Deira bus station to the hostel every 10 minutes from 6am until 11.45pm. The fare is Dh1. A taxi from central Deira will cost about Dh14.

GOLD PLAZA HOTEL Map pp208-9   *Hotel*

☎ 225 0240; Suq Deira St; s/d with balcony Dh125/150

A family hotel smack bang at the entrance to the Deira Gold Souq. The rooms are small and

have tiled floors. Some of the bathrooms need renovating, but otherwise it's not bad.

METRO HOTEL Map pp208-9   *Hotel*

☎ 226 0040; 32 St; s/d/tr Dh80/100/130

Located in an alley between Sikkat al-Khail and Al-Soor Sts, Metro has OK rooms, but accepts families only.

BUR DUBAI

Bur Dubai is fairly central and Deira is only a short *abra* (water taxi) ride away, but is mainly known for its hotel apartments, which can be good value if you're planning to stay for longer than a fortnight.

ASTORIA HOTEL Map pp212-13   *Hotel*

☎ 353 4300; astoria@astamb.com; Al-Nahda St; s/d Dh360/480

This large, rather ugly place has been around forever and is now popular with groups from Russia and the subcontinent. It is also home Pancho Villa's Mexican restaurant – one of the legends of Dubai's expat drinking scene.

CAPITOL HOTEL Map pp212-13   *Hotel*

☎ 346 0111; www.capitol-hotel.com; Al-Mina Rd, Satwa; s/d Dh370/480

A subtly tasteful hotel, popular with flight crews and business travellers, the huge rooms are beautifully furnished (and very quiet), and the neo–Art Deco lobby is stunning. Facilities are fine, although the less said about some of the entertainment on offer, the better.

FOUR POINTS SHERATON

Map pp212-13   *Hotel*

☎ 397 7444; www.starwood.com; Khalid bin al-Waleed Rd; s/d Dh720/840

A petite 125-room, four star oriented towards business travellers, this Sheraton is well located for sightseeing. The rooms are fairly standard, but it's a friendly hotel and the Viceroy bar on the 1st floor has agreeable leather couches to relax in. The hotel is also home to the fabulous Indian restaurant **Antique Bazaar** (p76).

GRAND HYATT DUBAI

Map pp206-7   *Hotel*

☎ 317 1234; www.dubai.grand.hyatt.com; Al-Qataiyat Rd; d from Dh1170

This recently opened resort-style hotel is the size of a small suburb. Dubbed Dubai's first city resort, it certainly matches the best beach resorts in terms of amenities, which include the Grand Spa. The rooms – all 674 of them – are conservatively but tastefully furnished, and facilities thoughtfully include broadband Internet and a 24-hour 'technology concierge' to help you get set up. The hotel was clearly designed with huge conferences in mind, but in some ways this just adds to the buzz. The best aspect is just wandering around the huge area that houses the eateries – all 14 of them. The chefs working in the open kitchens of the stylish restaurants, the massive indoor gardens (check those dhow hulls on the ceiling), and the sheer number of people out and about at all times of the day and night is enough to entice you out of your room just to see what's going on.

MÖVENPICK HOTEL BUR DUBAI
Map pp214-15 *Hotel*
☎ 336 6000; www.moevenpick-burdubai.com; 19 St, opposite American Hospital; s/d Dh850/950
Well positioned for shopping excursions, this modern hotel has fantastic business facilities including wireless Internet and smoke-free rooms, and is disabled-traveller friendly. There's a temperature-controlled rooftop pool as well as a fitness centre. Jimmy Dix and Fakhreldine restaurants are both very popular live-music venues. The hotel offers free airport pickup.

RAMADA HOTEL Map pp214-15 *Hotel*
☎ 351 9999; www.ramadadubai.com; Al-Mankhool Rd; s/d Dh960/1080
With its striking late-1970s stained-glass mural stretching the height of the atrium, the hotel is a bit of a throwback. The rooms are decent enough though, having been recently refurbished, and the hotel is well positioned for shopping and sightseeing.

REGAL PLAZA HOTEL
Map pp214-15 *Hotel*
☎ 355 6633; Al-Mankhool Rd; s/d from Dh225/275
Run by a reputable Indian hotel company, this hotel has modern rooms and facilities, including a swimming pool and gym. There are a couple of bars, such as **Bollywood Café** (p92), that play Hindi music at a volume that will make your ears bleed. The hotel boasts a good position and is well priced.

REGENT PALACE HOTEL
Map pp212-13 *Hotel*
☎ 396 3888; Sheikh Khalifa bin Zayed Rd; s/d from Dh300/360
Conveniently located opposite the BurJuman Centre, the quiet Regent Palace Hotel features a relaxing and leafy lobby area. The rooms are pleasant enough, although decorated in an old-fashioned style that bears no relation to the hotel exterior, but facilities are fine for the

Grand Hyatt Dubai (opposite)

price. The hotel also houses the infamous **Rock Bottom Café** (p93).

XVA Map pp212-13 *Boutique Hotel*
☎ 353 5383; xva@xvagallery.com; behind Basta Art Café, Al-Musallah Roundabout; r from Dh500

A welcome addition to the accommodation scene in Bur Dubai, this small hotel offers you a chance to stay in one of Dubai's recently restored traditional houses. The rooms, arranged around a central courtyard housing an art gallery and café, are uniquely furnished in an attractive but minimalist Oriental style (so there are no distractions like TVs in the rooms). It's a peaceful little area and it makes a wonderful retreat from the hectic pace of Dubai.

CHEAP SLEEPS

PACIFIC HOTEL Map pp208-9 *Hotel*
☎ 227 6700; www.pacifichotel-dubai.com; opposite Sabkha bus station; s/d Dh135/200

Close to the Creek action, the rooms are clean and the management friendly.

Shangri-La (opposite)

PANORAMA HOTEL Map pp212-13 *Hotel*
☎ 351 8518; panhotel@emirates.net.ae; Al-Mankhool Rd; s/d Dh250/350

This rather old apartment building set in a great location has large rooms, although they can be a bit noisy. The hotel bar is frequented by the Dubai demimonde – approach with caution.

TIME PALACE HOTEL
Map pp212-13 *Hotel*
☎ 353 2111; Al-Fahidi St; s/d Dh180/240

On the edge of Bur Dubai Souq, the rooms of Time Palace are small and slightly musty, but the sheets and bathrooms are kept clean. The entrance is in an alley just off 34 St.

SHEIKH ZAYED ROAD

Home to a new breed of fashionable five-star hotels, the Sheikh Zayed hotel strip also offers some great dining, nightlife and haute couture temptations. While it's an easy taxi ride to the beach resorts, keep in mind that the drive into Deira can be hellish at certain times of the day.

CROWNE PLAZA HOTEL
Map p218 *Hotel*
☎ 331 1111; www.dubai.crowneplaza.com; Sheikh Zayed Rd; s/d from Dh1100/1200

A very popular and long-standing business hotel, it has all the usual facilities you'd expect of this chain. The Crown Plaza is quite a large complex, with bars, restaurants and a shopping centre. The hotel's **Trader Vic's** (p81) restaurant and **Zinc** (p97) nightclub are extremely popular. If you can wrangle a good discount the executive floors are especially plush, in an ersatz French Restoration style.

DUSIT DUBAI Map p218 *Hotel*
☎ 343 3333; http://dubai.dusit.com/; Sheikh Zayed Rd, next to Interchange 1; r Dh850

This startling blue-glass edifice shaped like an upside-down Y adds yet another architecturally intriguing shape to the Sheikh Zayed Rd strip. The rooms are exceptionally comfortable with lush Thai furnishings, the service is excellent and there's a spectacular view from the rooftop pool on the 36th floor. But one of the best reasons to stay is so you can simply float back to your room after a hypnotic feast at **Benjarong** (p80).

Mina A'Salam, Madinat Jumeirah (p148)

EMIRATES TOWERS Map p218   *Hotel*
☎ 330 0000; www.emiratestowershotel.com; Sheikh Zayed Rd; d from Dh960

Located in the shorter of the stunning two towers, the hotel is a slick, ultramodern monument to Dubai's self-confidence. There's a real buzz about the place from the moment you enter the foyer – at least until the lobby pianist starts playing. The deluxe rooms – no standard rooms here – are splendid and it only get better (and more expensive, of course) as you head up the tower past the presidential suite into the royal suite. Joining the two towers at ground level is the **Emirates Towers Shopping Boulevard** (p131) – *haute couture*, anyone? – and some decent restaurants. At the top of the tower is **Vu's** (p82) and **Vu's Bar** (p94), which gives you a fantastic view of the Sheikh Zayed metropolis that's worth the price of a drink. Just.

FAIRMONT Map p218   *Hotel*
☎ 332 5555; www.fairmont.com; Sheikh Zayed Rd; d from Dh960

Cool and contemporary with some distinctly Arabian touches, the Fairmont is another landmark hotel on the strip that is easily recognisable at night with its illuminated four-poster towers and colour-cycling lighting scheme. The standard rooms are very comfortable and well appointed, and for something really special there are two floors of opulent Arabic-style or minimalist Japanese-style rooms as well as a spa. The food outlets are first-rate, especially **Spectrum on One** (p81) and the **Exchange** (p80), and staying at the hotel will hopefully help ease your path past the velvet ropes of the hip nightclub **Tangerine** (p96).

SHANGRI-LA Map p218   *Hotel*
☎ 343 8888; www.shangri-la.com; Sheikh Zayed Rd; d from Dh960

This chic new hotel, located on the upper levels of the Al-Jaber complex, is a welcome addition to the Sheikh Zayed strip. The ultra-stylish, roomy and comfortable rooms all have broadband Internet and stunning views of either the city or the sea. With one whole floor solely dedicated to the spa, this is one serious place to relax. The intimate **Hoi An** (p81) is a superb French-Vietnamese restaurant and **Marrakech** (p81), with its live music, makes for a good taste of Morocco.

WORLD TRADE CENTRE HOTEL
Map p218   *Hotel*
☎ 331 4000; www.worldtradecentrehoteldubai.com; Sheikh Zayed Rd; r from Dh550

Opened way back in 1978 (for Dubai that's like a century ago), it's decidedly old school, and attracts business clients and attendees of events at the adjacent Dubai World Trade Centre. Guests have access to the Jumeirah Beach Club facilities, at a charge. Check the website for up-to-date prices – they can be very reasonable.

Sleeping – Sheikh Zayed Road

14

An Oasis of Luxury

Al Maha Desert Resort (Map p150; ☎ 303 4224; www.al-maha.com; Margham; 2-person ste Oct-May Dh4448, Jun-Sep Dh2831) A genuine oasis in the desert, the Al Maha Resort, named after the endangered scimitar-horned oryx, is a luxurious ecotourism resort about 65km southeast of Dubai, off the Dubai–Al-Ain highway. The resort is set in a 25-sq-km wildlife reserve surrounded by a 165-sq-km buffer zone, a beautiful desert landscape area of peach-coloured dunes. Each guest room (there are 40 suites and two royal suites) is a luxurious, tent-style suite complete with Bedouin antiques and a chilled private plunge pool. Each suite has a guest-relations coordinator and wildlife field guide. The main building is in the style of a Hatta nobleman's house, while the bar resembles a colonial-era safari lodge.

The price includes all meals and activities, such as dune driving, camel trekking and falconry. The surrounding desert is home to its own ecosystem and is far from being a barren wasteland. The resort is located on a natural underground water table and the area is home to endangered species such as the aforementioned scimitar-horned oryx, the slender-horned gazelle, Arabian foxes and caracals. The resort uses recycled paper and packaging, biodegradable products and solar energy. There are also permanent exhibitions of paintings, sculptures and handicrafts by UAE artists. Private vehicles, visitors and children under 12 are not allowed at the resort.

JUMEIRAH

The luxury resort hotels are perfect for a relaxing beach holiday, but are a long way from the centre. While a view of Dubai expanding out over the desert is interesting, a sea view room is always superior – some of the more exclusive resorts only have sea views. Don't expect to find any budget accommodation here, but watch out for summer specials that can halve the price of some extraordinary digs.

BURJ AL ARAB Map pp206-7   *Hotel*
☎ 301 7000; www.burj-al-arab.com; Jumeirah Rd, Umm Suqeim; d from Dh6000
If the notion of paying the above amount to stay in the world's first 'seven-star' hotel (actually classified as five-star deluxe) doesn't raise any questions, book a room. For everyone else thinking, 'is it worth the money?', you're perhaps asking the wrong question. The hotel has gone far beyond just being a place to lay your head. In many ways it represents Dubai as an iconic visual symbol – it's now featured on Dubai's licence plates – and as the epitome of being brash, flash and not miserly with cash.

Built on an artificial island, 280m offshore from the Jumeirah Beach Hotel, the 320m-high hotel is home to 202 suites – each with their own private butler. The exterior of the hotel is visually stunning and at night, with its choreographed lightshow, it's as playful as it is audacious. The much-discussed interior redefines opulence but usually provokes a love-it or hate-it response – visitors either have a look of awe or horror written over their faces once inside. Think Versace on acid.

Regardless of whether you're considering staying at the hotel or not, a visit should be high on the list of anyone coming to Dubai.

DUBAI MARINE BEACH RESORT & SPA Map pp216-17   *Beach Resort*
☎ 346 1111; www.dxbmarine.com; Jumeirah Rd, Jumeirah; s/d Dh1000/1320
The somewhat dated rooms are set in a series of 33 villas among attractive tropical gardens, small fountains and ponds. There's a small but well-protected private beach, three pools, a spa and a well-equipped gym. The best aspect of the resort, however, is the myriad bars, restaurants and clubs – **Boudoir** (p95) and **Ginseng** (p92) are Dubaian favourites, so you certainly won't lack for nightlife if you stay here.

HILTON DUBAI JUMEIRAH
Map pp206-7   *Resort*
☎ 399 1111; www.hilton.com; Al-Sufouh Rd; s/d Dh1250/1350
While it's only a few years old, this resort is quite conservative in comparison to others along the strip. Most of the rooms have beach views, the suites are sensational, there's a spacious stretch of beach frontage and a fine pool area. It's quite a relaxing resort and the more casual nature of the eateries, combined with good facilities, makes it perfect for families.

JUMEIRAH BEACH CLUB
Map pp206-7   *Beach Resort*
☎ 344 5333; www.jumeirahbeachclub.com; Jumeirah Rd, Jumeirah; ste from Dh2880
This intimate resort has 48 junior suites and two larger suites in pavilions separated by lush

tropical gardens. The suites have a charming Southeast Asian feel to them (lots of wood and broad balconies), and there's an attractive swimming pool and stretch of beach where the chances of running into a visiting sporting celebrity are high – if they're not back in the suite watching a DVD from the private collection, or listening to a CD while relaxing in the Jacuzzi. So if seclusion, privacy and exclusivity is what you're after – this one's for you.

JUMEIRAH BEACH HOTEL
Map pp206-7   *Beach Resort*
☎ 348 0000; www.jumeirahbeachhotel.com; Jumeirah Rd, Umm Suqeim; s/d Dh1560/1650
This broad wave-shaped hotel may be somewhat overshadowed by its stablemate the Burj Al Arab, but certainly holds its own in terms of facilities. With over 600 large and well-equipped rooms it's a massive resort, but the amenities offered see guests happily fanning out to partake of the huge range of leisure activities. The water-based theme of the hotel is central to this and there's everything from nearly a kilometre of private beach to the Middle East's best water park, **Wild Wadi** (p60), and its own coral reef for diving trips. There are enough bars, cafés and restaurants to keep guests of all ages happy – it's a popular resort for families as well as business and conference guests.

LE MERIDIEN MINA SEYAHI RESORT
Map pp206-7   *Resort*
☎ 399 3333; www.lemeridien-minaseyahi.com; Al-Sufouh Rd; r with/without sea view from Dh1400/1200
This elegant and beautifully landscaped 210-room resort is a prime choice for water-sports enthusiasts as well as those who enjoy lazing by a gorgeous pool and exercising occasionally by swimming over to the wet bar. The standard rooms are large and the Royal Club rooms (mid-range) are big enough to park a car in without causing any inconvenience. The eateries are good and **Barasti Bar** (p92) is one of the best beach bars in Dubai. The hotel has two specially designed rooms for those with physical disabilities or special needs.

LE ROYAL MERIDIEN BEACH RESORT
Map pp206-7   *Resort*
☎ 399 5555; www.leroyalmeridien-dubai.com; Al-Sufouh Rd; s/d Dh1200/1440
This regal Arabian-influenced resort consists of three seemingly disconnected buildings. Tying it together is a variation of the customary Meridien landscaping and pools fronted by a vast private beach. The deluxe rooms are very well-appointed and from there on up it just gets better. There's a wide range of dining options – **Ossigeno** (p84), **Fusion** (p83) and **Prime Rib** (pp84-5) are notable and there are plenty of bars

Burj Al Arab (opposite) viewed from One&Only Royal Mirage (p148)

scattered around the leisure facilities so you're never too far from a cold beverage.

MINA A'SALAM, MADINAT JUMEIRAH

Map pp206-7   *Resort*
☎ 366 8888; www.minaasalam.com; Al-Sufouh Rd; s/d Dh2100/2220

Completing the extraordinary trinity of Jumeirah International resorts the Madinat Jumeirah is located adjacent to the Burj Al Arab and the Jumeirah Beach Hotel. Mina A'Salam is only the first of three hotels to open in the Madinat Jumeirah resort (see the boxed text on p137). The resort itself is set among 3km of winding waterways; the Mina A'Salam is right on the water and features attractive Arabic-style rooms facing the Burj or the lake. The resort is breathtakingly beautiful and any fears that it would be Disneyesque have been allayed. Sitting on the balcony of the hotel's **Bahri Bar** (p91), looking across the lake to the Burj Al Arab is an extraordinary sight. Also opening in late 2004 is the resort's shopping area Souq Madinat Jumeirah, which will have about 100 speciality shops and eateries. There are several more restaurants that should have opened by the time you read this; the fact that **Zheng He's** (p85) is booked up well in advance bodes well for the other eating options.

ONE&ONLY ROYAL MIRAGE

Map pp206-7   *Resort*
☎ 399 9999; www.oneandonlyresorts.com; Al-Sufouh Rd; s/d Dh1950/2160

Even with the new Mina A'Salam resort taking the Arabian theme to new heights, this is still the most gorgeous resort on the beach strip. Now consisting of three parts, the original Palace, the Residence & Spa and the Arabian Court, it's so vast that it has two separate main entrances. The Palace area and rooms lean towards a Moorish style, while the Arabian Court area and rooms are more pan-Arabian, but you'd happily stay in either. The Residence & Spa is more exclusive and the spa and *hammam* (bathhouse) are majestic. All rooms in the resort are sea-facing but you'll spend most of your time wandering around the resort discovering new alcoves and niches, restaurants and bars. Try sunset drinks at the **Rooftop Bar** (pp93-4), followed by dinner at **Eauzone** (p83) and clubbing at **Kasbar** (p95), and you've sampled some of the best dining and drinking options Dubai has to offer without having to leave the resort.

RITZ-CARLTON

Map pp206-7   *Beach Resort*
☎ 399 4000; www.ritz-carlton.com; Al-Sufouh Rd; r from Dh2050

The first Ritz-Carlton property in the Middle East, this Mediterranean-accented resort won't disappoint fans of the Ritz-Carlton style. The gardens and leisure areas are very attractive, the 138 rooms are furnished in a comfortable clubbish style and all rooms face the sea. There's a Balinese-themed spa, the well-regarded restaurant **La Baie** (pp83-4), and in the cooler months, the attractive and relaxing Amaseena Bedouin village is open, and features regional food, *sheesha* (water pipe) and live oud music.

Excursions

Strait of Hormuz

Tumb Kubra

Kumzar

Ras Sheikh Masud

Musandam
Peninsula

Khasab

Bukha

THE
GULF

Tibat

Sham

Abu Musa

Khor Khowair

O M A N

Rams

Gulf of Oman

Ras al-Khaimah

Habab

Al-Jazirah al-Hamra

RAS
AL-KHAIMAH

Digdagga

Umm
al-Qaiwain

Al-Rafaah

11

Hamraniyah

Habab

Dibba

Ras al-Khaiman
International
Airport

Dadna

FUJAIRAH

Aqqa

UMM
AL-QAIWAIN

Al-Uyaynah

Sharam

Hamriya

Bidiya

Az-Zora

AJMAN

Biatah

18

Tayyibah

Rifaisa
Dam

SHARJAH

Ajman

Hamadiyah

Al-Hilew

Nabgha

Khor Fakkan

Sharjah

Manama

AJMAN

O M A N

Qidfa

Sharjah
International
Airport

Al-Dhaid

88

Masafi

Madha

Mirbah

Dubai
International
Airport

Sharjah Natural
History Museum &
Desert Park

Siji

DUBAI

89

FUJAIRAH

SHARJAH

Bithnah

Al-Awir

Mileiha

Al-Hayl
Castle

Fujairah
International
Airport

Fujairah

66

Bahuth
Ruwayyah

Al-Haba

55

Kalba

Jebel Ali Port

Khor Kalba
Conservation
Reserve

Jebel Ali Village

Al-Madam

Fili

Jebel Ali Hotel
& Golf Resort

Hajar Mountains

SHARJAH

Khatmat
Malahah

Ghantoot Racing
& Polo Club

77

Al-Liseli

Margham

Big Red

RAS AL-
KHAIMAH

Wahlah

Jazira Hotel
& Resort

Al-Ghirefah

44

AJMAN

11

DUBAI

Muraqqab

Al Maha
Desert Resort

Mazeirah

DUBAI

Masfout

Al-Wajajah

Al-Samha

Ash-Shuayb

Hatta

Al-Faqa

Hatta Rock
Pools

To Abu Dhabi
(30km)

Sumayni

Ajban

Al-Haiyi

Fa'iyyah

O M A N

To Abu Dhabi
International Airport
(5km)

Al-Juwayf

Sharm

Zaymi

33

Sweihan

66

Mahidah

Al-Ohab

Al-Hijr al-Gharbi

ABU DHABI

Al-Ain
International
Airport

Buraimi

Wadi
al-Jizzi

To Abu Dhabi
(30km)

Al-Saad

Buraimi Oasis

Al-Khatam

Al-Khawrah

Al-Ain

Al-Wasit

Al-Khaznah

Zakhir

Al-Zahir

UNITED ARAB

Al-Zahir

EMIRATES

Jebel Hafit

(1160m)

Hafit

0   40 km
0   20 miles

150

Excursions

Dubai is dazzling – and difficult to leave. But if you're staying in Dubai for more than a few days or your threshold for shopping and swimming is low, there are plenty of excursions that can reveal the many facets of the UAE. You can witness the almost mythical haze at the edge of the Empty Quarter and jagged mountains painted in multiple shades of subtly changing colour, or pass camels and roadside mosques, visit an oasis city replete with palms burdened with dates, and swim at beaches with barely a hotel in sight.

All the trips mentioned here can be arranged with any tour company in Dubai (see p152), but – apart from visiting Sharjah, which can be reached by taxi – we suggest you hire a car (see pp170-2). One of the wonderful things about these excursions is how quickly the feel of your surroundings changes once outside the Dubai city limits. And no matter what type of experience you're craving, given the excellent road network in the UAE, nothing's further than a three-hour drive from Dubai.

DESERT SAFARIS

There's nothing like getting out into the desert, especially at sunset. You can take an afternoon or overnight safari – the silence under the stars is magic. Tours by the companies listed below all offer roughly the same experience: departing in the afternoon they travel across the desert and, after an exciting bit of 4WD 'dune-bashing', usually reach camp with enough time for a camel ride and sand boarding before sunset. After working up an appetite, you enjoy a barbecue dinner – Arabic and Lebanese food. While there is no alcohol provided, people have been known to sneak a bottle or two on the trip to drink under the stars. Dinner is followed by *sheesha* (water pipe) and a belly dancer before returning to Dubai. This costs

Do the Right Thing

Although tourism in Dubai has not reached the heights it has in other cities in the region, it does have an impact on the environment. There are a number of things you can do to be a responsible tourist and this list is particularly pertinent outside Dubai on an excursion.

- Preserve natural resources. Try not to waste water. Switch off the air-con when you go out – except in midsummer, of course!
- Ask before taking photographs of people, especially women. Don't worry if you don't speak Arabic. A smile and gesture will be understood and appreciated.
- Remember that the UAE is a Muslim country and although Dubai is the most international and cosmopolitan city of the Gulf, revealing clothes will still cause offence to most local people.
- Similarly, public displays of affection between members of the opposite sex are inappropriate.
- Learning something about Dubai's history and culture helps prevent misunderstandings and frustrations.

Be aware of environmental issues. Desert safaris in a 4WD make for a popular day excursion for visitors, but they are not environmentally sound activities. Expats are just as guilty of 'dune-bashing' the environment as tourists are, as the sport is becoming an increasingly popular weekend pastime. If you are taking part in any desert activities bear in mind the following guidelines.

- To minimise your impact on the land, stick to the tracks and avoid damaging the all-too-rare vegetation that is such an important part of the fragile desert ecosystem.
- Driving in wadis should be avoided where possible to ensure that they are not polluted with oil and grease. They are sometimes important sources of irrigation and drinking water.
- When diving or snorkelling, avoid touching or removing any marine life, especially coral.
- If you plan to camp out, remember to take your own wood – don't pull limbs from trees or uproot shrubs. Plants in the desert may look dead but usually they are not.

Coffeepot Roundabout, Al-Ain (p163)

around Dh270 per person and if you haven't experienced the desert before, it's a wonderful afternoon and evening. Even if you're a time-poor traveller, the trip is worthwhile because you can tick off several must-do activities in one hit. If you really want that Bedouin experience, you can stay overnight in the camp or under the stars for an extra fee.

The following tour companies can arrange desert safaris.

Arabian Adventures (Map pp206-7; ☎ 343 9966; www.arabian-adventures.com; Emirates Holidays Bldg, Interchange No 2, Sheikh Zayed Rd, Dubai)

Net Tours & Travels (Map pp210-11; ☎ 266 8661; www.nettoursdubai.com; Al-Bakhit Centre, Abu Baker al-Siddiq Rd, Hor al-Anz)

Orient Tours (Map pp210-11; ☎ 282 8238; www.orienttours.co.ae; Al-Garhoud Rd, Deira)

MOUNTAIN RETREAT

Set deep in the rugged Hajar Mountains is the scenic town of **Hatta** (pp156-8). Half the fun of Hatta is getting there – driving on a freeway surrounded by great, red-tinged dunes is definitely part of the adventure.

CULTURAL JOURNEY

While Dubai's architecture and resort ideas keep getting wilder, **Sharjah** (pp153-6) opts for a different kind of creative outlet. Dubai's neighbour has positioned itself as the cultural capital of the UAE and was named by Unesco as the cultural capital of the Arab world. Galleries and artists abound and Sharjah even hosts the Sharjah International Biennale.

DESERT OASIS

A trip to **Al-Ain** (pp162-6) will provide you with that 'oasis in the desert' feel as both Al-Ain and neighbouring Buraimi in Oman lie within the Buraimi Oasis. While the road to Al-Ain is excellent, it passes through enough sand dunes to give you a feeling of just how welcome the oasis must have been after a couple of weeks' travel by camel. The cooler, drier temperature and fantastic dates don't hurt either.

BEACHES & FISHING VILLAGES

The scenic drive over to the **East Coast** (pp158-62) takes you to some fine beaches and rocky headlands, that are home to a string of dive sites, fishing villages, rugged wadis, sturdy forts and the busy ports of **Khor Fakkan** (p160) and **Fujairah** (p158).

SHARJAH

With its numerous excellent museums and galleries **Sharjah's** (Map p150) title of cultural capital of the Arab world is well-deserved, but it's an ironic choice considering that there is a deepening conservatism in the emirate (see the boxed text on p155). In addition to the cultural highlights, Sharjah offers excellent souq shopping and many souvenirs are cheaper here than in Dubai. Most visitors to Dubai tend to miss out on Sharjah, but it's easy to get to and well worth a visit. The main sites can be covered in just half a day and an excursion to the nearby **Sharjah Natural History Museum & Desert Park** (see p156) is also recommended.

The centre of town is the area between the Corniche and Al-Zahra Rd, from the Central Market to Sheikh Sultan bin Saqr al-Qasimi Rd. It's not a huge area and it's pretty easy to get around on foot if the heat's not too debilitating.

Sharjah can be hellish to navigate when driving. Al-Wahda Rd, the main link with Dubai, is gridlocked during peak hours, especially at the King Faisal Sq overpass. The proliferation of roundabouts, lengthy street names and the absence of directions to Ajman or Dubai make it easy to get lost. Street signs tend to be written in very small print and have similar-sounding names – Sheikh Mohammed bin Sultan al-Qasimi Rd versus Sheikh Khalid bin Mohammed al-Qasimi Rd, for example. The website www.sharjah-welcome.com is a comprehensive resource aimed at tourists and has a decent map that's worth printing.

One of the first places to visit in Sharjah is the **Heritage Area** and the first stop should be the **Al-Hisn Fort**. This double-storey, three-towered fort sits somewhat forlornly in the middle of Al-Borj Ave and was the residence of the ruling family of Sharjah. Originally built in 1820, it has been fully restored and houses a fascinating collection of artefacts, documents and photographs, many from the 1930s, showing members of the ruling Al-Qasimi family and the British Trucial Oman Scouts who were stationed here at the time. As you enter the fort there is a room on your left showing footage of the first Imperial Airways flights from London, which landed here in 1932 on their way to India. The difference between Sharjah then and now is astonishing. Other rooms have displays of weapons (including a rifle called Abu Futilah, 'Father of Rifles', which was the first gun brought to the fort), jewellery, currency and items used in the pearl trade.

The buildings in the Heritage Area block, just inland from the Corniche, between Al-Borj Ave and Al-Mina St, have all been faithfully reconstructed and incorporate traditional designs and materials such as sea rock and gypsum. Coming from Al-Borj Ave the first place you arrive at is **Literature Sq**. At the **House of Poetry**, facing the square, public poetry readings are sometimes held. The **Sharjah Heritage Museum** is housed in an historic building that is the former home of the Al-Nabooodah family. The museum has traditional living rooms and displays of clothing and jewellery; and the architecture is typical of dwellings in the region. There is also a documentary on the history of Sharjah that is worth watching.

Next door to this is the **Sharjah Islamic Museum**, which is a must. It includes a large collection of coins from all over the Islamic world and a number of handwritten Qurans

Transport

Distance from Dubai 10km.

Direction Northeast.

Travel Time 10 to 40 minutes, traffic dependent.

Car Firstly avoid peak hours (8am to 10am, 1pm to 2pm and 4pm to 7pm), which are horrendous. Take Al-Ittihad Rd, which is signposted E11 (the 'E' represents an interemirate highway and this one takes you up the coast, as well as back through to Abu Dhabi).

Taxi & Minibus Minibuses (Dh5) go from the Deira minibus and taxi station (Map pp208-9) on Omar ibn al-Khattab Rd. A taxi will cost you about Dh25. You won't be able to get a minibus back to Dubai – take a taxi from the stand at the north end of Rolla Sq; this should cost around Dh30.

and writing implements. There are ceramics from Turkey, Syria and Afghanistan, as well as a display on the covering of the Kaaba stone at Mecca, the most sacred shrine for Muslims, which includes a copy of the embroidered cloth. Next to the cloth is the original holy key bag, which once held the key to the Kaaba. There's also a remarkable map of the region made 1200 years ago, which is quite accurate once you realise that south is at the top.

Next stop should be the **Souq al-Arsah**, on the south side of Al-Borj Ave, which was restored by the government after large sections fell to pieces during the 1970s and '80s. *Arsah* means a large open space or courtyard and this place was originally a stop for travellers. The *areesh* (palm frond) roof and wooden pillars give it a traditional feel, and it's a lovely place to wander around and look for Arabic and Bedouin souvenirs. Despite the efforts to recreate a traditional atmosphere you can buy all kinds of non-Arabic souvenirs here too. There is also a traditional **coffeehouse** and **restaurant**, as well as a beautifully restored house that is now the charming little **Dar al-Dhyafa** hotel.

There are more restored old buildings north of the Sharjah Heritage Museum, towards the Corniche; admission is free and they keep the same hours as the museum. The **Majlis of Ibrahim Mohammed al-Midfa** is known for having the only round wind tower in the Gulf. Ibrahim al-Midfa started the first newspaper in the UAE in 1927 and was an advisor to the ruling family. The main **Al-Midfa House**, across from the *majlis* (meeting room), has an elephant engraved on its door that's worth a peek.

Tucked away on the other (north) side of Al-Borj Ave is the Arts Area, where the excellent **Sharjah Art Museum** houses a permanent collection of Orientalistic painting and contemporary art. The museum also hosts the cutting-edge Sharjah International Biennale and is by far the finest art gallery in the UAE. Of the 72 different small galleries, eight hold a permanent collection of 19th-century European paintings and lithographs from Sheikh Sultan bin Mohammed al-Qasimi's own collection. There's a library and smart coffee shop at the museum.

A couple of doors down from the museum is the **Very Special Arts Centre**, which is both a workshop and a gallery for disabled artists, and the **Emirates Fine Arts Society**, which also displays the works of local artists.

The **Sharjah Archaeological Museum**, near Cultural Sq, covers the earliest archaeological finds in the emirate (dating from 5000 BC) up to the beginning of the Islamic era. Video and audio are used effectively to avoid the crushingly dull experience often associated with

Central Market (p155)

Decency Laws

In 2001 Sharjah's government introduced new laws on decency and public conduct. These are the strictest laws governing dress in the UAE and, along with Sharjah's ban on alcohol, they represent a deepening conservatism in the emirate. For men the new laws mean no bare chests or short shorts in public or in commercial or public offices (knee-length shorts are OK, if not exactly acclaimed). For women the laws forbid clothing that exposes the stomach, upper arms, shoulders and back, clothing above the knee, and 'tight and transparent clothing that describes the body'. Obviously, swimwear can't be worn in the streets, and only conservative swimwear can be worn on Sharjah's public beaches.

The new laws also forbid 'a man and woman who are not connected by a legally acceptable relationship to be alone in a vehicle, in public places or in suspicious times or circumstances'. No-one quite knows how widely this law applies. It doesn't seem to include looking around, say, the Arts Area with someone who isn't your sibling, parent or spouse, but you certainly could not share a hotel room with an unrelated member of the opposite sex. The interpretation of the laws is up to Sharjah's police and courts and the police, government employees, security officers and building guards have been charged with their enforcement. These regulations apply to all of Sharjah territories, including Khor Fakkan, Dibba and Kalba on the East Coast.

archaeological museums. The first hall has an interesting display on the science of archaeology, while the other five galleries cover different eras: fishermen, hunters and herders (5000–3000 BC); farmers, traders and craftspeople (3000–1000 BC); Wadi Suq (2000–1300 BC); oasis dwellers (1300–300 BC); and greater Arabia (300 BC–AD 600). Displays include reconstructions of tombs and houses, as well as weapons, pottery, tools, coins and jewellery. The café has sandboxes where kids can dig for 'artefacts'.

The **Central Market** (Blue Souq) is located on the Corniche near the King Faisal Mosque. It consists of two grand halls connected by an overhead bridge. It has the lowest prices and best selection of carpets in the country, as well as dozens of shops selling souvenirs and antiques from Oman, India, Thailand and Iran. The gold-domed **Al-Majarrah Souq**, on the Corniche, houses about 50 shops that sell textiles, perfumes and clothes. The **Gold Centre**, on the corner of Sheikh Zayed and Al-Wahda Rds, is home to about 40 shops selling jewellery, diamonds, gold coins and everything else that glitters. The **Fruit & Vegetable Souq**, **Animal Souq**, **Plant Souq** and **Fish Souq** are worth a visit if you have time to spare.

Sights & Information

To telephone from outside Sharjah, you need to use the area code (☎ 06).

Al-Hisn Fort (☎ 06 537 5500; Al-Borj Ave; 🕙 9am-1pm & 5-8pm Tue-Sun, 5-8pm Fri, women only Wed)

Al-Majarrah Souq (Sharjah Creek, close to Holiday Inn Resort; 🕙 9am-1pm & 4.30-10pm)

Central Market (Blue Souq; Al-Majaz, end of Corniche, close to Sharjah Creek; 🕙 9am-1pm & 4-11pm Sat-Thu, 4-11pm Fri)

Gold Centre (Al-Yarmook, cnr of Al-Qassimia & Al-Wahda Rds; 🕙 10am-1pm & 4.30-10pm)

Sharjah Archaeological Museum (☎ 06 566 5466; Al-Hizam al-Akhdar Rd, near Cultural Sq; 🕙 9am-1pm & 5-8pm Mon-Sat, 5-8pm Fri, women only Wed afternoon)

Sharjah Art Museum (☎ 06 568 8222; Al-Shuwaiheyn, behind Souq al-Arsah, close to Al-Borj Ave; 🕙 9am-1pm & 5-8pm Sat-Thu, 5-8pm Fri, women only Wed afternoon)

Sharjah Heritage Museum (☎ 06 551 2999; between the waterfront & Al-Borj Ave; 🕙 9am-1pm & 5-8pm Tue-Sun, 5-8pm Fri, women only Wed)

Sharjah Islamic Museum (☎ 06 568 3334; Al-Gharb; 🕙 9am-1pm & 5-8pm Tue-Sun, 4.30-8.30pm Fri)

Souq al-Arsah (Al-Muraija, close to Heritage Area; 🕙 9am-1pm & 4.30-8.30pm, some shops open later)

Eating

Al-Fawar (☎ 06 559 4662; King Faisal Rd; mezze Dh8-12, mains Dh20-40) A popular, long-standing Lebanese restaurant, with a cheaper cafeteria-style section next door that also offers takeaway.

Sanobar Restaurant (☎ 06 528 3501; Al-Khan Rd; mezze Dh10, mains Dh15-40) An excellent seafood restaurant close to Sheikh Sultan al-Awal Rd. The atmosphere is reminiscent of a Greek taverna, with prices far lower than what you find in Dubai. It also offers Lebanese dishes.

Souq al-Arsah Coffeehouse (Al-Muraija, near Heritage Area) A great Sharjah experience. For Dh10 you get a large biryani and fresh dates for dessert. There are backgammon sets and sweet tea is served out of a huge urn.

Thriveni Restaurant (Rolla Sq; meals around Dh5) This cheap Indian eatery has agreeable surroundings and has a pleasant view out onto the square.

Detour: Sharjah Natural History Museum & Desert Park

The **Sharjah Natural History Museum & Desert Park** (Map p150; ☎ 06 531 1411; Sharjah–Al-Dhaid Rd; adult/child Dh5/2; ☉ 9am-5.30pm Sat-Wed, 11am-5.30pm Thu, 2-5.30pm Fri) is a great family attraction that's both entertaining and educational. The first segment of the park, the **Natural History Museum**, is an interesting and well-planned museum. It covers the evolution of the planet and also features dioramas of Sharjah's various ecosystems and environments. The museum may appeal to kids more than adults, but the gardens are worth anyone's time and include a botanic garden with more than 120 types of wild flower.

The second part of the park is the **Children's Farm** (☎ 06 531 1127), which has farm animals – including goats, camels and ducks – that kids can feed, pony rides and even eggs and cheese on sale. The third part is the nearby **Arabia's Wildlife Centre** (☎ 06 531 1999). This modern, well laid-out centre is a breeding centre and zoo for many of the species found on the Arabian Peninsula. Animals include a rather active family of puff adders (safely behind glass), wispy sand snakes, desert monitors and Jayakar's sand boas, which spend their life wriggling beneath the surface of the sand. There are also rooms for nasties such as scorpions and the nightmarish camel spider. A highlight is the massive indoor aviary, home to flamingos, Houbara bustards and Indian rollers. The aviary also houses rock hyraxes, rabbit-sized critters distantly related to elephants. The cave area has a host of Egyptian fruit bats. There's also a section with several species of indigenous rodent – check out the gorgeous, bandy-legged lesser jerboas. Outdoor enclosures are home to sacred baboons, striped hyenas, Arabian wolves and the splendid Arabian leopard.

Don't miss the wildlife centre's **restaurant**, which looks out over a large open-range area with flamingos, Nubian ibexes, Arabian oryxes, ostriches and sand gazelles. They're fed food and water near the windows so they can watch the humans feeding behind glass inside. It certainly makes for a better zoological experience – and a less depressing one – than the **Dubai Zoo** (p57).

The complex is 26km out of Sharjah (past Intersection No 8), towards Fujairah. There's no public transport. A taxi out here would cost about Dh100 – you'd be better off hiring a car for the day.

Sleeping

Dar al-Dhyafa (☎ 06 528 3501; Souq al-Arsah; d/ste Dh550/735) If you're enchanted by the ambience of the souq area, this boutique style hotel offers a wonderful way to enjoy it overnight. The bridal suite is the pick of the rooms on offer, but all are decorated in a traditional style and Emirati food is served in the *majlis*.

HATTA

An enclave of Dubai Emirate nestled in the Hajar Mountains, **Hatta** (Map p150) is a popular weekend getaway – so if you want to explore it peacefully avoid going on Friday. Hatta also makes a good overnight stop on a two- or three-day itinerary. It is 105km from Dubai by road, about 20km of which runs through Omani territory. There is no customs check as you cross the border, but remember that if you are driving a rental car your insurance does not cover accidents in Oman (see p156). This mountain town was once an important source of tobacco, as well as a vital staging post on the trade route between Dubai and Oman. Today, Hatta's main drawcards are its relatively cool, humidity-free climate and the dramatic mountain scenery. The magnificent rock pools near Hatta are one of the UAE's highlights. Hatta makes a good base for off-road trips through the mountains.

Hatta's main attraction is the **Heritage Village**, which is a re-created traditional mountain village. In the complex is a restored fort and traditional buildings dedicated to weaponry, local songs and dances, palm-tree products and social life, plus other exhibits on facets of the old village society and economics. Most buildings have videos and mannequins to explain their theme. Climb up some stairs to the top of the watchtower for some great views over the valley. There is a functioning *falaj* (traditional irrigation

Insurance Warning

Unless you make specific arrangements, your hire-car insurance will not cover you when in Oman. This means that if you go to Hatta, which involves passing through about 20km of Omani territory, or visit Buraimi on an excursion to Al-Ain, you will not be covered for any accident while in Omani territory. Coverage for Oman increases the insurance rate as well as increasing the hire rate significantly.

channel) watering small but lush agricultural plots just below the Heritage Village. The traditional handicrafts building is across the road from the main complex and features displays on crafts such as weaving, cosmetics, perfumes and traditional dress. The turn-off for the village is signposted to the left off the main street, about 3km from the Fort Roundabout and 500m from the bus stop.

With your own 4WD you can bump up the wadi to a **dam** above Hatta village. The turn-off is just after the mosque near the Heritage Village. This road soon deteriorates into a steep graded track. Don't try to get a 2WD car up this road; the rental company won't thank you for it. The dam lies 2km up the rugged wadi.

Most people come to Hatta to visit the **Hatta rock pools** (Map p150), which are about 20km south of Hatta town. They are actually across the border in Oman, but access is from Hatta. This intricately carved miniature canyon has water year-round, and it's an amazing experience to swim through these narrow rock corridors and play at the waterfalls. Although it is beautiful, the area gets very busy at weekends and unfortunately you will find some litter and graffiti scattered around.

Transport

Distance from Dubai 105km.

Direction Southeast.

Travel Time 90 minutes.

Car Head south out of Dubai along Sheikh Zayed Rd (E11). Take the exit near Nad al-Sheba – there are signs for Hatta and Oman – and head inland. The road becomes Emirates highway E44 – follow it all the way to Hatta.

Public Transport From Dubai buses leave Deira bus station (Map pp208-9) for Hatta every hour from 6.10am to 9pm (Dh10, one hour). In Hatta, buses depart for Dubai from the red bus shelter near the Hatta Mountains Restaurant every hour from 6am to 9pm (buy tickets from the driver). Shared/engaged taxis leave from Bur Dubai bus station (Map pp212-13) in Bur Dubai and cost Dh25/100.

You don't *need* a 4WD to get to the rock pools from Hatta, but it's strongly advised. If you want to continue past the pools and on to Al-Ain we advise you to attempt it only with a 4WD and an experienced driver behind the wheel.

To get to the impressive rock pools, turn right at the Fort Roundabout on the edge of town and head into the centre. After driving down this road for 2.7km take the turn-off to the left for the Heritage Village. Then turn left when you get to the T-junction at the mosque, 50m past the entrance to the Heritage Village. Follow this road for 900m as it bends around to the left. At this point take the turn-off onto the tarmac road to the right. This will take you past a row of identical houses, along a stretch riddled with lots of speed bumps. Continue along this road for 6.5km until the tarmac road ends. At this point there is a turn-off to the right onto a graded track (there is a stop sign here as well). Follow the graded track for 6km, passing blue-and-white road signs to the Omani villages of A'Tuwayah, Al-Karbi al-Gharbiyah, Al-Qarbi a'Sharqiyah and Al-Bon. Along this road is some wonderful scenery, particularly the striking layers of folded sedimentary rock on the

Rock pools (p158), Hatta

hillsides. Watch out for oncoming traffic, as it can be a bit dangerous. After the sign to Al-Bon the road continues over a steep hill – the track to the pools' parking area is a sharp left turn at the bottom of the road. The parking area is about 600m away, at the edge of a *falaj*, and the pools are a short walk from here.

If you don't have your own transport, the Hatta Fort Hotel (see p158) offers a 4WD safari to the rock pools. A three-hour trip for six people costs Dh600, including soft drinks and towels. A seven-hour trip for six people costs Dh1400 and includes a picnic lunch.

Sights & Information

Heritage Village (☉ 8am-7.30pm Sat-Thu, 3-9pm Fri)

Sleeping & Eating

Hatta Fort Hotel (☎ 04 852 3211; www.jebelali-international.com; r Sat-Wed/Thu & Fri Dh524/780) The only place to stay in Hatta. The hotel is renowned for its setting, with lovely gardens and mountains (bird-watchers flock here to look for Indian rollers and other species). There are extensive sports facilities, including a modest nine-hole golf course. The coffee shop (mains about Dh30) is a popular lunch stop, but the food is ordinary. The hotel's Jeema Restaurant (meals Dh200 to Dh300) serves French cuisine.

Diversions: Around Hatta

Midway between Dubai and Hatta the highway cuts right through a towering peach-coloured dune system and a 100m-high dune known as Big Red. This is a hugely popular spot for local 4WD fanatics to let down their tyres and tackle the slopes. On weekends, dozens of vehicles crawl up and down the soft sands. On the Hatta side, **Al-Badayer Motors** (☎ 050 655 5447) hires out quad bikes for Dh40 for 30 minutes (try bargaining), so you can tear up the dunes on one of these offensively noisy vehicles (before participating, read the boxed text Do the Right Thing on p151). Presumably any wildlife here has long since fled. On the Dubai side, **Al-Ramool Motors** (☎ 050 453 4401/050 698 5678) hires out quad bikes for the same price. Both are open from 8am until sunset daily. Assuming you don't get run over by quad bikes and 4WDs, it takes about 20 minutes to walk from the highway to the top of the dunes.

There is a huge rug market at the village of **Mazeirah** (Map p150), about 12km west of Hatta on the main highway. This is the only large country market apart from the one at **Masafi** (p159). If you're looking for rugs, it's worth a stop as you can pick up great bargains.

EAST COAST

The East Coast is one of the most beautiful parts of the UAE. The Hajar Mountains provide a stunning backdrop to the waters of the Gulf of Oman. It's very green here. There are wadis to explore in the mountains and waterholes that are full year-round. The area north of Khor Fakkan is well known for diving and snorkelling, but south of Khor Fakkan the sea is less inviting. The port at Fujairah is the second-busiest bunkering (refuelling) port in the world and at any time there are dozens if not hundreds of ships queued up offshore – the line runs the entire length of the coast! It seems that some ships illegally empty out their holds before they head into the Gulf to pick up another load of oil. The degree of pollution varies according to the currents, but most days you're likely to pick up a sticky sheen if you touch the water. The effects on local fisheries and wildlife can be imagined.

The prosperous little city of **Fujairah** (Map p150) is the capital of the emirate of the same name. There isn't a great deal to see in Fujairah itself, but it makes a good base for exploring the rest of the East Coast.

The main business strip is Hamad bin Abdullah Rd, between the Fujairah Trade Centre and the coast. Along this road, just west of the Fujairah Trade Centre, is the Etisalat office, the 48-storey Fujairah Tower, banks and, at the intersection with the coast road, the Central Market. The main post office is on Al-Sharqi Rd, just off Hamad bin Abdullah Rd.

The **old town** is best described as spooky. Of interest is the cemetery and a 300-year-old fort (under restoration) which overlooks the ruins of old Fujairah. There is a shanty settlement here whose residents don't especially like tourists walking around.

The **Fujairah Museum** has exhibits on maritime activities, archaeological finds from around the emirate (such as items from tombs near Qidfa dating from 1500 BC), displays of heritage jewellery and a collection of photographs showing local life in the preoil era.

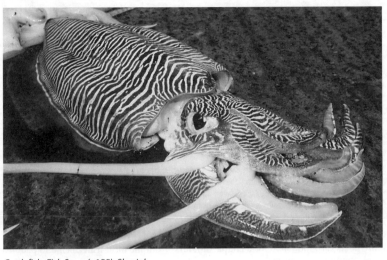

Cuttlefish, Fish Souq (p155), Sharjah

Ain al-Madhab Garden, on the edge of town, is nothing special, but the swimming pools here are clean, cool and segregated into men's and women's sections. There is a small **Heritage Village** (admission free; 9am-6pm) across from the garden, fenced with palm fronds. Here you'll find a reconstructed coastal desert village, complete with a real cow.

The small town of **Masafi** (Map p150), an enclave of Ajman Emirate, 35km from Fujairah, is at the junction where the road from Dubai splits into two and heads north to Dibba and south to Fujairah. Known as the location of the Masafi water-bottling factory, the town is also famous for its **Friday market**. Despite its name, the market is actually open every day of the week and has an enormous range of carpets, plants and souvenirs for sale. Some of the carpets send the kitsch-meter off the scale, such as those featuring Sheikh Zayed and others featuring Lolitaesque girls. You are sure to get a bargain here, but you have to work at it – aim to pay 40% to 50% of the asking price.

The traditional fishing village of **Kalba** (Map p150) is just south of Fujairah and remains true to what life would have been like on the Gulf coast during the early part of the 20th century. *Shashas* (small fishing boats made from palm fronds) and crayfish baskets line the beach; fishermen can be seen setting out each morning and pulling in their nets each evening.

Kalba is part of the Sharjah Emirate. The *khor* (inlet), just south of town, is part of the **Khor Kalba Conservation Reserve** (Map p150) and the site of the oldest mangrove forest in Arabia. Bird life is particularly abundant in the reserve, which is the only place in the world that the Khor Kalba white-collared kingfisher is found; there are reported to be 44 pairs of the birds here. It's possible

Transport

Distance from Dubai 130km.

Direction East.

Travel Time 90 minutes.

Car Take Emirates highway E11 towards Sharjah and then E88 in the direction of Al-Dhaid. At Masafi you can take the road heading north to Dibba or south to Fujairah.

Public Transport Minibuses leave from the Deira minibus and taxi station (Map pp208-9) and cost Dh25. Long-distance taxis cost Dh25 in a shared taxi or Dh150 in an engaged taxi. In Fujairah the taxi station is on the road to Sharjah and Dubai. Minibuses from Dubai continue as far as Khor Fakkan. A shared/engaged taxi costs Dh5/20 from Fujairah to Khor Fakkan and Dh20/100 to Dibba, although you should be able to negotiate a discount.

Bullfighting, Fujairah Style

Every Friday, at around 4.30pm, Fujairah's special brand of bullfighting gets under way at a site next to the road to Kalba, near the Al-Rughailat Bridge. There are no prancing matadors; this contest is bull against bull, but the horns of the opponents are blunted and bloodshed is very rare. The bulls lower their heads almost to the ground and mostly head-butt and shove each other around. Sooner or later one bull forces another out of the ring, or else one tires of the struggle and walks away. Usually there are four or five contests, after which the competitors are led into pick-up trucks and driven home.

One tradition has it that the Portuguese introduced bullfighting to Fujairah, though other sources say that the bullfights predate the arrival of Islam. A more colourful legend holds that long ago two young men came into conflict over their desire to marry the same woman, so their families decided to let battling bulls settle the matter.

The beasts are descended from Brahman bulls brought from India to turn waterwheels (camels, common in the other emirates, are rare on the East Coast). Today pumps do the job but Fujairah's landowners still keep bulls to fight against each other. Prize fighters are said to be pampered with a diet of dates, honey and butter, costing up to Dh2000 a month. There's no gambling on the result; victory simply confers honour on the bull's owner. A champion bull can be worth as much as Dh50,000. Fujairah's bullfights won't please animal-rights activists but it's hugely popular with locals, and visitors are very welcome to watch the spectacle.

---

to hire boats (around Dh50 for a couple of hours) from the local fishermen and paddle up the inlets into the mangroves.

You'll need a 4WD to get to the ruins of **Al-Hayl Castle** (Map p150), set among mountain peaks in Wadi Hayl, 13km from Fujairah. This was once the site of the summer palace of the ruling Al-Sharqi family of Fujairah. The ruins of the palace, complete with freestanding pillars and watchtowers, look stunning against the mountains and the cultivated valley floor is a pleasant place to wander.

Coming from Fujairah towards Dubai, the signposted turn-off for Al-Hayl Castle is on the left, about 2km past the main roundabout, on the outskirts of town. Follow the tarmac road for 4km, then turn left towards the quarries. The turn-off is 700m past the first roundabout. Take a right after 1km and drive up the wadi. The paved road runs out after 3km; take the main graded track straight ahead. The castle lies a bumpy 3km further on. There's a much rougher route back to Fujairah: returning along the main track, take the left-hand track down into the wadi, about 800m from the fort. This route bounces along the wadi floor down to Hayl village. Once through the village there's tarmac all the way back to Fujairah. Allow half a day for a trip to Al-Hayl Castle from Fujairah.

One of Sharjah Emirate's enclaves, **Khor Fakkan** (Map p150) is the largest town on the East Coast after Fujairah and sits on the prettiest bay in the UAE. While the port has proved to be a roaring success, the development of tourism has been somewhat held back by Sharjah's ban on alcohol.

The sweeping Corniche is bounded by the port and fish market at the southern end and the Oceanic Hotel to the north; there is nice beach between. The beach is fronted by a leafy strip of parkland, ideal for strolling. **Sharq Island**, at the entrance to the bay of Khor Fakkan, is a popular diving spot –

It's PADI Time!

To check out the wonderful sea life in this region it's best to go diving with Professional Association of Diving Instructors (PADI) approved dive centres. As well as a full open-water diving course (costing around Dh1700), they offer 'discover diving' courses that include instruction, pool diving and often a shallow open-water dive for around Dh250. Below is a list of PADI-certified dive centres on the East Coast.

Al-Boom Diving (☎ 09 204 4925; www.alboom diving.com; Le Meridian Al Aqah Beach Resort, Al-Aqah Beach)

Divers Down Khor Fakkan Dive Centre (☎ 09 237 0299; Oceanic Hotel, Khor Fakkan)

Sandy Beach Diving Centre (☎ 09 244 5555; www.sandybm.com; Sandy Beach Motel, Al-Aqah Beach)

Scuba International Diving College (☎ 09 220 0060; www.scubainternational.net; Fujairah International Marine Club) contact any of the diving operators listed (see p160) to arrange a diving excursion. And don't worry, *sharq* means 'east' in Arabic.

If you have your own transport it's worth a drive to **Rifaisa Dam** (Map p150), which is in the mountains above the town. This mountain lake is supposed to have a village submerged beneath it, which you can see when the water is clear. It's a very peaceful spot. To get to the dam, turn inland from the main street at the Emarat petrol station, then go left at the T-intersection (there should be a red-and-white radio tower on your left). Turn right onto the graded track after the mosque but before the bridge. The track divides after 300m or so; stick to the right. Follow this road up the valley for 4.7km to the dam. You'll notice a couple of ruined watchtowers atop hills along the way.

The charming fishing village of **Bidiya** (Map p150), 8km north of Khor Fakkan, is one of the oldest towns in the Gulf. Archaeological digs have shown that the site of the town has been settled more or less continuously since the 3rd millennium BC. Today it is best known for its **mosque**, a small structure of stone, mud brick and gypsum, which is still in use and has recently been restored. It is said to have been built around AD 640, although other sources date it to AD 1449, and is the oldest mosque in the UAE. It is built into a low hillside along the main road just north of the village, and on the hillside above and behind it are several restored **watchtowers**.

Just offshore from the Sandy Beach Motel, about 6km north of Bidiya, is **Snoopy Island**, a popular diving and snorkelling spot. There are stonefish around the island, so wear shoes while paddling. Don't be alarmed by the family of reef sharks here; they're friendly. Access to the hotel's beach and Snoopy Island costs Dh25 per day.

Sights & Information

Ain al-Madhab Garden (admission with/without swimming Dh5/2; ☺ gardens 10am-10pm, swimming pools 10am-7pm Sun-Fri)

Fujairah Museum (admission Dh1; ☺ 8.30am-1.30pm, 4.30-6.30pm Sun-Thu, 2-6.30pm Fri)

Eating

Al-Meshwar (☎ 09 222 9255; King Faisal Rd; mezze Dh7-12, mains Dh12-25) An upmarket, medium-priced Lebanese restaurant in the block behind the Diner's Inn.

Diner's Inn (☎ 09 222 6351; Al-Faseel Rd; meals from Dh8) Across from the Hilton Fujairah, Diner's Inn serves

Spices

Major Diversion: Musandam Peninsula

The **Musandam Peninsula** (Map p150) is spectacular – rugged, wild and beautiful and a boat trip is the best way to see it properly. The peninsula is part of Oman and the UAE separates it from Oman proper. While you can drive there, insurance is a problem (see the boxed text on p156 for details), so the best way to see it is to organise a trip through a travel agent.

Khasab is the capital of the province and is a busy harbour, with all sorts of activities being undertaken in several different languages. The old souq is interesting and there is a fort or two to explore. But the real attraction here is to get on a dhow and explore the *khors* of the **Strait of Hormuz**. The landscape is extraordinary and the fjordlike appearance has seen the area nicknamed the 'Norway of Arabia'. While on a boat trip you may be accompanied by a dolphin or 10 and the fishing and diving in the area are top-notch.

Contact the Dubai office of **Khasab Travel & Tours** (☎ 04 266 9950; www.khasabtours.com) for more information. It will handle visa arrangements as well as your boat trip and sightseeing.

reasonably large helpings of good cheap Indian and Chinese food.

Fusion (☎ 09 244 9000; Le Meridien Al Aqah Beach Resort, Al-Aqah Beach; mains from Dh45) Open for dinner only, it's the best restaurant in the whole region, mainly offering decent Thai specialties. Reservations essential.

Lebanon Cafeteria (☎ 09 238 5631; Corniche, Khor Fakkan; mains Dh20) A good option for a meal, offering a range of grills and Lebanese mezze as well as the usual Indian fare of biryanis and tikka dishes.

Taj Khorfakkan Restaurant (☎ 09 222 5995; inland from the Central Market, across from the Saheel Market shop, Khor Fakkan; mains Dh10-15) A nicely decorated restaurant with reasonably priced food, mostly Indian with some Chinese dishes.

Taj Mahal (☎ 09 222 5225; Hamad bin Abdullah Rd, Fujairah, back of bldg opposite Etisalat; mains from Dh10) Good quality Indian and Chinese food. It is clean, cool and comfortable and the service is good.

Sleeping

Hilton Fujairah (☎ 09 222 2411; www.hilton.com; Al-Faseel Rd, Fujairah; s/d Dh750/805) This low-rise complex has pleasant gardens, a decent gym, fine pool area and

beachfront bar. Check the website for excellent discounts off the rack rate.

Le Meridien Al Aqah Beach Resort (☎ 09 244 9000; www.lemeridien-alaqah.com; Al-Aqah Beach; s/d from Dh1035) Easily the best hotel on the East Coast, it has large and luxurious sea-facing rooms that overlook the beautiful beach and amazing leisure area of the hotel, which includes the largest pool in the UAE. The standard rooms are excellent, but the superior rooms are worth the extra money. There are plenty of water-sports opportunities as well as a full gym and tennis courts. The Fusion restaurant serves up good Thai seafood. Finishing the night with a *sheesha* (water pipe) at the outdoor café/bar by the water is a must. Book ahead and get excellent Internet deals from the website.

Oceanic Hotel (☎ 09 238 5111; www.oceanichotel .com; Khor Fakkan; s/d Dh460/575) This 1970s hotel at the northern end of the Corniche is looking a bit worn around the edges. The beach in front is clean and secluded.

Sandy Beach Motel (☎ 09 244 5555; www.sandybm .com; outside Bidiya, near the village of Aqah; d from Dh380) Thanks to the lovely beach, lush gardens and relaxed atmosphere, guests tend to forgive the high prices and very average food and rooms.

AL-AIN & BURAIMI

The border between the UAE and Oman wriggles through a collection of interconnected oases; **Al-Ain** (Map p150) and **Buraimi** (Map p150) lie within the Buraimi Oasis. In the days before the oil boom, the oasis was a five-day overland journey by camel from Abu Dhabi. Today the trip takes 90 minutes on a tree-lined freeway. In barely 30 years Al-Ain (in Abu Dhabi Emirate on the UAE side of the border) has been transformed from a series of rustic villages into a suburbanised garden city. It's best to make an overnight trip, but if you are really pressed for time you could get there, zip around the sites and get back to Dubai in a day, as long as you get an early start. Once in the oasis, you can cross freely between the UAE and Oman – the official frontier post to enter Oman is 50km east of Buraimi at Wadi al-Jizzi. UAE currency is accepted in Buraimi at a standard rate (at the time of writing) of OR1 to Dh9.55.

Entrance, Hili Gardens & Archaeological Park (p165)

One of Al-Ain's main attractions during summer is its dry air, which is a welcome change from the humidity of the coast. The temperate climate has ensured that many sheikhs from around the Emirates have their summer palaces here. The cool and quiet date-palm oases located all over town are pleasant to wander through at any time of the year.

Distances in both Al-Ain and Buraimi are large, but taxis are abundant and cheap. It's fairly easy to find most of the things worth seeing in Al-Ain by following the big, purple tourist signs. Almost everyone travels by taxi in Al-Ain as they are so cheap: most trips around the centre will only cost you Dh3. It's better to use the gold-and-white Al-Ain taxis rather than the orange-and-white Buraimi ones, which don't have meters.

The **Eastern Fort & Al-Ain Museum** are in the same compound, southeast of the overpass near the Coffeepot Roundabout in the heart of town. This is one of the best museums in the country and is a highlight of a visit to Al-Ain. The fort was the birthplace of the UAE's president, Sheikh Zayed. As you enter the museum, take a look at the *majlis* and be sure to see the display of photographs of Al-Ain in the 1960s – it's unrecognisable. Other exhibits cover traditional education, flora, fauna, weapons and Bedouin life. A large portion of the museum is dedicated to the archaeology of the area.

You can see the entrance to the **livestock souq** from the museum and fort parking lot. The souq, which sells everything from Brahman cows to Persian cats, attracts people from all over the eastern UAE and northern Oman. Don't be surprised if you see an Emirati loading goats into the back

Transport

Distance from Dubai 160km.

Direction Southeast.

Travel Time 90 minutes.

Car Head south out of Dubai along Sheikh Zayed Rd (E11). Take the exit near Nad Al-Sheba – there are signs to Al-Ain (E66). This Emirates highway goes all the way to Al-Ain.

Public Transport Minibuses (Dh30, 90 minutes) to Al-Ain leave from the main Bur Dubai bus station (Map pp212-13) in Bur Dubai. A shared/engaged taxi from the Bur Dubai bus station costs Dh30/150. To return to Dubai you'll need to catch a shared taxi (the taxi stand is next to the bus station), as the minibuses don't take passengers in the other direction. Shared taxis take four to seven passengers to Dubai (Dh30); an engaged taxi will cost about Dh130 to Dh150, depending on your negotiation skills.

The Date Palm

If you visit Al-Ain, Dubai or Abu Dhabi in early summer, one of the things you will be struck by is the enormous number of date clusters hanging off date palms lining many of the streets and parks. The ubiquitous date palm has always held a vital place in the life of Emiratis. For centuries dates were one of the staple foods of the Bedouin, along with fish, camel meat and camel milk. Not a great deal of variety you may say, but consider the fact that there are 80 different kinds of date in the UAE. Dates are roughly 70% sugar which prevents them from rotting, making them edible for longer than other fruits.

Apart from being a major food source, the date palm was also used to make all kinds of useful items. Its trunk was used to make columns and ceilings for houses, while its fronds (called *areesh*) were used to make roofs and walls. The date palm provided the only shade available in desert oases. Livestock were fed with its seeds and it was burned as fuel. Palm fronds were, and still are, used to make bags, mats, *shashas* (boats), shelters, brooms and fans.

seat of a late-model Mercedes. The souq is at its busiest before 9am, when trading is heaviest, but remember to ask before you take any photos.

The beautifully restored **Jahili Fort & Park** is set inside a walled park, next to the public gardens and near the Al-Ain Rotana Hotel. Built in 1898 the fort is a handsome piece of traditional architecture; look out for the main corner tower, which is graced with three concentric rings of serrated battlements. The fort itself is not open to visitors, but you can wander around the pleasant gardens.

Another thoroughly restored fort, the **Al-Khandaq Fort** in Buraimi is said to be about 400 years old. Be sure to climb one of the battlements for a view of the surrounding oasis. Unusually for an Omani fort, there are both inner and outer defence walls. Once you get into the courtyard head directly across it and slightly to the left to reach a large, well-restored room. This was the *majlis*, where the fort's commander would have conducted his official business. The large enclosed yard just east of the fort is Buraimi's **Eid prayer ground**, where people gather to pray during the holidays marking the end of Ramadan and the end of the pilgrimage season.

The **Buraimi Souq** is housed in the large brown building at the Horse Roundabout and sells fruit, vegetables, meat and household goods. The enclosed (concrete) part of the souq houses a few shops that sell Omani silver jewellery and *khanjars*, the ornate daggers worn by many Omani and some Emirati men (see p123), although the selection is not great.

Camel and calf

The **Hili Gardens & Archaeological Park**, about 8km north of the centre of Al-Ain, off the Dubai road, consists of a public park and archaeological site. The main attraction is the **Round Structure**, a building dating from the 3rd millennium BC. It has two porthole entrances and is decorated with relief carvings of animals and people. Although it's referred to as a tomb locally, it may not have ever been one at all: no bones were ever found here, just remnants of pottery, and there are suggestions that it may have been a temple. Excavations on a tomb (dating to somewhere between 2300 and 2000 BC), adjoining the older Round Structure, have uncovered more than 250 skeletons.

In an Arab Home

If you are invited into someone's home, the following tips may be useful:

- It is appropriate to take a small gift such as sweets or pastries.
- Do not sit in such a way that the soles of your feet are pointing at someone else.
- Do not eat or offer things with your left hand.
- It is considered polite to let your host set the pace in any conversation.
- Be wary of openly admiring any of your host's belongings. It is an Arab custom to make a gift of anything that a guest admires.
- It is polite to take a second or third helping, but don't leave your plate completely empty. This implies that you are still hungry and that your host has not been attentive to your needs.
- It's considered very impolite to refuse an offer of coffee or tea in any social or business setting. After finishing your drink hold out the cup in your right hand for more. If you have had enough, rock the cup gently back and forth to indicate that you're done. It's generally considered impolite to drink more than three cups, unless the conversation drags on for an extended period.
- Don't overstay your welcome. If you are dining at someone's house it's best to leave soon after coffee is served.

Sights & Information

Al-Khandaq Fort (750m past the border, near Buraimi Souq; ⌚ 8am-6pm Sat-Wed, 8am-1pm & 4-6pm Thu & Fri)

Eastern Fort & Al-Ain Museum (☎ 03 764 1595; Sultan bin Zayed St; admission 50 fils; ⌚ 8am-1pm & 3.30-5.30pm Mon-Thu, 9-11.30am Fri, 8am-1pm Sat Nov-Apr; 8am-1pm & 4.30-6.30pm Mon-Thu, 9-11.30am Fri, 8am-1pm Sat May-Oct)

Hili Gardens & Archaeological Park (8km north of Al-Ain centre, off the Dubai road; admission Dh1; ⌚ 9am-10pm)

Jahili Fort & Park (next to the public gardens, near the Al-Ain Rotana Hotel; admission Dh1; ⌚ 9am-10pm)

Eating

Al-Ain Oasis Restaurant (☎ 03 766 5340; Al-Ain Oasis; mains Dh15-30) In a beautiful setting in the heart of the oasis, the restaurant is about a 500m walk from the Al-Ain Museum. The menu includes mixed grills and fish biryani.

Al-Mallah (☎ 03 766 9928; Khalifa St; mains Dh20-40) Serves generous portions of Lebanese cuisine. Mezzes cost around Dh7, *shish tawooq* (grilled, skewered chicken pieces) Dh20, and fish and prawn dishes cost about Dh40.

Golden Fork (☎ 03 766 9033; Khalifa St; mains Dh7-15) A branch of the ubiquitous Filipino restaurant chain, it offers noodle dishes and mixed grills.

Golden Gate Restaurant (☎ 03 766 2467; Al-Ain St; mains Dh15-25) A little more upmarket than the Golden Fork, it serves respectable Chinese and Filipino food.

Hut (☎ 03 751 6526; Khalifa St) A Western-style coffee shop offering good cappuccino (Dh5) and other coffees as well as a wide selection of cakes, pastries and sandwiches.

Luce (☎ 03 768 6686; Al-Ain InterContinental, Khalid bin Sultan St; mains Dh50) Easily the best Italian food in town.

Trader Vic's (☎ 03 751 5111; Al-Ain Rotana Hotel, Mohammed bin Khalifa St; mains Dh50) A branch of the venerable French-Polynesian restaurant group – just watch those famed cocktails, they're lethal.

Sleeping

Note that none of the hotels in Buraimi serve alcohol.

Al-Ain InterContinental (☎ 03 768 6686; www.ichotelsgroup.com; Khalid bin Sultan St; s/d Dh671/700) With spacious gardens, a huge pool area and lots of sports facilities it's a good choice. The restaurants are first-rate and it's also home to Al-Ain's most popular expat bar, the Horse & Jockey.

Al-Ain Rotana Hotel (☎ 03 751 5111; www.rotana.com; Mohammed bin Khalifa St; s/d Dh760/814) The newest of the three 'name' hotels, it's a fine place with all of the expected facilities.

Al-Dhahrah Hotel (☎ 00968 650 492; sirshirt@omantel.net.om; Abu Bakr al-Siddiq St, Buraimi; s/d Dh130/160) A few doors north of the Hamasa Hotel, it has clean rooms and bathrooms and is fine for the price.

Diversions: Jebel Hafit

South of Al-Ain is **Jebel Hafit** (Map p150), a jagged 1160m-high limestone mountain that rears out of the plain. The views across the desert from the top of this mountain are worth the effort of the rather twisty drive up. The summit is about 30km by road from the centre of Al-Ain.

To get there, head south from the Clock Tower Roundabout, turn right at Khalid bin Sultan St and follow the purple tourist signs. There are no buses to Jebel Hafit. A taxi will cost around Dh50 for the round trip.

Al-Masa Hotel (☎ 00968 653 007; Abu Bakr al-Siddiq St, Buraimi; s/d Dh200/300) A new mid-range hotel about 500m from the border, on the left as you enter Buraimi from Al-Ain. All rooms have satellite TV and a small balcony.

Hamasa Hotel (☎ 00968 651 200, in the UAE 050 619 4248; Abu Bakr al-Siddiq St, Buraimi; s/d Dh120/150) The better of the two cheap hotels in Buraimi, it sits about 100m north of the border, on your right as you enter Buraimi from Al-Ain. The rooms are larger than the nearby Al-Dhahrah Hotel, though not quite as clean.

Hilton Al-Ain (☎ 03 768 6666; www.hilton.com; Khalid bin Sultan St; s/d Dh600/670) The oldest of the three 'name hotels' and, while perfectly, comfortable it doesn't quite match its rivals.

Directory

Directory

TRANSPORT

AIR

You can fly direct to Dubai from most of Europe and Asia. Flights from North America involve changing flights in Europe or Asia. Dubai's reputation as the travel hub of the Gulf, and increasingly as the major stopover between Europe and Asia was built on a combination of easy landing rights for aircraft in transit and a large, cheap duty-free centre at the airport.

For general airport information in Dubai call ☎ 224 5555; for flight inquiries dial ☎ 206 6666.

The national carrier is Emirates Airlines, which flies to about 50 destinations in the Middle East, Europe, Australia, Africa and the subcontinent. The secondary carrier is the regional airline Gulf Air. It flies to many of the same destinations as Emirates, although all flights go via Bahrain. Emirates has a perfect safety record, whereas Gulf Air doesn't. There is also a new kid on the aviation block, Air Arabia (www.airarabia.com), which is based in neighbouring Sharjah (with a bus link from Dubai); a return trip to Beirut, for example, will cost you around Dh290 – about a quarter of the price of Emirates.

Remember when buying air tickets that direct flight routes are generally more expensive than nondirect routes. This means that flying Emirates or British Airways between London and Dubai, for instance, is going to be more expensive than flying Gulf Air via Bahrain or Qatar Airways via Doha. Sometimes, however, connecting flights can be more trouble than they're worth and you should check how long you'll be stuck at an airport before you buy that cheaper ticket. For all the talk of free markets, air fares out of the UAE are just as strictly regulated as anywhere else. There are no bucket shops.

High season for air travel varies from airline to airline. Generally, it is from late May or early June to the end of August, and from the beginning of December to the end of January. Low season is generally any other time. Regardless, special fares are offered throughout the year by different travel agents and airlines, so it pays to shop around.

Airlines

The following is a selection of carriers that fly to and from Dubai. Many of them also have desks at the **Dubai National Air Travel Agency Airline Centre** (DNATA; Map pp210-11) on Al-Maktoum Rd in Deira.

Air France (Map p210-11; ☎ 294 5991; Al-Shoala Complex, cnr Al-Maktoum Rd & 9 St, Deira)

Air India (Map pp210-11; ☎ 227 6787; Al-Maktoum Rd, Deira)

Alitalia (Map pp210-11; ☎ 224 2257; 16th fl, Green Tower, Baniyas Rd, Deira)

British Airways (Map p218; ☎ 307 5555; 10th fl, Kendah House, Sheikh Zayed Rd)

Cathay Pacific Airways (Map pp210-11; ☎ 295 0400; Al-Shoala Complex, cnr Al-Maktoum Rd & 9 St, Deira)

Czech Airlines (Map pp210-11; ☎ 295 9502; Al-Maktoum Rd, Deira)

EgyptAir (Map pp210-11; ☎ 224 7055; Al-Maktoum Rd, Deira)

Emarat Link Aviation (Map pp210-11; ☎ 295 9779; 3rd fl, Al-Yamamah Towers, cnr Baniyas Rd & 9 St, Deira)

Emirates Airlines (Map pp210-11; ☎ 295 1111; DNATA Airline Centre, Al-Maktoum Rd, Deira)

Emirates Airlines (☎ 214 4444; Sheikh Zayed Rd, near Interchange No 2)

Ethiopian Airlines (Map pp208-9; ☎ 228 4338; 2nd fl, Pearl Bldg, 18 St, Deira)

Gulf Air (Map pp208-9; ☎ 271 3111; Salahuddin Rd, Deira)

Iran Air (Map pp210-11; ☎ 224 0200; Al-Salemiyah Tower, Baniyas Rd, Deira)

Iran Asseman (Map pp208-9; ☎ 299 6611; Al-Maktoum Rd, near the InterContinental Dubai, Deira)

KLM (Map pp214-15; ☎ 335 5777; 9th fl, Gulf Towers, cnr Oud Metha Rd & 20 St, Oud Metha)

Lufthansa Airlines (Map pp206-7; ☎ 343 2121; 2nd fl, Lufthansa Bldg, Sheikh Zayed Rd)

Malaysia Airlines (Map pp212-13; ☎ 397 0250; 1st fl, National Bank of Umm al-Qaiwain Bldg, Khalid bin al-Waleed Rd, Bur Dubai)

Middle East Airlines (Map pp208-9; ☎ 203 3761; 3rd fl, Dubai Tower, Baniyas Sq, Deira)

Oman Air (Map pp212-13; ☎ 351 8080; mezzanine fl, Al-Rais Centre, Al-Mankhool Rd, Bur Dubai)

Qatar Airways (Map pp208-9; ☎ 221 4448; Doha Centre, Al-Maktoum Rd, Deira)

Royal Brunei Airlines (Map pp212-13; ☎ 351 4111; 3rd fl, Rais Hassan Saadi Bldg, Al-Mankhool Rd, Bur Dubai)

Singapore Airlines (Map pp208-9; ☎ 223 2300; 3rd fl, Pearl Bldg, 18 St, Deira)

SriLankan Airlines (Map pp210-11; ☎ 294 9119; 3rd floor, DNATA Airline Centre, Al-Maktoum Rd)

Swiss (Map pp210-11; ☎ 294 5051; 1st fl, Al-Yamamah Towers, cnr Baniyas Rd & 9 St, Deira)

Thai Airways International (Map pp210-11; ☎ 268 1702; Al-Muraqqabat Rd, Deira)

Airport

Dubai International Airport (Map pp210-11) is the busiest airport in the Middle East, with over 18 million passengers passing through the airport in 2003. By 2010 this is expected to rise to 30 million passengers a year, so the airport authority is launching another building programme costing US$2.5 billion, which is due to be completed in 2006. The new structures will be for the exclusive use of Emirates Airlines, including a new underground third terminal and a doubling in size of the concourse. A third concourse will be built to accommodate the new A380 super jumbo aircraft.

All the major international airlines, including Emirates, use Terminal 1, the main terminal. Smaller airlines, mostly en route to East Africa or the countries of the former Soviet Union, use the much smaller Terminal 2.

To get to/from the airport you can choose from Dubai municipality buses, airport buses or taxi. If you're staying at one of the beach hotels along the Jumeirah strip, remember to ask about transfers when booking your accommodation. All transport leaves outside the arrivals hall and the areas (bus, taxi, limo etc) are signposted. Unlike most other Middle Eastern destinations, there's virtually no spruiking.

Airport bus No 401 goes via DNATA Airline Centre, Union Sq, Baniyas Rd, Sabkha bus station and Deira bus station. Airport bus No 402 goes via Deira City Centre and Karama. The airport buses cost Dh3.

Dubai municipality buses leave from the **Deira bus station** (Map pp208-9), bus Nos 4, 11 and 15 go to the airport every 15 to 20 minutes and the trip costs Dh1.50. From the **Bur Dubai bus station** (Map pp208-9), bus Nos 33 and 44 go to the airport for a cost of Dh2, but No 44 takes a circuitous route via Karama. Only bus No 2 goes to Terminal 2, leaving from the Deira Gold Souq, but there's a shuttle service between the two terminals.

Only the sand-coloured Dubai Transport Company taxis are allowed to pick up passengers from the arrivals area. There's an extra charge levied on these taxis for the run from the airport (welcome to Dubai!), and while you could try to save money by heading to the departures area and trying to flag down a taxi after a drop-off, taxis are not allowed to pick up passengers here. A ride to the Deira souq area will cost about Dh30 while to Bur Dubai it costs about Dh37. A taxi ride from the Deira souq area to the airport costs Dh12; from Bur Dubai it's about Dh17. A ride to a Jumeirah area hotel starts at around Dh60.

BICYCLE

While you can now hire bicycles in Dubai we can't really recommend cycling as a way of getting around the city. With drivers more concerned with the mobile phone held in one hand, the cigarette in the other and knee-steering across three lanes in as many metres, you, dear cyclist (and pedestrian for that matter), are way down the list of driver priorities. You will see cyclists around and if you do want to ride remember to monitor your fluid intake in the heat and humidity. And always yield to cars. For hire and repairs contact **Wolfi's Bike Shop** (Map pp206-7; ☎ 339 4453; Sheikh Zayed Rd).

BOAT

Scores of *abras* (small motorboats) cross the Creek from early morning until around midnight, taking two routes. One route links **Bur Dubai abra station** (Map pp212-13), near the Bank of Baroda Building, with the **Deira Old Souq abra station** (Map pp212-13) at the intersection of Old Baladiya St and Baniyas Rd. The other route, further up the Creek, connects the **Dubai Old Souq abra station** (Map pp212-13; at Bur Dubai Souq) with the **Sabkha abra station** (Map pp212-13) on the Deira side, at the intersection of Al-Sabkha and Baniyas Rds.

Like shared taxis, *abra*s leave when they are full, but it never takes more than a few minutes for one to fill up. The fare is just a measly 50 fils.

Note that it can be quite tricky getting on and off the *abra*s – not something to attempt wearing high heels.

BUS

Local buses operate out of the two main stations in Deira and Bur Dubai. The **Deira bus station** (Map pp208-9) is off Al-Khor St, near the Deira Gold Souq. The **Bur Dubai bus station** (Map pp212-13), Dubai's main bus station, is on Al-Ghubaiba Rd. In the official timetables the two stations appear as Gold Souq Bus Station and Al-Ghubaiba Bus Station, respectively. Numbers and the routes are posted on the buses in English as well as Arabic. Fares range from Dh1 to Dh3.50, depending on the distance that is travelled. You pay the driver, so keep some change handy. A free schedule and route map can be picked up from either bus station, or from the Department of Tourism & Commerce Marketing (DTCM) office on Baniyas Sq.

Note that on Friday most buses begin and end their days a bit later. You can count on there being no Friday service from about 11.30am until about 1.30pm (except on route Nos 16, 90 and 91) while noon prayers, the most important of the week, are under way. From Saturday to Thursday, buses run from approximately 5.45am to 11.15pm, at intervals of about 15 to 20 minutes.

If you're going to regularly use the buses, get an e-Go Card. The card costs Dh5 to purchase and then you must recharge it with credit – Dh20 for the first time and multiples of Dh10 after that. The amount for each bus ride is deducted each time you use the ticket machine on the bus. Purchase the e-Go Cards from the major bus stations.

For information on public buses you can call the 24-hour **Dubai Municipality hotline** (☎ 800 4848).

CAR & MOTORCYCLE

If you are planning on taking a day or overnight excursion from Dubai, hiring a car is the best and cheapest way to do it. If you decide to hire a car to get around the city, remember that traffic congestion in Dubai can be a real problem at peak hours, which occur three times a day: between 7am and 9am, 1pm and 2pm and most of the evening from 6pm onwards. The worst congestion is around the approaches to Al-Maktoum and Al-Garhoud Bridges, and along Al-Ittihad Rd towards Sharjah.

It is compulsory to wear seatbelts when sitting in the front and it is illegal to use a hand-held mobile phone while driving (not that this stops anyone!).

As you would expect, Dubai is not short on petrol stations. Petrol is sold by the imperial gallon (an imperial gallon is just over 4.5L). Regular petrol costs Dh4 per gallon and premium is Dh4.56.

It is not possible to hire motorcycles in Dubai – probably just as well. Before you drive in Dubai, read the boxed text Motoring Mayhem on p171 for some important safety messages.

Hire

Like most countries, a credit card makes hiring a car much easier in Dubai. If you do find a car-hire company that will take a cash deposit instead, not only will you probably have to leave your passport with them, they may not offer full insurance. Some agencies insist on a credit card deposit as well as your passport. Find another agency if this is the case. You do not have to leave your passport with them. A photocopy of it is sufficient. The reason for all this security is to protect themselves against customers who run up traffic violations and then leave town without paying them.

For tourists, most foreign driving licences are accepted in Dubai so long as you are either a citizen or a resident of the country that issued the licence. Some companies insist on an international licence, however, so it's worth getting one of these before you leave home.

At large international agencies, small cars such as a Toyota Corolla start at about Dh120 per day with another Dh20 to

Motoring Mayhem

Driving in Dubai is not for the faint of heart. Although it's not as bad as in other parts of the Middle East, drivers tend to cut in front of you, turn without indicating and view roundabouts as a laneless free for all. Out on the freeway, driving in the lane closest to the centre of the road at speeds of less than 160km/h will invoke some serious headlight flashing from the latest model Mercedes trying to break the Dubai–Abu Dhabi land speed record.

So it's no surprise that the UAE has one of the world's highest rates of road deaths per capita. Inappropriate speed and reckless driving are the major causes. The worst aspect of this is that there doesn't seem to be a sufficient incentive not to drive badly. Although speeding fines are meted out, most of the population view speed cameras as toll booths you don't have to stop at! Causing a death through an accident requires the payment of *dhiyya* (blood money) to the victim's family. Although this is a large sum (up to Dh200,000), nationals are insured against it. This often means that the only punishment for causing death or injury through reckless driving is an increased insurance premium.

If you're used to counting drinks down at the local to see whether you're over the alcohol limit or not, we'll make it easy – if you've had one, you've had one too many. Dubai has a zero tolerance policy on drink-driving and if your vehicle is stopped and you're found to have been driving under the influence of alcohol, you'll be a guest of the Dubai Police for at least one night. If you have been involved in an accident and have been drinking, you're insurance will be voided whether you were responsible for the accident or not.

Dh25 for collision damage waiver (CDW) insurance. These rates fall to about Dh120 per day including insurance for a week's hire, and around Dh85 to Dh95 per day with insurance for a month. If you have taken out CDW, the larger agencies do not charge an excess in the case of an accident that is your fault. Always call the police if you are involved in an accident (see the boxed text Accident Alert on p172 for more details).

At the smaller agencies, you should be able to negotiate a net rate of around Dh120 per day, including CDW insurance. With these agencies, no matter what they tell you, you may still be liable for the first Dh1000 to Dh1500 of damage in the event of an accident that is your fault, even if you have CDW. Sometimes this excess is only Dh200 if you have paid CDW. Ask questions and read the small print on the contract carefully.

The first 100km or 150km per day are usually free, while additional kilometres cost 40 or 50 fils each. If you rent a car for more than three days you should be given unlimited mileage.

Most agencies have free pick-up and delivery within Dubai, either to/from a hotel or the airport. They also offer a chauffeur service, but you'll pay around Dh180 per eight hours for this privilege. If you are just moving around Dubai for the day it is much cheaper to use taxis.

Although smaller agencies are generally cheaper than the larger chain companies, it's worth considering the convenience of being able to contact the local office of a reliable company if you are driving out of Dubai and something goes wrong. It's also worth ensuring complete insurance cover (zero liability).

There are dozens of car-hire firms in Dubai, including all the major international chains as well as plenty of local companies. The highest concentrations of local hire companies are on Abu Baker al-Siddiq Rd, just north of the Clock Tower Roundabout, and on Omar ibn al-Khattab Rd. They are also found opposite the minibus and taxi station on Omar ibn al-Khattab Rd in Deira, on the Bur Dubai side of the Creek on Sheikh Khalifa bin Zayed Rd, just north of Al-Adhid Rd, and on Kuwait St in Karama. The major companies listed below will generally deliver the car to you.

Avis (Map pp210-11; ☎ 295 7121; www.avis.com; Al-Maktoum Rd, Deira)

Avis (Map pp210-11; ☎ 224 5219; airport arrivals hall; ☿ 24hr)

Budget (Map pp210-11; ☎ 282 3030; www.budget.com; Airport Rd, just before Cargo Village)

Budget (Map pp210-11; ☎ 224 5192; airport arrivals hall; ☿ 24hr)

Diamondlease (Map p218; ☎ 331 3172; www.diamond lease.com; Sahara Towers, Sheikh Zayed Rd)

Europcar (☎ 352 0033) Desks at the Crowne Plaza Hotel (Map p218), InterContinental Dubai (Map pp208-9), Al-Bustan Rotana Hotel (Map pp210-11) and Hyatt Regency Dubai (Map pp208-9).

Hertz (Map pp210-11; ☎ 282 4422; www.hertz-uae .com; Airport Rd, just before Cargo Village)

Hertz (Map pp210-11; ☎ 224 5222; airport arrivals hall; ☼ 24hr)

Thrifty (☎ 355 6732; thrifty@emirates.net.ae) Desks at Golden Sands 3 (Map pp212-13) and Hilton Dubai Jumeirah (Map pp212-13) hotels.

Thrifty (Map pp210-11; ☎ 224 5404; airport arrivals hall; ☼ 24hr)

Road Rules

Drive on the right in Dubai. The speed limit is 60km/h on city streets and 80km/h on major city roads. On Sheikh Zayed Rd and on other dual-lane highways around the UAE the official speed limit is 100km/h on some sections, but otherwise it's 120km/h. If you are caught speeding, you will be fined, but in some cases you will simply be sent a bill in the mail by the police. For this reason, most car-hire companies require customers to sign a statement acknowledging that they are aware of this and authorising the hire

company to charge their credit card for any tickets that turn up after they have left town. There are also speed cameras on the major highways.

Increasingly the busier city streets have a strictly enforced four-hour limit on parking. Tickets must be purchased from one of the numerous orange ticket-dispensing machines and displayed on your dashboard. Rates start at Dh2 for an hour. Parking rates apply from 8am to 1pm and from 4pm to 9pm Saturday to Thursday. Parking in the centre of Dubai is free on Friday and holidays. Fines for not buying a ticket start at Dh100 and you can't reregister your car until you've paid up.

TAXI

Dubai has a large, modern fleet of taxis with meters, and you can usually find one without too long a wait. The starting fare is Dh3 plus Dh1.43 per kilometre, rising to Dh3.50 plus Dh1.70 per kilometre between 10pm and 6am. Drivers are sometimes very keen to round up to the nearest five dirhams, so keep some smaller notes (fives and 10s) and coins handy for taxi trips. There are still a few taxis without meters, but these are slowly disappearing as their licences expire and are not renewed. If you do happen to get in a taxi that doesn't have a meter, save yourself the hassle and simply get out and wait for another one.

Dubai Transport Company has women taxi drivers and if you book in advance it can provide wheelchair-accessible taxis.

Taxi companies:

Cars Taxis (☎ 269 3344)

Dubai Transport Company (☎ 208 0808)

Metro Taxis (☎ 267 3222)

National Taxis (☎ 336 6611)

PRACTICALITIES

ACCOMMODATION

Accommodation in the Sleeping chapter (p135) is listed by neighbourhood, with mid-range and top-end places listed alphabetically, followed by budget 'cheap sleeps'. With well over 400 hotels and a new one seemingly announced every week, Dubai doesn't lack for accommodation options; except for cheap sleeps, which are still thin on the ground. Accommodation prices quoted in the Sleeping chapter are rack rates (the standard published rates) and you can expect to pay these rates during any of the holidays, festivals and events that frequently occur in Dubai (see p9 for details). During summer hotels drop their rates as the tourist traffic really drops off, so from mid-May to mid-September you can often receive a discount of up to 50% off the published rack rate. Always ask for the best price or whether there are any deals on – generally the hotels won't tell you these unless you ask. The hotels publish specials on their websites (if there are none currently available that generally means occupancy is high), or you can try Expedia (www.expedia.com) or Lastminute.com (www.lastminute.com).

BUSINESS

Dubai's physical location places it in a strong position to attract both regional and multinational companies, and the Dubai government has been very successful in their strategy of luring companies from other capital cities in the Middle East to base operations in Dubai. Their innovative, 'can do' style of dealing with businesses has really set them apart from other Middle Eastern centres.

Business Hours

Business hours and even working days are not fixed in Dubai. Government departments generally work Saturday to Wednesday between 7am and 2pm, but offices that deal with the public often have extended business hours and are sometimes open on Thursday. Private companies generally work an 8am-to-5pm or 9am-to-6pm day but may take Friday and Saturday as the weekend or even just Friday alone. Meetings in Dubai take a little getting used to as you're expected to arrive punctually, but can end up waiting a long time for your host. Meetings, when they do eventually start, can go for hours without seemingly achieving anything tangible. See the boxed text Top Survival Guides on p174 for more info.

Centres

Business is spread over a huge area in Dubai. All of the big media players congregate at Dubai Media City, trading companies at the Jebel Ali free zone. Most large hotels are set up for conferences and incentives meetings better than those in the West, but for some strange reason they end up at a hotel near a golf course.

CHILDREN

As in most Gulf cities, families are well catered for in Dubai and there are plenty of activities for children. All the parks mentioned in this book (see the Neighbourhoods chapter, p45) have kids' playgrounds and plenty of grassy stretches where they can expend energy – just make sure the kids are getting enough fluids in the heat. All the shopping centres have nurseries or play areas for little kids though most of the time you won't be able to leave them unattended. For the best children's activities, check the Top Five for Children boxed text (p47). *Kids Explorer* (Dh25) lists dozens of fun things for kids to do around the UAE. Lonely Planet's *Travel with Children* by Cathy Lanigan is a useful book that prepares you for the joys and pitfalls of travelling with the little ones.

Top Survival Guides

Globalisation may have provided Dubai with a multicultural workforce, but it's proven no match for traditional Arab customs. Business, social and cultural practices are still noticeably different from those of the West. To avoid embarrassment in a social situation or even blowing a business deal through poor meeting etiquette, here are nine books that will help:

- *The Arab Way: How to Work More Effectively with Arab Cultures* by Dr Jehad Al Omari. Want to know how to make small talk or avoid confrontation? This excellent cross-cultural guide provides practical tips to avoid faux pas while addressing Western misconceptions of Arabs, Islam and the Arab world.
- *Culture Shock! United Arab Emirates: a Guide to Customs and Etiquette* by Gina Crocetti. Created primarily for expats and business travellers with good detail on UAE culture, society, customs and etiquette.
- *Don't They Know it's Friday* by Jeremy Williams. Straightforward advice on social and business etiquette written by an expat who has worked all over the Gulf and runs courses on doing business with Arabs – compulsory reading for those moving to the UAE.
- *Live and Work in Saudi and the Gulf* by Louise Whetter. Aimed at people looking for work, starting a business or buying a home in the Gulf – details on jobs and how to get them, the way of life, law, health and education systems.
- *Living and Working in the Gulf States and Saudi Arabia* by Robert Hughes, Graeme Chesters and Jim Watson. A detailed guide for anyone planning to move to Dubai, it covers everything you need to know about living, working and studying in the Gulf.
- *Serve Them Right* by Kate Dickens. A very practical guide to working with and serving Dubai's multicultural population.
- *Teach Yourself Islam* by Ruqaiyyah Waris Maqsood. Written by a practising Muslim, this basic introduction to Islam, its teachings and Islamic society is an easy read and a must for travellers to the UAE.
- *UAE: a Meed Practical Guide*. A comprehensive guide to the country with helpful background on UAE business, finance and trade.
- *Understanding Arabs: a Guide for Westerners* by Margaret K Nydell. A superb cross-cultural handbook for people who want to better appreciate Arab culture, society, beliefs and values.

Baby-Sitting

Most of the large hotels have baby-sitting services. These are reliable as they are very used to large numbers of children visiting.

CLIMATE

For most of the year Dubai's weather is warm and humid; the sky is rarely cloudy. The summer months (May to September) are extremely hot with daytime temperatures in the low to mid-40s (Celsius). July and August are the hottest months, with average temperatures around 43°C with 85% humidity. Sometimes the heat reaches 48°C and the humidity 95%. The sea temperature in the height of summer (June to August) is about 37°C, which provides no relief, and hotel swimming pools have to be cooled during this time so that they don't turn into hot baths.

During October, November, March and April the weather is much more bearable, with temperatures in the low to mid-30s. In winter (December to February) Dubai enjoys perfect weather with an average temperature of 24°C, though it can get quite windy. Unlike the desert area inland, Dubai doesn't get too cold on winter nights, the lowest temperature hovering around 15°C. It doesn't rain often, or heavily, but when it does (usually in December or January) getting around can suddenly become difficult as streets turn into rivers and traffic becomes chaotic. Drivers here are not used to wet road conditions, and the city planners decided Dubai didn't need a drainage

DUBAI 5m (16ft)

Average Max/Min

Temp/Humidity | Rainfall

system, so there are no gutter or storm-water drains. The average annual rainfall is about 6.5cm per year (and it rains only five days a year on average), but rainfall varies widely from one year to the next. In winter there can be fog in the early mornings.

Sandstorms can occur during March and April, although Dubai is protected from the swirling dust and sand to some degree by its many tall buildings.

COURSES
Language Courses

Most language courses on offer are for learning English. There are only a few places where English speakers can study Arabic. This is because of the great demand from national students and expats from the subcontinent who want to improve their employment opportunities in the business world, which is dominated by the English language.

Arabic Language Centre (Map p218; ☎ 308 6036; alc@dwtc.com; World Trade Centre, Sheikh Zayed Rd) Runs five courses a year in Arabic from beginner to advanced levels.

Berlitz Language School (Map pp216-17; ☎ 344 0034; Jumeirah Rd) Offers courses in a number of languages, including Arabic and Urdu. The latter is useful to know to some extent as this is the language of so many of the Pakistani expats in the UAE.

Polyglot Language Institute (Map pp208-9; ☎ 222 3429; www.polyglot.co.ae; Al-Masaeed Bldg, Al-Maktoum Rd, Deira) Beginner courses and conversation classes in Arabic, French, German and English. A 10-week Arabic course with three classes per week costs Dh1000.

CUSTOMS

The duty-free allowances for tobacco are huge: 2000 cigarettes, 400 cigars or 2kg of loose tobacco (there is no cracking down on smoking here). Non-Muslims are allowed to import 2L of wine and 2L of spirits. Note that if you are entering the UAE through Sharjah, where alcohol is prohibited, you won't be able to bring any in to Dubai. You are generally not allowed to bring in alcohol if you cross into the UAE by land. No customs duties are applied to personal belongings. If videos are found in your bag, officials will remove them and check them. Officials have a list of banned videos and

other materials. It is also illegal to bring into the UAE any materials that insult Islam (this includes books such as Salman Rushdie's *The Satanic Verses*) or materials that might be used to convert Muslims to any other religions.

DISABLED TRAVELLERS

Dubai's **Department of Tourism & Commerce Marketing** (DTCM; ☎ 223 0000; www.dubaitourism .co.ae) has a highly detailed list of facilities offered at dozens of hotels for disabled people, which it will fax to you on request. All the major shopping centres have wheelchair access, but ramps in car parks and into most buildings in the city are few and far between. There are a number of car parks for disabled drivers.

Dubai Transport Company (☎ 208 0808) has taxis that can accommodate wheelchairs. The airport has facilities for disabled travellers, including low check-in counters, but things do get more difficult once you are out of the airport. While many hotels in Dubai now claim that they are disabled-friendly, we have noted the hotels that have specifically paid attention to the details of what this actually means. These are **Le Meridien Mina Seyahi Resort** (p147) and **Mövenpick Hotel Bur Dubai** (p143). Dubai Museum has ramps, but other tourist attractions are difficult for disabled visitors to get around on their own. Dubai airport has modern facilities for people with disabilities, including lounges and carts for getting around the concourse.

ELECTRICITY

The electric voltage is 220V AC. British-style three-pin wall sockets are used, with most electical appliances are sold with two-pin plugs. Adaptors are inexpensive and available in small grocery stores and supermarkets. The two-pin plugs will fit into the three-pin sockets, but it involves a technique that won't be seen in a workplace safety video anytime soon.

EMBASSIES & CONSULATES

It's important to realise what your own embassy can and can't do to help you if you get into trouble.

Generally speaking, it won't be much help in emergencies if the trouble you're in is remotely your own fault. Remember that you are bound by the laws of the UAE. Your embassy will not be sympathetic if you end up in jail after committing a crime locally, even if such actions are legal in your own country.

In genuine emergencies you might get some assistance, but only if other channels have been exhausted. For example, if you need to get home urgently, a free ticket home is exceedingly unlikely – the embassy would expect you to have insurance. If you have all your money and documents stolen, it might assist with getting a new passport, but a loan for onward travel is out of the question.

Some embassies used to keep travellers' letters and stock home newspapers, but the mail-holding service has generally been stopped and the newspapers tend to be out of date.

Embassies & Consulates in Dubai

Most countries have diplomatic representation in the UAE. Dubai is home to the consulates and one embassy, the UK embassy; other embassies are in Abu Dhabi and are listed in the front pages of the Dubai phone book. The telephone area code for Dubai is ☎ 04 (drop the 0 if calling from outside the UAE).

Australia (Map p218; ☎ 321 2444; 1st fl, Emarat Atrium Bldg, Sheikh Zayed Rd; ☒ 8am-3.30pm Sat-Tue, 8am-2.45pm Wed)

Canada (Map pp212-13; ☎ 352 1717; dubai@dfait-maeci.gc.ca; 7th fl, United Bank Bldg, Khalid bin al-Waleed Rd, Bur Dubai; ☒ 8-11.30am Sat-Wed)

Egypt (Map pp212-13; ☎ 397 1122; 11 St, Bur Dubai; ☒ 9am-noon Sat-Wed)

France (Map p218; ☎ 332 9040; fransula@emirates.net.ae; 18th fl, API World Tower, Sheikh Zayed Rd, Za'abeel; ☒ 8.30am-1pm Sat-Wed)

Germany (Map pp214-15; ☎ 379 0002; aadubai@emirates.net.ae; 1st fl, Sharaf Bldg, Khalid bin al-Waleed Rd, near BurJuman Centre, Bur Dubai; ☒ 9am-noon Sat-Wed)

India (Map pp214-15; ☎ 397 1222; cgidubai@emirates.net.ae; 7B St, Bur Dubai; ☒ 8am-4.30pm Sun-Thu)

Iran (Map pp216-17; ☎ 344 4717; irancons@emirates.net.ae; cnr Al-Wasl Rd & 33 St, Jumeirah; ☒ 8am-1pm Sat-Wed)

Italy (Map p218; ☎ 331 4167; consulit@emirates.net.ae; 17th fl, World Trade Centre, Sheikh Zayed Rd, Za'abeel; ☒ 9am-1pm Sat-Wed)

Jordan (Map pp214-15; ☎ 397 0500; jorconslt@emirates.net.ae; 11 St, Bur Dubai; ☒ 8am-12.30pm Sat-Wed)

Kuwait (Map pp208-9; ☎ 228 4111; kuwait@emirates.net.ae; Baniyas Rd, Deira; ☒ 8.30am-2.30pm Sat-Wed)

Lebanon (Map pp214-15; ☎ 397 7450; lebconsd@emirates.net.ae; 3 St, Bur Dubai; ☒ 9am-noon Sat-Wed)

Netherlands (Map pp212-13; ☎ 352 8700; nlgovdba@emirates.net.ae; 5th fl, ABN-Amro Bank Bldg, Khalid bin al-Waleed Rd, Bur Dubai; ☒ 9am-3pm Sat-Wed)

Oman (Map pp214-15 ☎ 397 1000; general@ocodubai.com; 11 St, Bur Dubai; ☒ 8am-2pm Sat-Wed)

Pakistan (Map pp214-15; ☎ 397 0412; parepdub@emirates.net.ae; 11 St, Bur Dubai; ☒ 8am-noon Sat-Wed)

Qatar (Map pp214-15; ☎ 398 2888; qatar98@emirates.net.ae; cnr Al-Adhid Rd & 52 St, Al-Jafiliya; ☒ 8-11.30am Sat-Wed)

Saudi Arabia (Map pp212-13; ☎ 266 3383; 28 St, Hor al-Anz; ☒ 8.30-11.30am Sat-Wed)

South Africa (Map pp214-15; ☎ 397 5222; sacons@emirates.net.ae; 3rd fl, Sharaf Bldg, Khalid bin al-Waleed Rd, near BurJuman Centre, Bur Dubai; ☒ 8.30am-12.30pm Sat-Wed)

Syria (Map pp206-7; ☎ 266 3354; cnr 15 & 10C Sts, Al-Wuheida, Deira; ☒ 8.30am-2.30pm Sat-Wed)

Turkey (Map p218; ☎ 331 4788; tcdubkon@emirates.net.ae; 11th fl, World Trade Centre, Sheikh Zayed Rd, Za'abeel; ☒ 9am-noon Sat-Thu)

UK (Map pp212-13; ☎ 397 1070; britemb@emirates.net.ae; Al-Seef Rd, Bur Dubai; ☒ 8am-1pm Sat-Wed)

USA (Map p218; ☎ 311 6000; 21st fl, World Trade Centre, Sheikh Zayed Rd, Za'abeel; ☒ 8.30am-5pm Sat-Wed)

Yemen (Map pp214-15; ☎ 397 0131; 7B St, Bur Dubai; ☒ 8.30-11.30am Sat-Wed)

UAE Embassies & Consulates

Here are contact details for UAE diplomatic missions:

Australia (☎ 02-6286 8802; 36 Culgoa Circuit, O'Malley, ACT 2606)

Bahrain (☎ 723 737; House No 221, Rd 4007 - Complex 340, Manama)

Egypt (☎ 023-609 722; 4 Ibn Seena St, Giza, Cairo)

France (☎ 01 45 53 94 04; 3 Rue de Lota, 75116 Paris)

Germany (☎ 022-826 7070; Erste Fahrgasse, D-54113, Bonn)

India (☎ 011 687 2822; EP 12 Chandra Gupta Marg, Chanakyapuri, New Delhi 11002)

Iran (☎ 021-878 8515; Wali Asr St, Shaheed Waheed Dastakaardi St No 355, Tehran)

Kuwait (☎ 252 1427; Al-Istiqlal St, Qaseema 7, Al-Assaffa, PO Box 1828, Kuwait 13019)

Oman (☎ 600302; Al-Khuwair, PO Box 551 code 111, Muscat)

Qatar (☎ 483 8880; 22 Al-Markhiyah St, Khalifa Northern Town, PO Box 3099, Doha)

Saudi Arabia (☎ 01-482 6803; Abu Bakr al-Karkhi Zone, Amr bin Omayad St, PO Box 94385, Riyadh 11693)

UK (☎ 020-7581 1281/4113; 30 Princes Gate, London SW1)

USA (☎ 202-338 6500; 3000 K St NW, Suite 600, Washington DC 20007)

EMERGENCY

Ambulance (☎ 998/999)

Electrical faults (☎ 991)

Fire department (☎ 997)

Operator (☎ 181)

Police (☎ 999)

GAY & LESBIAN TRAVELLERS

Officially homosexuality is illegal in the UAE and can incur a jail term. Gay travellers, however, have no trouble travelling in the UAE. You will see men walking hand in hand but that's no indication of sexual orientation. Women walking hand in hand are not as commonly seen.

Dubai has made a huge effort to promote itself as a tolerant, safe tourist destination, and gay and lesbian travellers won't face any discrimination or legal trouble, short of staging a gay-pride march down Sheikh Zayed Rd. Basically authorities don't want bad publicity, so there's generally only a problem when a situation is played out in the public sphere. For example, one nightclub that had a strong gay following crossed the line when it posted flyers around the city calling

on local gays and drag queens to come out. Only then were the authorities compelled to take action. Note that any specifically gay-focussed websites are blocked in the UAE.

Jules (p93), near Le Meridien Dubai, has a reputation as a gay-friendly place to mingle, especially on Thursday night.

HOLIDAYS

See the table of Islamic Holidays (p177) for the approximate dates of the religious holidays observed in Dubai. Lailatul Miraj is the celebration of the Ascension of Prophet Mohammed. Eid al-Fitr is a three-day Festival of Breaking the Fast that occurs after Ramadan, and Eid al-Adha is a four-day Feast of Sacrifice that marks the haj, the pilgrimage to Mecca.

Secular holidays are New Year's Day (1 January) and National Day (2 December). The death of a minister, a member of the royal family or the head of state of another Arab country is usually marked by a three-day holiday. These holidays are announced in the newspaper on the day they occur. If a public holiday falls on a weekend (ie Thursday or Friday), the holiday is usually taken at the beginning of the next working week.

The Islamic calendar starts at the year AD 622, when Prophet Mohammed fled Mecca for the city of Medina. It is called the Hejira calendar (hejira means 'flight'). As it is a lunar calendar, it's 11 days shorter than the Gregorian (Western) calendar, which means that Islamic holidays fall 11 days earlier each year. This is not a fixed rule, however, as the exact dates of Islamic holidays depend upon the sighting of the moon at a particular stage in its cycle. This can be as informal as a group of elderly imams being taken on a night-time drive into the desert to confer on whether or not the new moon is visible. This is why Islamic holidays are not definitely announced until a day or two

Islamic Holidays

Hejira Year	New Year Birthday	Prophet Mohammed's	Ramadan	Eid al-Fitr	Eid al-Adha
1425	22.02.04	02.05.04	15.10.04	14.11.04	21.01.05
1426	10.02.05	21.04.05	04.10.05	03.11.05	10.01.06
1427	31.01.06	11.04.06	24.09.06	24.10.06	31.12.06
1428	20.01.07	31.03.07	13.09.07	13.10.07	20.12.07

before they occur, and why they differ from country to country.

Ramadan

This is the month during which Muslims fast from dawn until dusk. Government offices ease back to about six hours' work per day. Bars and pubs are closed until 7pm each night, live music is prohibited and dance clubs are always closed throughout the month. Camel racing ceases too. Some restaurants do not serve alcohol. Everyone, regardless of their religion, is required to observe the fast in public. That not only means no eating and drinking but no smoking in public as well.

Some hotels still serve breakfast and lunch to guests, but most of the time eating during the day means room service or self-catering. Non-Muslims offered coffee or tea when meeting a Muslim during the day in Ramadan should initially refuse politely. If your host insists, and repeats the offer several times, you should accept so long as it does not look as though you are going to anger anyone else in the room who may be fasting.

INSURANCE

A travel insurance policy to cover theft, loss and medical problems is a good idea. Some policies offer lower and higher medical-expense options; the higher ones are chiefly for countries such as the USA, which have extremely high medical costs. There are a wide variety of policies available, so check the small print. Some policies specifically exclude 'dangerous activities', which can include scuba diving and motorcycling.

You may prefer a policy that pays doctors or hospitals directly rather than you having to pay on the spot and claim later. If you have to claim later make sure you keep all

documentation. Some policies ask you to call back (with reverse charges) to a centre in your home country where an immediate assessment of your problem is made.

Check that the policy covers ambulances or an emergency flight home.

INTERNET ACCESS

Etisalat is theoretically the sole provider of Internet access in Dubai. For private dwellings, dial-up accounts are quite cheap at Dh20 per month for rental and an off-peak rate of Dh1 per hour for use. For a cashed-up monopoly, the introduction of faster Internet services such as ADSL has been handled haphazardly with both software and line quality issues. In the UAE the Internet is accessed through a proxy server in an attempt to block out pornography and other 'unsuitable' material. Many hotels and hotel residences offer Internet access to their guests, though sometimes this is only available to executive guests who are paying a premium for their rooms. Broadband is now becoming common in hotels and there are a couple of hotels offering wireless access – these have been noted in the hotel reviews. Hotels do have the necessary cables to get connected, but many can't offer help past that.

If you wish to access the Internet with your own modem, Etisalat has a 'Dial 'n Surf' service at ☎ 500 5555; all you need is a modem and a phone line. No account number or password is needed. It is charged at 15 fils per minute directly to the telephone you are connected to. If you're staying at a hotel you should check whether the hotel will charge you an additional fee for using their phone line.

There are a few specialist Internet cafés around the city, and you'll find small cafés in the shopping centres that have a few terminals. Rates are around Dh10 to Dh15 per hour. Some reliable Internet cafés:

Al-Jalssa Internet Café (Map pp212-13; ☎ 351 4617; Al-Ain Centre, Al-Mankhool Rd; ☉ 9-1am) Has wireless.

Formula One (Map pp216-17; ☎ 345 1232; Palm Stripe, Jumeirah Rd; ☉ 10am-10pm) Decked out in racing car décor.

French Connection (Map p218; ☎ 351 4617; Wafa Tower, Sheikh Zayed Rd; ☉ 9am-1am) Has wireless. There is another branch at Al-Ain Centre on Al-Mankhool Rd.

Inet (Map pp210-11; ☎ 344 2602; Hamarain Centre, Abu Baker al-Siddiq Rd, Rigga)

Internet Cafe (Map pp216-17; ☎ 345 3441; Al-Dhiyafah Rd, Jumeirah; ✆ 10-3am Sat-Thu, 2pm-3am Fri)

LEGAL MATTERS

Dubai maintains the death penalty for drug importation, although the penalty usually ends up being a very long jail term. Jail sentences for being involved in drugs by association are also likely. That means that even if you are in the same room where there are drugs, but are not partaking, you could be in as much trouble as those who are. The UAE has a small but growing drug problem and the authorities are cracking down hard on it. The secret police are pervasive and they include officers of many nationalities. Theft and writing bad cheques are also taken pretty seriously and usually involve jail and deportation.

If you are arrested you have the right to a phone call, which you should make as soon as possible (ie before you are detained in a police cell or prison pending investigation, where making contact with anyone could be difficult). Call your embassy or consulate first. If there is an accident, it's a case of being guilty until proven innocent. This means that if you are in a road traffic accident, you may be held under police guard until an investigation reveals whose fault the accident was.

Note that drinking alcohol in a public place that is not a licensed venue is illegal. The penalties vary from a warning to a fine. If the police should come across you when you're camping, put away any alcohol.

MAPS

Maps of Dubai are available from the bigger bookshops around town. The maps mentioned here should also be available in the bookshops at five-star hotels. The *Dubai Tourist Map* (Dh45), published by the municipality, is the best of the local maps. Geoprojects publishes a map of Dubai which is not bad, but it's becoming increasingly outdated and it doesn't include the names of all the minor streets. It is available from most bookshops and hotels for Dh30.

MEDICAL SERVICES

There are pharmacies on just about every street in Dubai. See the *Gulf News* for a list of pharmacies that are open 24 hours on

that particular day or if you need to get to a pharmacy urgently, call ☎ 223 2323, a hotline that will tell you where the nearest open pharmacy is located. As a visitor you will receive medical care, but you will be charged for it. It's important to have health cover for your trip as a lengthy stay in a hospital in Dubai will be expensive. Generally the standard of medical services is good.

The following government hospitals have emergency departments:

Al-Maktoum Hospital (Map pp208-9; ☎ 222 1211; Al-Maktoum Hospital Rd, near cnr of Omar ibn al-Khattab Rd, Rigga)

Al-Wasl Hospital (Map pp214-15; ☎ 324 1111; Oud Metha Rd, south of Al-Qataiyat Rd, Za'abeel)

New Dubai Hospital (Map pp208-9; ☎ 222 9171; Abu Baker al-Siddiq Rd, near cnr of Al-Khaleej Rd, Hor al-Anz)

Rashid Hospital (Map pp214-15; ☎ 337 4000; off Oud Metha Rd, near Al-Maktoum Bridge, Bur Dubai)

If you need nonurgent care, ask your consulate for the latest list of recommended doctors and dentists. Some are listed here in case you need to find one and your consulate is closed:

Al-Zahra Private Medical Centre (Map p218; ☎ 331 5000; Zaabeel Tower, Sheikh Zayed Rd)

Dubai London Clinic (Map pp216-17; ☎ 344 6663; Al-Wasl Rd, Jumeirah) The clinic also has an emergency section.

General Medical Centre (Map pp216-17; ☎ 349 5959; 1st fl, Magrudy's Shopping Centre, Jumeirah Rd) The clinic also has an emergency section.

Manchester Clinic (Map pp216-17; ☎ 344 0300; Beach Centre, Jumeirah Rd) Just north of McDonald's.

MONEY
ATMs & Credit Cards

There are globally linked ATMs all over Dubai, at banks, shopping centres and at some of the hotels and hotel 'residences'. If you need an ATM in central Deira look for Emirates Bank International, which has a branch on **Baniyas Rd** (Map pp208-9), near Al-Khaleej Hotel; another on **Al-Maktoum Rd** (Map pp208-9), near the Metropolitan Palace Hotel; and another on **Al-Souq St** (Map pp212-13) in Bur Dubai. Its ATMs are tied into the Electron, Cirrus, Switch and Global Access systems. ATMs at branches of HSBC are linked to the Global Access system. You'll find one on **Baniyas Sq** (Map pp208-9) and another in Bur Dubai, near the **Moneychangers Souq** (Map pp212-13). The highest concentration of international banks is along Khalid bin al-Waleed Rd in Bur Dubai, east of Al-Mankhool Rd.

Visa, MasterCard and Amex are widely accepted at shops, hotels and restaurants throughout Dubai.

Changing Money

Don't exchange money at the airport; the rates are terrible. Once in the city, there is no shortage of banks and exchange houses. In central Deira, especially along Sikkat al-Khail St and around Baniyas Sq, every other building seems to contain a bank or a money-changer. In Bur Dubai there are plenty of moneychangers (though most of them only take cash and not travellers cheques) around the *abra* dock. Thomas Cook Al-Rostamani has a number of branches around the city, including one on **Sheikh Zayed Rd** (Map p218), south of the Crowne Plaza Hotel; on Al-Fahidi Rd in Bur Dubai; and on **Rd 14** (Map pp208-9) in Deira, near Al-Khaleej Hotel.

If you are changing more than US$250 it might pay to do a little shopping around. Moneychangers sometimes have better rates than banks, and some don't charge a commission. The problem with moneychangers is that some of them either will not take travellers cheques or will take one type only. Some places will only exchange travellers cheques if you can produce your original purchase receipt. If you don't have the receipt try asking for the manager.

Currencies of neighbouring countries are all recognised and easily changed with the exception of the Yemeni riyal.

American Express (Amex) is represented in Dubai by **Kanoo Travel** (Map pp214-15; ☎ 336 5000; Za'abeel Rd, Karama; ☿ 8.30am-1pm & 3-6.30pm Sat-Thu). The office is on the 1st floor of the Hermitage Building, next to the main post office. It won't cash travellers cheques but will hold mail for Amex clients. Address mail to: c/o American Express, Client's Mail, PO Box 290, Dubai, UAE.

Currency

The UAE dirham (Dh) is divided into 100 fils. Notes are produced in denominations of five, 10, 20, 50, 100, 200, 500 and 1000. There are Dh1, 50 fils, 25 fils, 10 fils and 5 fils coins (although the latter two are rarely

used today). A few years ago the government issued new coins, which are smaller than the old ones. Both types remain legal tender, but you should look at your change very closely as the new Dh1 coins are only slightly smaller than the old 50 fils coins. The coins only show the denomination in Arabic, so it's a great way to learn (turn to p189 for a table of Arabic numerals).

The UAE dirham is fully convertible and – for better or worse depending where you're coming from – pegged to the US dollar. See the Quick Reference page on the inside front cover for a list of exchange rates.

NEWSPAPERS & MAGAZINES

Gulf News, *Khaleej Times* and *Gulf Today*, all published in Dubai, are English-language newspapers. They cost Dh2 each and carry pretty much the same international news, though *Gulf News* is the best of an average bunch. Local news consists largely of 'business' stories, which are little more than recycled press releases masquerading as news. The local papers tend to have fairly comprehensive coverage of the Indian, Pakistani and Filipino political and entertainment scenes. *Gulf Business* (Dh15) is a glossy business magazine published locally, as is the English-language fashion and lifestyle magazine *Emirates Woman* (Dh15).

International newspapers and news magazines, such as the *International Herald Tribune* (Dh15) and the *Economist* (Dh28), are fairly easy to find in Dubai, although they are sometimes several days or a week out of date. Many newsagencies and bookshops sell Indian newspapers, such as *Malayalam Manorama* and the *Times of India* (Dh2 to Dh3).

The Arabic dailies are *Al-Bayan* (published in Dubai), *Al-Khaleej* and *Al-Ittihad* (both published in Abu Dhabi). Foreign newspapers are available in larger bookshops and hotels as well as Spinney's and Choithram's supermarkets.

Time Out Dubai is produced monthly and has decent listings and stories featuring upcoming events. It costs Dh10 although you'll find it free in Dubai's better hotel rooms. *What's On* (Dh10) is another listings monthly, although it's not as 'hip' as *Time Out Dubai*.

Connector, which is produced monthly, is aimed at Western expatriats and includes plenty of advertisements but useful listings pages in the green section at the back of the book.

POST

There are post boxes at most of the major shopping centres. There are also a number of fax and postal agencies dotted along the small streets around the Deira souqs and Bur Dubai Souq. Letters up to 20g cost Dh3 to Europe and most African countries; Dh3.50 to USA, Australia and the Far East; Dh2.50 to the subcontinent; Dh1.50 to Arab countries; and Dh1 within the Gulf. Double these rates for letters weighing 20g to 50g. For letters weighing 50g to 100g, rates to these destinations are about Dh13/11/9/6/4. Postcard rates are Dh2 to Europe, Africa, the USA, Australia and Asia; Dh1 to Arab countries; and 75 fils within the Gulf.

Parcels weighing between 500g and 1kg cost Dh68 to the USA, Australia and the Far East; Dh45 to Europe and Africa; Dh36 to the subcontinent; Dh34 to other Arab countries; and Dh23 within the Gulf. For parcels weighing between 1kg and 2kg, the rates to the these destinations are Dh130/85/68/64/45. Rates for surface mail are roughly half those for airmail. Here are the most useful post offices in Dubai:

Al-Musalla post office (Map pp212-13; Al-Fahidi Roundabout, Bur Dubai; 🕑 8am-1pm & 4-7pm Sat-Thu)

Al-Rigga post office (Map pp210-11; near the Clock Tower Roundabout; 🕑 8am-1pm & 4-7pm Sat-Thu)

Deira post office (Map pp208-9; Al-Sabkha Rd; 🕑 8am-midnight Sat-Wed, 8am-1pm & 4-8pm Thu) Near the intersection with Baniyas Rd.

Main post office (Map pp214-15; Za'abeel Rd; 🕑 8am-11.30pm Sat-Wed, 8am-10pm Thu, 8am-noon Fri) On the Bur Dubai side of the Creek in Karama. Has a philatelic bureau.

Satwa post office (Al-Satwa Rd; 🕑 8am-1pm & 4-7pm Sat-Thu)

Mail generally takes around a week to 10 days to reach Europe or the USA and eight to 15 days to reach Australia. There does not, however, seem to be any way of tracing packages that have gone missing. Mumtaz Speed Post is available at post offices (Dh100 to send a letter to Australia). If you need to send something in a hurry it will cost you half as much to use a courier company, and it will come and collect the package from you. Recommended courier agencies:

Aramex (☎ 286 5000)

DHL (☎ 800 4004)

FedEx (☎ 800 4050)

Poste restante facilities are not available in Dubai. As the local postal service doesn't at present deliver to residential properties, most residents get their mail posted via the post office box of their place of work. There are plans to introduce a mail delivery service in the near future. The Amex office will hold mail for Amex clients (see p180). If you are staying at a five-star hotel, the reception desk will usually hold letters and small packages for two or three days prior to your arrival. It's a good idea to mark these 'Guest in Hotel' and, to be sure, 'Hold for Arrival'.

RADIO

The emirate's English-language radio station, Dubai FM, is at 92FM, while Ajman's Channel 4FM (also English-language) is on 104.8FM. Both have DJs playing mainstream chart music alongside occasional speciality music programmes featuring classical pieces or country and western tunes. Emirates FM's music station, EFM1 is at 104.1FM and 100.5FM, and carries much of the same music and style as the others, while EFM2 at 99.3FM and 106FM tends towards a mix of news and talk shows. The music played on these stations used to be a bit stale – endless classic rock – but now they've discovered urban music things have changed a little. Generally on Wednesday, Thursday and Friday night you can hear cutting-edge dance music.

It's worth searching through the dial as there are stations playing Hindi, Arabic and Indian regional music, as well as stations where you can hear recitations of the Quran – very soothing when you're stuck in Dubai's horrific traffic.

SAFETY

On the whole, Dubai is a very safe city, but you should exercise the same sort of caution with your personal safety as you would anywhere. One very real danger in Dubai is the bad driving (see the boxed text Motoring

Mayhem on p171). We don't recommend that you swim, water-ski or jet-ski in the Creek. The tides in the Gulf are not strong enough to flush the Creek out on a regular basis so it is not a clean waterway, despite what the tourist authorities might tell you. Also, be careful when swimming in the open sea. Despite the small surf, currents can be very strong and drownings are not uncommon.

TAXES & REFUNDS

When people say there is 'no tax' in Dubai, what they are referring to is the fact that there is no tax on incomes in Dubai – at this time. Prices for most goods are generally cheaper as there is less tax on goods before they arrive in shops. Prices on many items in Dubai's shops are cheaper than at Dubai Duty Free and there is no tax refund that applies when you depart.

TELEPHONE

The UAE has an efficient telecommunications system. Calls within Dubai Emirate, not including Hatta, are free of charge. The state telecommunications monopoly is held by **Etisalat** (Map pp208-9; cnr Baniyas & Omar ibn al-Khattab Rds; ☽ 24hr), recognisable by the giant, white golf ball on top of its headquarters. There is another office in **Al-Khaleej Shopping Centre** (Map pp212-13; Al-Mankhool Rd).

If you need to make a call from the airport, there are telephones at the far end of the baggage-claim area. Some of the lounges at the gates in the departures area also have phones from which you can make free local calls. Coin phones have almost completely been taken over by cardphones. Phonecards are available in denominations of Dh30 from various places including grocery stores, supermarkets and petrol stations – do not buy them from street vendors as they are often 'recycled' and don't work. Note that there are two phonecards, one for cardphones and ones for mobile phones operating on the Wasel Global System of Mobile Communications (GSM) service.

To phone another country from the UAE, dial ☎ 00, followed by the country code. If you want to call the UAE, the country code is ☎ 971. The area code for Dubai is ☎ 04, although if you are calling from outside the UAE you drop the zero.

There are Home Country Direct services to 43 countries. Dialling these codes connects you directly to an operator in the country being called. A list of access codes to these countries is in the Etisalat Services section of the phone book.

Call Charges

The following are some direct-dial rates per minute from the UAE:

To	Peak (Dh)	Off-peak (Dh)
Australia	2.69	1.91
Canada	2.12	1.37
France	2.12	1.37
Germany	2.12	1.37
India	2.40	1.89
Japan	2.95	2.43
Netherlands	2.12	1.37
UK	2.69	1.91
USA	2.12	1.37

There is a complete list of call rates in the green pages section at the back of the Dubai phone book. The off-peak rates apply from 9pm to 7am every day and all day on Friday and national holidays. Note that direct-dial calls are much cheaper than operator-assisted calls.

Faxes

Most Etisalat offices are equipped to send and receive faxes. They may ask for a local address and contact number before they'll send a fax. The service is fairly good and it costs about Dh10 per page to most international destinations. Most typing and photocopying shops also have fax machines you can use. You'll find the highest concentration of these just north of the Clock Tower Roundabout on Abu Baker al-Siddiq Rd.

Mobile Phone

Mobile numbers begin with 050 in the UAE. Often people will give their seven-digit mobile number without mentioning this prefix as mobiles have become the standard means of communication in Dubai.

If you don't have a worldwide roaming service and want to use your mobile phone in Dubai, you can buy a prepaid SIM card from Etisalat. This Wasel GSM service costs Dh185 and includes the SIM card and Dh10 free credit. Recharge cards are available in denominations of Dh30 from grocery stores, supermarkets and petrol stations – and once again do not buy them from street vendors.

The UAE has introduced Wireless Application Protocol (WAP) services, which is available to Wasel GSM users as well as to normal UAE-based GSM subscribers. All you need to do is dial 125 and follow the instructions. Details on actually setting up access is available from Etisalat (www.etisalat .co.ae). Once you have done this, as long as you have credit on the Wasel account, WAP services are available.

TELEVISION

Channel 33 shows an English-language film and a couple of American sitcoms most days of the week, as well as news in English. It can be picked up on 33 UHF. Dubai TV, the Arabic channel, features religious and educational programmes as well as the occasional variety show or drama serial from Egypt or Lebanon. It can be picked up on 2 and 10 VHF or 30, 38 or 41 UHF. The Dubai Business Channel covers business around the world with a particular focus on business in Asia and the Middle East. It broadcasts continuously from 6pm until 2pm the next day.

Most hotels, even the smaller ones, have satellite TV. This usually consists of the standard package of four channels from Hong Kong–based Star TV: a music video channel, a sports channel, a movie channel and the BBC World Service. There may also be one or two Indian or Pakistani services (Zee TV/PTV) and sometimes one or more of the Arabic satellite services (MBC, Dubai Satellite Channel, Nilesat, ART).

TIME (GMT)

Dubai is four hours ahead of GMT. The time does not change during the summer. Not taking daylight saving into account, when it's noon in Dubai, the time elsewhere is:

City	Time
Auckland	8pm
Hong Kong, Perth	4pm
London	8am
Los Angeles	midnight
New York	3am
Paris, Rome	9am
Sydney	6pm

TIPPING

Tips are not generally expected since a service charge is added to your bill (this goes to the restaurant, however, not to the waiter). If you want to leave a tip, 5% to 10% is sufficient for good service.

TOILETS

The best advice is to go when you have the opportunity. The very few public toilets on the streets are usually only for men. Public toilets in shopping centres, museums, restaurants and hotels are Western style and are generally well maintained. On an excursion outside Dubai you might have to contend with 'hole in the ground' loos at the back of restaurants or petrol stations.

TOURIST INFORMATION
Local Tourist Offices

Dubai's **Department of Tourism & Commerce Marketing** (DTCM; ☎ 223 0000; www.dubaitourism .co.ae) is the official tourism board of the Dubai government. It is also the sole regulating, planning and licensing authority for the tourist industry in Dubai. It has three main welcome bureaus (as well as the smaller offices also listed here) that you can call for information or for help in booking hotels, tours and car hire: airport arrivals area (just after customs, on your left), Baniyas Sq and way down Sheikh Zayed Rd on the way to Abu Dhabi (around 40km out of Dubai). The quality of information they give largely depends on the enthusiasm of the person behind the desk but things are getting more professional.

Airport (Map pp210-11; ☎ 224 5252/224 4098; ⓨ 24hr)

Baniyas Sq (Map pp208-9; ☎ 228 5000; ⓨ 9am-11pm)

BurJuman Centre (Map pp212-13; ☎ 352 0003; ⓨ 10am-10pm)

Deira City Centre (Map pp210-11; ☎ 294 8615; ⓨ 10am-10pm)

Sheikh Zayed Rd (☎ 883 3397; ⓨ 9am-9pm)

Wafi City Mall (Map pp214-15; ☎ 324 0499; ⓨ 10am-10pm)

The Dubai National Travel & Tourist Authority (DNATA) is the quasi-official travel agency in Dubai; it has the monopoly on travel services at wholesale level. The **DNATA** head office (Map pp210-11; ☎ 295 1111; Al-Maktoum Rd, Deira) is at the DNATA Airline Centre. There are other branches opening around the city.

Tourist Offices Abroad

The DTCM has a number of branches overseas that are vigorously promoting Dubai as an upmarket tourist destination. Those listed below service their surrounding regions. These branches go by the name of the Dubai Tourism & Commerce Promotion Board:

Australia (☎ 02-9956 6620; dtcm_aus@dubaitourism.ae; Level 6, 75 Miller St, North Sydney, NSW 2060)

France (☎ 01 44 95 85 00; dtcm-france@dubai.fr; 15 bis, rue de Marignan, 75008 Paris)

Germany (☎ 069-710 0020; dtcm_ge@dubaitourism.ae; Bockenheimer Landstrasse 23 D_60325, Frankfurt-am-Main)

Hong Kong (☎ 2827 5221; dtcm_hk@dubaitourism.ae; 19th fl, 148 Electric Rd, North Point)

India (☎ 022-2283 3497/2283 7765; dtcm_in@dubai tourism.ae; 51 Bajaj Bhavan, 5th fl, Nariman Point, Mumbai 400 021)

Italy (☎ 02 8691 3952; dtcm_it@dubaitourism.ae; Foro Buonaparte, 70, 20121, Milan)

Japan (☎ 03 3379 9311; dtcm_ja@dubaitourism.ae; 4th fl, One-Win Yoyogi Bldg 3-35-10, Yoyogi, Shibuya-ku, Tokyo 151-0053)

Russia (☎ 095-933 67 17; dtcm_cis@dubaitourism.ae; Philippovskiy pereulok, 13, bldg 1 - Office 201, 119019, Moscow)

South Africa (☎ 011 785 4600; dtcm_sa@dubaitourism .ae; 51 Orchard Lane, PO Box 698, Rivonia 2128 Johannesburg)

Sweden (☎ 08 411 11 35; dtcm_sca@dubaitourism.ae; Skeppsbron 30, SE-111 30, Stockholm)

Switzerland (☎ 043 255 44 44; dtcm_ch@dubaitourism .ae; Schaffhauserstrasse 121, CH-8302 Kloten-Zürich)

UK (☎ 020-7839 0580; dtcm_uk@dubaitourism.ae; 125 Pall Mall, London SW1Y 5EA, UK)

USA (☎ 215 751 9750; dtcm_usa@dubaitourism.ae; 8 Penn Center, Philadelphia PA 19103, USA)

VISAS

To visit Dubai your passport must have at least two months validity left from your date of arrival. Visit visas valid for 60 days are available on arrival in the UAE at approved ports of entry, including all airports and ports, for citizens of most developed countries. These include all Western European countries (except Malta and Cyprus), Australia, Brunei, Canada, Hong Kong, Japan, Malaysia, New Zealand, Singapore, South Korea and the USA. Tourist visas are valid for 60 days despite the fact that the stamp on your passport, which is in Arabic, says it is valid for 30 days. Perhaps this will change when immigration officials are issued with the new stamps. No fee is charged for tourist visas.

Citizens of other Gulf Cooperative Council (GCC) countries do not need visas to enter the UAE, and can stay pretty much as long as they want. For citizens of other countries, a transit or tourist visa must be arranged through a sponsor. This can be a hotel, a company or a resident of the UAE. Most hotels charge a fee for arranging a visa of around Dh100.

Officially, you will be denied entry if your passport shows any evidence of travel to Israel, although we've heard from several travellers who report that in practice this isn't an issue.

For up-to-date visa information, follow the links on Lonely Planet's website at www.lonelyplanet.com/subwwway.

Visa Extensions

Visit visas can be extended once for 30 days by the **Department of Immigration and Naturalisation** (Map pp214-15; ☎ 398 1010; Sheikh Khalifa bin Zayed Rd), near the Za'abeel Roundabout, for Dh500 and a fair amount

Vis-à-vis Oman

Coming from Dubai, many nationalities can enter Oman without visa charges if they have tourist visas or entry stamps issued by Dubai authorities. They are also free to depart for, or return from, a third destination through land or air facilities in either country. If you are visiting Oman on a tourist visa, these same nationalities can enter the UAE by land, air or sea without visa charges. The latest information on this arrangement is available from the Royal Oman Police website (www.rop.gov.om).

of paperwork. You may be asked to provide proof of funds.

For longer periods, you have to leave the country and come back to get a new stamp. People have been known to stay in Dubai for a year or more simply by flying out to Bahrain, Doha or Kish (an island off the Iranian coast) every two months and picking up a new visa on return at a total cost of about Dh400 per trip. Due to a fatal aeroplane accident at Sharjah, which involved people returning from a 'visa run', this requirement was being reviewed at the time of research.

Visas can only be extended in the city or emirate you arrived in, so if you landed in Sharjah you can't get your visa extended in Dubai.

WOMEN TRAVELLERS
Attitudes Towards Women

In general, Dubai is one of the best locations in the Middle East for women travellers. Checking into hotels is not usually a problem, though unaccompanied women might want to think twice about taking a room in some of the budget hotels in Deira and Bur Dubai. They are renowned for accommodating prostitutes from the Commonwealth of Independent States (CIS) and Africa, and you may run the risk of being mistaken for one.

Although things might be better in Dubai than in other parts of the Gulf, it does not mean that some of the problems that accompany travel in the Middle East will not arise here as well, such as unwanted male attention and long, lewd stares. You may be beeped at by men in passing cars, but most times these are taxi drivers touting for business. Try not to be intimidated; it helps to retain a sense of humour.

Safety Precautions

Dubai is a very liberal place and people here are used to Western women. While it is liberal, try to dress conservatively if you will be among local Emiratis.

It's once you're out of Dubai that you might encounter a different attitude. Don't wear tight or revealing clothes. Women should always sit in the back seat of taxis. You'll find that you'll often be asked to take the front seat in buses or be asked to sit next to other women. This is so you can avoid the embarrassment of men's stares.

In banks, Etisalat offices, post offices and libraries there are usually separate sections or windows for women – great when there's a queue. In small Arab and Indo-Pakistani restaurants you will often be ushered into the 'family room'. You don't have to sit here but the room is there to save you from being stared at by men.

Useful Organisations

The green pages at the back of *Connector* magazine list a variety of cultural and social groups, from gardening clubs to support groups for single mothers. Listed here are some of the larger organisations which women travellers may find useful.

American Women's Association (☎ 050 768 8657) This is a 300 member–strong social and philanthropic club, which meets once a month. Sporting activities and outings are also arranged. You can only become a full member if you or your spouse has a US passport or green card; a number of associate memberships are also available.

Dubai & Sharjah Women's Guild (☎ 394 5331) This is a social group of predominantly Western women who meet twice a month to hear a guest speaker or to go on an excursion. It's also a fundraising organisation that donates to various local and overseas charities.

German Women's Club (☎ 050 444 5709; dfk_dubai@ yahoo.de) This is a club for German-speaking women in Dubai. Similar to the American Women's Association, it puts on social events and provides support to members.

International Business Women's Group (☎ 345 2282; ibwg_dxb@emirates.net.ae) With over 200 members, this is a networking support group for women in the UAE who are in senior management or who own their own companies. It meets on the second Monday of each month and is open to all nationalities.

WORK

You can prearrange work in the UAE, but if you enter the country on a visit visa and then find work, you will have to leave the country for one day and re-enter under your employer's sponsorship.

If you have arranged work in Dubai you will enter the country on a visit visa sponsored by your employer while your residence visa is processed. This process involves a blood test for HIV/AIDS and lots of paperwork. Those on a residence visa who are sponsored by a spouse, who is in turn sponsored by an employer, are not officially permitted to work. This rule is often broken and it is possible to find work in the public or private sector. If you are in this situation, remember that your spouse, and not the company you work for, is your sponsor. One effect of this is that you may only be able to apply for a tourist visa to another Gulf Arab country with a consent letter from your spouse. In some cases you will need to be accompanied by your spouse who has company sponsorship. Similarly, if you want to apply for a driving licence you will also need a consent letter from your spouse.

If you obtain your residence visa through an employer and then quit because you've found something better, you may find yourself under a six-month ban from working in the UAE. This rule is designed to stop people from job hopping.

If you are employed in Dubai and have any work-related problems you can call the **Ministry of Labour Helpline** (☎ 269 1666) for advice.

Finding Work

While plenty of people turn up in Dubai on a visit visa, decide they like the look of the place and then scout around for a job, this isn't really the most effective way to go about it. Employers in Dubai and the UAE in general are fond of people with qualifications – it's of little consequence which higher learning establishment you attended, it's of lesser importance than the paper it's written on. Teachers, nurses and those in engineering are highly valued in Dubai and very well paid.

The *Khaleej Times* and the *Gulf News* publish employment supplements several times a week. When you find a job, you will be offered an employment contract written in English and Arabic. Get the one in Arabic translated before you sign it. Besides the recruitment agencies listed below, there's an extensive list on the Web at www.godubai .com/citylife/empagencies.asp.

Business Aid Centre (☎ 337 5747; www.bacdubai.com; PO Box 8743, Dubai)

Clarendon Parker (☎ 331 1702; www.clarendonparker .com; PO Box 26359, Dubai)

SOS Recruitment Consultants (☎ 396 5600; www.sos .co.ae; PO Box 6948, Dubai)

Language

Language

It's true – anyone can speak another language. Don't worry if you haven't studied languages before or that you studied a language at school for years and can't remember any of it. It doesn't even matter if you failed English grammar. After all, that's never affected your ability to speak English! And this is the key to picking up a language in another country. You just need to start speaking.

Learn a few key Arabic phrases before you go. Write them on pieces of paper and stick them on the fridge, by the bed or even on the computer – anywhere that you'll see them often.

You'll find that locals appreciate travellers trying to speak Arabic, no matter how muddled you may think you sound. So don't just stand there, say something!

SOCIAL
Meeting People
Hello.
al-salaam alaykum
Hello. (response)
wa alaykum e-salaam
Welcome.
ahlan wa sahlan/marHaba
Goodbye.
fl'man ullah or ma'al salaama
Goodbye. (response)
(to a man) alla ysalmak
(to a woman) alla ysalmich
Goodbye.
(to a man) Hayyaakallah
(to a woman) Hayyachallah
Goodbye. (response)
(to a man) alla yHai'eek
(to a woman) alla yHai'eech
Please.
(to a man) min fadhlak
(to a woman) min fadhlich
Thank you (very much).
mashkur (woo ma ghasart)
You're welcome.
al-afu
Excuse me.
(to a man) lau tismaH
(to a woman) lau tismaHin
Yes.
aiwa/na'am
No.
la'
Do you speak English?
titkallam ingleezi?
Do you understand (me)?
Hal bitifhaam (alay)?
I understand.
(by a man) ana fahim
(by a woman) ana fahma

I don't understand.
(by a man) ana mu fahim
(by a woman) ana mu fahma

Could you please ...?
mumkin min fadhlak ...?

repeat that	a'id Hatha
speak more slowly	takalam shwai shwai
write it down	iktbHa lee

Going Out
What's on ...?
maza yaHdos ...?

locally	mahaleeyan
this weekend	fee nihayet Hatha alesboo'a
today	al-yom
tonight	al-layla

Where are the ...?
wayn el ...?

clubs	nawadi al-layleeya
gay venues	amaken el-gay
places to eat	maHalat al-aakl
pubs	bar/khamarat

Is there a local entertainment guide?
Hal yoojad kitab daleel mahalee leel Hafalat?

PRACTICAL
Question Words

Who?	mnu?
What?	shnu?
When?	mata?
Where?	wayn?
How?	chayf?
How many?	cham?

Numbers & Amounts

0	sifr
1	waHid
2	ithneen
3	thalatha
4	arba'a
5	khamsa
6	sitta
7	sab'a
8	thimania
9	tis'a
10	ashra
11	Hda'ash
12	thna'ash
13	thalathta'ash
14	arba'ata'ash
15	khamista'ash
16	sitta'ash
17	sabi'ta'ash
18	thimanta'ash
19	tisi'ta'ash
20	'ishreen
21	waHid wa 'ishreen
22	ithneen wa 'ishreen
23	thalatha wa 'ishreen
30	thalatheen
40	arbi'een
50	khamseen
60	sitteen
70	saba'een
80	thimaneen
90	tis'een
100	imia
101	imia w-aHid
102	imia wa-ithneen
103	imia wa-thalatha
200	imiatain
300	thalatha imia
1000	alf
2000	alfayn
3000	thalath-alaf

Days

Monday	yom al-ithneen
Tuesday	yom al-thalath
Wednesday	yom al-arbaa'
Thursday	yom al-khamis
Friday	yom al-jama'a
Saturday	yom as-sabt
Sunday	yom al-Had

Banking

I want to ...
ana areed an ...

cash a cheque
asref el-chek
change money
asref beezat
change some travellers cheques
asref chekat siyaHeeya

Where's the nearest ...?
wayn aghrab ...?
    automatic teller machine (ATM)
    alet saref/sarraf alee
    foreign exchange office
    maktab al-serafa

Post

Where is the post office?
wayn maktab el-bareed?

I want to send a ...
ana areed an arsell an ...

fax	faks
parcel	barsell/ta'rd
postcard	beetaga bareediya/kart

I want to buy ...
ana areed an ashtaree ...

an aerogram	reesala jaweeya
an envelope	zaref
a stamp	tab'eh bareed

Phones & Mobiles

I want to buy a (phone card).
ana areed ashtaree (beetaget Hatef/
   kart telefon)

I want to make a call (to ...)
ana areed an atsell (bee ...)
I want to make a reverse-charge/collect call.
ana areed taHweel kulfet al-mukalama ila
   al-mutagee

Where can I find a/an ...?
wayn mumkin an ajed ...?
I'd like a/an ...
ana areed ...
   adaptor plug
   maakhaz tawseel
   charger for my phone
   shaHen leel Hatef
   mobile/cell phone for hire
   mobail ('mobile') leel ajar
   prepaid mobile/cell phone
   mobail moos baq aldaf'
   SIM card for your network
   seem kart lee shabaket al-itsalaat

Internet

Where's the local Internet café?
wayn magHa al-internet?

I'd like to ...
ana abga an ...
check my email	chayk al-emayl malee
get online	ahsaal ala khat internet

Transport

When does the ... leave?
mata yamshi ...
When does the ... arrive?
mata yusal ... (m)
boat	il-markab
train	il-qittar

mata tusal ... (f)
bus	il-bas
plane	il-tayara

What time's the ... bus?
mata ... bas?
first	awal
last	akhar

What time's the next bus?
mata il-bas al-thani?
Are you free? (taxi)
anta fathee?
Please put the meter on.
lau samaHt shagal al-addad
How much is it to ...?
bcham la ...?
Please take me to (this address).
lau samaHt wasalni la (Hadha elonwan)

FOOD

breakfast	futtoor
lunch	ghadha
dinner	asha
snack	akal khafif

eat	kol
drink	ishrab

Can you recommend a ...
mumkin an tansaHanee ala ...?
bar/pub	baar
café	magha
restaurant	mata'am

Is service/cover charge included in the bill?
Hal al-fattoora tashmole al-khadma aidan?

For more detailed information on eating and dining out, see 'Eating' on p67.

EMERGENCIES

It's an emergency!
Halet isa'af!
Could you please help me/us?
mumkin an toosaadnee min fadhlak?
Call the (police/a doctor/an ambulance)!
etasell bil (shurta/tabeeb/sayyaret al-isa'af)!
Where's the police station?
wayn marekaz al-shurta?

HEALTH

Where's the nearest ...?
wayn aghrab ...?
chemist (night)	saydalee (laylee)
dentist	tabeeb asnan
doctor	tabeeb
hospital	mustashfa

Symptoms

I have (a) ...
ana andee ...
diarrhoea	is-haal
fever	sukhoona
headache	suda or waja' ras
pain	alam/waja'

Glossary

This glossary contains a list of Arabic terms that you may hear on your travels through Dubai. For terms of foods you'll commonly find in the city, check out the Lebanese Food Lingo 101 (p15) and Persian Plates (p16) boxed texts.

abeyya – woman's full-length black robe
abra – small, flat-decked boat; water taxi
agal – headropes used to hold a *gutra* in place
areesh – palm fronds used to construct houses

attar – perfume
ayyalah – Bedouin dance
azan – call to prayer

baggara – traditional pearling boat
baglah – large *dhow* used for long-distance journeys
baiti – romantic Arabic poetry style
barasti – traditional Gulf method of building palm-leaf houses; house built with palm leaves
bateel – large *dhow* used for long-distance journeys
boom – large *dhow* used for long-distance journeys
burj – tower

dalla – traditional copper coffeepot
dhow – traditional sailing vessel of the Gulf
dishdasha – man's shirt-dress

falaj – traditional irrigation channel

galalif – dhow builder
gutra – white headcloth

habban – Arabian bagpipes
haj – Muslim pilgrimage to Mecca
halal – meat from animals killed according to Islamic law
hammam – bathhouse
hamour – common species of fish found in Gulf waters
haram – forbidden by Islamic law
hawala – written order of payment
housh – courtyard

imam – prayer leader, Muslim cleric

jasr – drum covered with goatskin, which is slung around the neck and hit with sticks
jebel – hill, mountain

kandoura – casual shirt-dress worn by men and women
khaleeji – traditional Gulf-style music
khanjar – traditional curved dagger
khor – inlet or creek

liwa – traditional dance performed to a rapid tempo and loud drumbeat; it is usually sung in Swahili and most likely brought to the Gulf by East African slaves
luban – frankincense

majlis – formal meeting room or reception area
Majlis – parliament
manior – percussion instrument of a belt decorated with dried goat hooves
masayf – traditional summer house incorporating a *wind tower*

mashait – traditional winter house incorporating a courtyard
masjid – mosque
mathaf – museum
mihrab – niche in a mosque indicating the direction of Mecca
mimzar – oboelike instrument
mina – port
Muallaqat – collection of pre-Islamic Arabic odes
muezzin – mosque official who sings the *azan*
mullah – Muslim scholar, teacher or religious leader

nabati – Arabic vernacular poetry

qibla – the direction of Mecca, indicated in a mosque by the *mihrab*

Ramadan – Muslim month of fasting

sambuq – boat mainly used for fishing
shasha – small fishing boat made of palm fronds
sheesha – tall, glass-bottomed smoking implement; also called a water pipe or hubble-bubble
sheikh – venerated religious scholar, tribal chief, ruler or elderly man worthy of respect
sheikha – daughter of a *sheikh*
somok – wooden incense

tafila – prose-style Arabic poetry
tamboura – harplike instrument with five horse-gut strings that are plucked with sheep horns
Trucial States – former name of the United Arab Emirates; also called Trucial Coast, Trucial Oman and Trucial Sheikdoms

wind tower – architectural feature of *masayf* houses designed to keep the house cool
wudu – practice of ritual washing before daily prayer
wusta – influence gained by way of connections in high places

Behind the Scenes

THE LONELY PLANET STORY

The story begins with a classic travel adventure: Tony and Maureen Wheeler's 1972 journey across Europe and Asia to Australia. There was no useful information about the overland trail then, so Tony and Maureen published the first Lonely Planet guidebook to meet a growing need.

From a kitchen table, Lonely Planet has grown to become the largest independent travel publisher in the world, with offices in Melbourne (Australia), Oakland (USA), London (UK) and Paris (France).

Today Lonely Planet guidebooks cover the globe. There is an ever-growing list of books and information in a variety of media. Some things haven't changed. The main aim is still to make it possible for adventurous travellers to get out there – to explore and better understand the world.

At Lonely Planet we believe travellers can make a positive contribution to the countries they visit – if they respect their host communities and spend their money wisely.

THIS BOOK

This edition was written by Terry Carter and Lara Dunston. The previous (2nd) edition was revised and updated by Richard Plunkett. The 1st edition was researched and written by Lou Callan. This guide was commissioned in Lonely Planet's Melbourne office, and produced by:

Commissioning Editors Will Gourlay & Emma Koch
Coordinating Editor Helen Christinis
Coordinating Cartographer Daniel Fennessy
Coordinating Layout Designer Pablo Gastar
Editor David Andrew
Cartographers Karen Fry & Chris Thomas
Layout Designers Tamsin Wilson & Jacqui Saunders
Cover Designer Wendy Wright
Series Designer Nic Lehman
Series Design Concept Nic Lehman & Andrew Weatherill
Managing Cartographer Shahara Ahmed
Mapping Development Paul Piaia
Project Manager Eoin Dunlevy
Language Editor Quentin Frayne
Regional Publishing Manager Kate Cody
Series Publishing Manager Gabrielle Green

Thanks to Jennifer Garrett, Melanie Dankel & Martine Lleonart

Cover photographs The Burj Al Arab, Neil Setchfield/Lonely Planet Images (top); Deira Gold Souq, Walter Bibikow/Photolibrary (bottom); man drinking coffee at Heritage Village, Shindagha, Phil Weymouth/Lonely Planet Images (back).

Internal photographs by Phil Weymouth/Lonely Planet Images except for the following:

p21, p152, p163 Chris Mellor/Lonely Planet Images; p154 Christine Osborne/Lonely Planet Images; p157 Clint Lucas/Lonely Planet Images; p159 Guy Moberley/Lonely Planet Images.

THANKS
TERRY CARTER & LARA DUNSTON

A big thanks to the following people for their time and advice for this book: Dimitri, Hadia, Latifa and the Emirati fashionistas, Luca, Noel and Roberto. A big thank you to Will from LP for his book-juggling skills over the past few months. And finally, thanks to everyone in Dubai who thought we were being particularly nosy, but were too polite to ask what the hell we were doing.

PHIL WEYMOUTH

The photos in this book would have not been possible without the wonderful assistance of Sue Ann Miller and Maher Jelfar, both from the Government of Dubai's Department of Tourism & Commerce Marketing, and Eddie Lim. Thanks to all of you.

OUR READERS

Many thanks to the travellers who used the last edition and wrote to us with helpful hints, useful advice and interesting anecdotes. Your names follow:

SEND US YOUR FEEDBACK

We love to hear from travellers – your comments keep us on our toes and help make our books better. Our well-travelled team reads every word on what you loved or loathed about this book. Although we cannot reply individually to postal submissions, we always guarantee that your feedback goes straight to the appropriate authors, in time for the next edition. Each person who sends us information is thanked in the next edition – and the most useful submissions are rewarded with a free book.

To send us your updates – and find out about LP events, newsletters and travel news – visit our award-winning website: www.lonelyplanet.com.

Note: We may edit, reproduce and incorporate your comments in Lonely Planet products such as guide-books, websites and digital products, so let us know if you don't want your comments reproduced or your name acknowledged. For a copy of our privacy policy visit www.lonelyplanet.com/privacy.

Sven Berger, Jacqueline Black, Philip Bowell, Ken & Rosemary Brooks, JW Byron, Burt Candy, Magdalena Dral, John Lee Fagence, Brian Furner, Dede Ghiradi, M Harris, Peter Hore, Trygve & Karen Inda, Lin Lee, Thorsten Luttger, Astrid & Heidi Marshall, Nick Massey, Rachel Metcalfe, Rolf Palmberg, Prakash Parmar, Simon Peters, Ceri Powell, Henryk Sadura, Carla Santos, Beate Schamhl, Maggie Seeliger, Guelsah Taskin, Miquel Trujillo, Shabnam Walji.

Notes

Notes

Notes

Index

See also the separate indexes for Eating (p203), Shopping (p203) and Sleeping (p204).

000 map pages
000 photographs

Index

000 map pages
000 photographs

MAP LEGEND

ROUTES

Tollway	One-Way Street
Freeway	Unsealed Road
Primary Road	Mall/Steps
Secondary Road	Tunnel
Tertiary Road	Walking Tour
Lane	Walking Tour Detour
Under Construction	Walking Trail
Track	Walking Path
Emirate-Route	Dubai-Route

TRANSPORT

Ferry	Rail
Bus Route	Cable Car, Funicular

HYDROGRAPHY

River, Creek	Canal
Intermittent River	Water
Swamp	Lake (Dry)
	Lake (Salt)

BOUNDARIES

International	Regional, Suburb
State, Provincial	Ancient Wall
Disputed	Cliff

AREA FEATURES

Airport	Cemetery, Christian
Area of Interest	Cemetery, Other
Beach, Desert	Land
Building, Featured	Mall
Building, Information	Park
Building, Other	Sports
Building, Transport	Urban

POPULATION

CAPITAL (NATIONAL)	**CAPITAL (STATE)**
Large City	**Medium City**
Small City	Town, Village

SYMBOLS

Sights/Activities	Drinking	Information
Beach	Drinking	Bank, ATM
Castle, Fortress	Café	Embassy/Consulate
Christian	**Entertainment**	Hospital, Medical
Hindu	Entertainment	Information
Jewish	**Shopping**	Internet Facilities
Islamic	Shopping	Police Station
Monument	**Sleeping**	Post Office, GPO
Museum, Gallery	Sleeping	Telephone
Ruin	**Transport**	
Sikh	Airport, Airfield	**Geographic**
Swimming Pool	Border Crossing	Lookout
Zoo, Bird Sanctuary	Bus Station	Mountain, Volcano
Eating	Parking Area	National Park
Eating	Taxi Rank	Oasis

Map Section

A B C D

1

THE
GULF

2

SIGHTS & ACTIVITIES (pp45–60)
Al-Boom Tourist Village................................1 F3
Al-Mamzar Park..2 H2
Arabian Adventures...............................(see 45)
Bounty Charters..(see 9)
Burj Al Arab...(see 31)
Dhow-Building Yard......................................3 F3
Dubai Camel Racecourse...............................4 E3
Dubai Country Club.......................................5 E4
Dubai Desert Extreme....................................6 F3
Dubai Equestrian Centre................................7 E4
Dubai Exiles Rugby Club................................8 E3
Dubai International Marine Club.....................9 A2
Dubai Road Runners..............................(see 21)
Dubai Water Sports Association.....................10 F3
Emirates Golf Club.......................................11 A2
Fatima Sports...12 C2
Formula One...(see 18)
Givenchy Spa...(see 40)
Jumeirah Beach Hotel..................................13 C2
Jumeirah Beach Park....................................14 D2
Majlis Ghorfat Um-al-Sheef...........................15 D2
Montgomerie..16 A2
Mushrif Park...17 H5
Nad al-Sheba Club.......................................18 E4
One&Only Royal Mirage...............................19 A2
Pilates Studio..20 E2
Safa Park..21 D2
Total Arts...22 C2
Umm Suqeim Public Beach............................23 C2
Wild Wadi Waterpark...................................24 C2

EATING (pp67–86)
Al Mahara...(see 31)
Andiamo!..(see 33)

Apartment...(see 36)
BiCE...(see 34)
Celebrities...(see 40)
Chinese Kitchen.......................................(see 25)
Choithrams...25 D2
Colonnade...(see 36)
Der Keller...(see 36)
Eauzone...(see 40)
Fusion..(see 38)
Go West...(see 36)
Indochine...(see 33)
La Baie...(see 41)
La Parilla...(see 36)
Marina Seafood
    Market...(see 36)
Nina's..(see 40)
Ossigeno..(see 38)
Peppercrab...(see 33)
Prime Rib...(see 38)
Retro...(see 37)
Safestway...26 E2
Spinney's..27 D2
Tagine..(see 40)
Union Co-op Society...............................(see 25)
Venezia..28 D2
Zheng He's..(see 39)

DRINKING (pp90–5)
Apartment...(see 36)
Bahri Bar...(see 39)
Barasti Bar...(see 37)
Kasbar...(see 40)
Rooftop Bar...(see 40)
Skyview Bar..(see 31)
Uptown...(see 13)

ENTERTAINMENT (pp87–98)
Al-Areesh Restaurant.................................(see 1)
Grand Cineplex.......................................(see 33)
Mix...(see 33)
Reem Al Bawadi..29 D2
Shisha Courtyard.....................................(see 19)

SHOPPING (pp117–34)
Gold & Diamond Park..................................30 C2
Palm Lane Market...................................(see 21)

SLEEPING (pp135–48)
Burj Al Arab...31 C2
Dubai Youth Hostel.....................................32 H3
Grand Hyatt Dubai......................................33 F3
Hilton Dubai Jumeirah..................................34 A2
Jumeirah Beach Club.....................................35 C2
Jumeirah Beach Hotel...................................36 C2
Le Meridien Mina Seyahi Resort.....................37 A2
Le Royal Meridien Beach Resort.....................38 A2
Mina A'Salam, Madinat
    Jumeirah...39 C2
One&Only Royal Mirage...............................40 A2
Ritz-Carlton..41 A2

TRANSPORT (pp168–9)
Lufthansa Airlines..42 D2
Wolfi's Bike Shop..43 D2

INFORMATION
Syrian Consulate...44 G2

OTHER
Emirates Holidays Building............................45 E2
Wollongong University..................................46 C2

0 |=========| 4 km
0 |=========| 2 miles

E   **F**   **G**   **H**

1

See Jumeirah Road Map (pp216–17)

See Bur Dubai (North) Map (pp212–13)

See Deira (North) Map (pp208–9)

Port Rashid

Al-Khaleej Rd

Hamriya Port

Al-Mamzar Park

Khor al-Mamzar

JUMEIRAH   **BUR DUBAI**   **DEIRA**   Corniche   2

Jumeirah Rd   **MANKHOOL**   **AL-MATEENA**   Public Beach   2

Al-Wasl Rd

SATWA   **AL-JAFILIYA**   **RIGGA**   **SHARJAH**

Sheikh Zayed Rd   Sheikh Khalifa bin Zayed Rd   **KARAMA**   **HOR AL-ANZ**

58A   26 20

See Sheikh Zayed Road Map (p218)

Interchange No 1   *Horse Racecourse*   Al-Khebisi Rd   Umm Hureir Rd   Banyas Rd   Al-Ittihad Rd   To Sharjah Art Museum (1km); Sharjah Cricket Stadium (1km); Ajman (15km); Umm al-Qaiwain (35km); Ras al-Khaimah (90km)   32

2nd Za'abeel Rd   **ZA'ABEEL**   *Creekside Park*   Airport Rd

See Bur Dubai (South) Map (pp214–15)   **AL-QUSAIS**

Dhine Rd   Oud Metha Rd   Al-Qataiyat Rd   33   6   See Deira (South) Map (pp210–11)

AL-MARQADH   **JADDAF**   1   **AL-GARHOUD**   Al-Twar Rd   Al-Nahda Rd   Baghdad Rd   3

Khor Dubai Wildlife & Waterbird Sanctuary   3   *Dubai International Airport*

Dubai Camel Racecourse   10   *Dubai Creek (Khor Dubai)*   *Dubai Festival City Site*   **AL-RAMOOL**   Rabat Rd   Beirut Rd

4   8

7   18   5   **RAS AL-KHOR**   *Cemetery*

NAD AL-SHEBA   Ras al-Khor Rd   Nadd al-Hamar Rd   **RASHIDIYA**   Ring Rd   Tunis Rd   4

Dubai Al-Ain Rd   Rabat Rd   **AL-MIZHAR**

MIRDIF   Al-Khawaneej Rd

AL-WARQAA   *Mushrif Park*   17   5

WARSAN   **AL-KHAWANEEJ**

Ring Rd   66   Al-Awir Rd   44

To Al Maha Desert Resort (40km); Al-Ain (105km)   To Big Red (25km); Sharjah Desert Park (32km); Hatta (70km); Fujairah (110km)   6

207

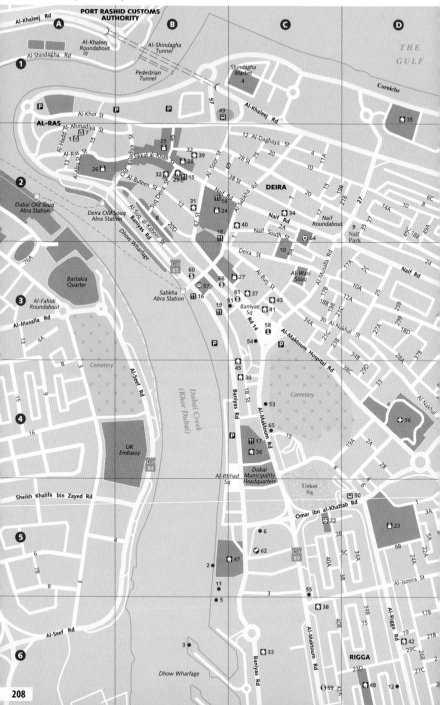

PORT RASHID CUSTOMS
AUTHORITY

Al-Khaleej Rd

A   **B**   **C**   **D**

Al-Khaleej Rd

Al-Khaleej Roundabout

Al-Shindagha Rd

1

Al-Shindagha Tunnel

Pedestrian Tunnel

Shindagha Market
4

THE GULF

Corniche

Al-Khor St

P   P   P

49

Al-Khaleej Rd

35

AL-RAS

Al-Ahmadiya St

7

Al-Hadd

1

15

12 Al-Daghaya St

25

Sikkat al-Khail St

32

39

28

DEIRA

4A
11A

20

10

15

2

Dubai Old Souq
Abra Station

Al-Ras St

Al-Buteen St

26

32

29

15

38 St

Al-Soor St

28 St

Al-Sabkha Rd

20

Deira Old Souq
Abra Station

Old Baladiya St

Naif St

14

34

Naif
Rd

Naif
Roundabout

19B
21B

27

14A

10

6C

Al-Suq al-Kabeer St

31

24

40

Naif South St
2A

64

9
35
37

Naif
Park

Al-Musalla Rd

Banyas Rd

18

Deira St

10

Al-Wasi
Souq

Al-Nakhal St

Naif Rd

24

45C 18B

49A

3

Al-Fahidi
Roundabout

85

60

66

27

Al-Burj St

17A

2C

10A

25

17B

18B

12A

27A

23B

29B

23B

18D

Sabkha
Abra Station

57

16

61

51

37

43

41

34A
30
34A

29C
2C

7A

28A

37B

Al-Musalla Rd

13   4A

8   3

Cemetery

Al-Seef Rd

19

Baniyas
Sq
Rd 1A

58

54

Al-Maktoum Hospital Rd

34B

38C
29D

33

4

15

9

16

Dubai Creek
(Khor Dubai)

Baniyas Rd

45

30

18 St

53

65

Cemetery

15

56

19A

2A

34B

Al-Nakhal St

UK
Embassy

84

17
36

Al-Maktoum Rd

Dubai
Municipality
Headquarters

2B

5

Sheikh Khalifa bin Zayed Rd

Al-Ittihad
Sq

Union
Sq

50

Omar Ibn al-Khattab Rd

22

23

1

3A

6   7B

4

6

62

85

40A

34A

5B

24A

5A
22A

8

3

2

47

11

40A

3B

Al-Jazeira St

5

3

55

38

34B

15

40B

17B

42

21B

6

Al-Seef Rd

Dhow Wharfage

3

33

Baniyas Rd

Al-Maktoum Rd

RIGGA

23C
26B

27C

23D

59

48

12

19

23C

42A

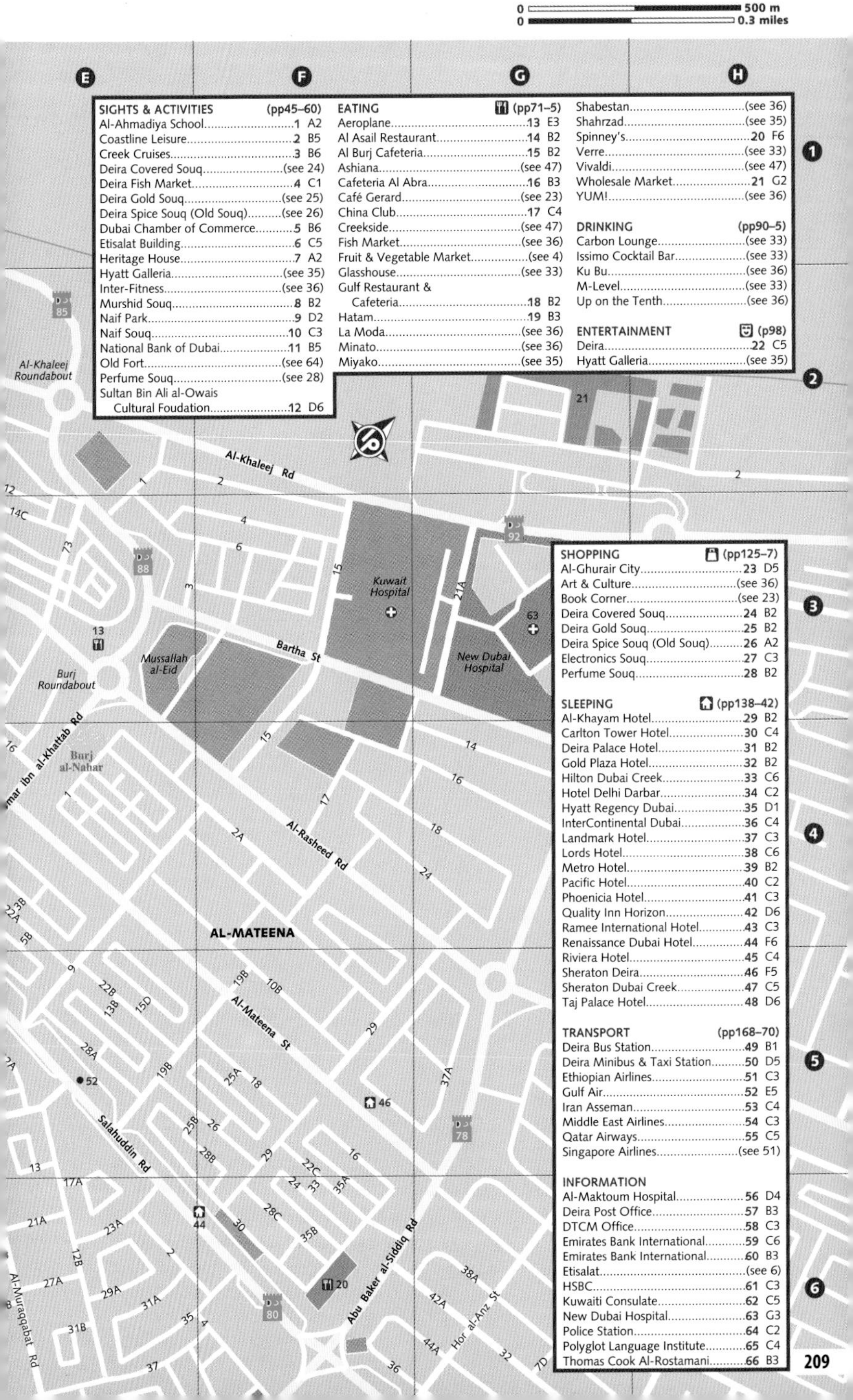
0 500 m
0 0.3 miles
E
F
G
H
1
2
3
4
5
6
Al-Khaleej Roundabout
Al-Khaleej Rd
Bartha St
Kuwait Hospital
New Dubai Hospital
Mussallah al-Eid
Burj Roundabout
Burj al-Nahar
Umar ibn al-Khattab Rd
Al-Rasheed Rd
AL-MATEENA
Al-Mateena St
Salahuddin Rd
Abu Baker al-Siddiq Rd
Hor al-Anz St
Al-Muraqqabat Rd

SIGHTS & ACTIVITIES (pp45–60)
- Al-Ahmadiya School....1 A2
- Coastline Leisure....2 B5
- Creek Cruises....3 B6
- Deira Covered Souq....(see 24)
- Deira Fish Market....4 C1
- Deira Gold Souq....(see 25)
- Deira Spice Souq (Old Souq)....(see 26)
- Dubai Chamber of Commerce....5 B6
- Etisalat Building....6 C5
- Heritage House....7 A2
- Hyatt Galleria....(see 35)
- Inter-Fitness....(see 36)
- Murshid Souq....8 B2
- Naif Park....9 D2
- Naif Souq....10 C3
- National Bank of Dubai....11 B5
- Old Fort....(see 64)
- Perfume Souq....(see 28)
- Sultan Bin Ali al-Owais Cultural Foudation....12 D6

EATING (pp71–5)
- Aeroplane....13 E3
- Al Asail Restaurant....14 B2
- Al Burj Cafeteria....15 B2
- Ashiana....(see 47)
- Cafeteria Al Abra....16 B3
- Café Gerard....(see 23)
- China Club....17 C4
- Creekside....(see 47)
- Fish Market....(see 36)
- Fruit & Vegetable Market....(see 4)
- Glasshouse....(see 33)
- Gulf Restaurant & Cafeteria....18 B2
- Hatam....19 B3
- La Moda....(see 36)
- Minato....(see 36)
- Miyako....(see 35)
- Shabestan....(see 36)
- Shahrzad....(see 35)
- Spinney's....20 F6
- Verre....(see 33)
- Vivaldi....(see 47)
- Wholesale Market....21 G2
- YUM!....(see 36)

DRINKING (pp90–5)
- Carbon Lounge....(see 33)
- Issimo Cocktail Bar....(see 33)
- Ku Bu....(see 36)
- M-Level....(see 33)
- Up on the Tenth....(see 36)

ENTERTAINMENT (p98)
- Deira....22 C5
- Hyatt Galleria....(see 35)

SHOPPING (pp125–7)
- Al-Ghurair City....23 D5
- Art & Culture....(see 36)
- Book Corner....(see 23)
- Deira Covered Souq....24 B2
- Deira Gold Souq....25 B2
- Deira Spice Souq (Old Souq)....26 A2
- Electronics Souq....27 C3
- Perfume Souq....28 B2

SLEEPING (pp138–42)
- Al-Khayam Hotel....29 B2
- Carlton Tower Hotel....30 C4
- Deira Palace Hotel....31 B2
- Gold Plaza Hotel....32 B2
- Hilton Dubai Creek....33 C6
- Hotel Delhi Darbar....34 C2
- Hyatt Regency Dubai....35 D1
- InterContinental Dubai....36 C4
- Landmark Hotel....37 C3
- Lords Hotel....38 C6
- Metro Hotel....39 B2
- Pacific Hotel....40 C2
- Phoenicia Hotel....41 C3
- Quality Inn Horizon....42 D6
- Ramee International Hotel....43 C3
- Renaissance Dubai Hotel....44 F6
- Riviera Hotel....45 C4
- Sheraton Deira....46 F5
- Sheraton Dubai Creek....47 C5
- Taj Palace Hotel....48 D6

TRANSPORT (pp168–70)
- Deira Bus Station....49 B1
- Deira Minibus & Taxi Station....50 D5
- Ethiopian Airlines....51 C3
- Gulf Air....52 E5
- Iran Asseman....53 C4
- Middle East Airlines....54 C3
- Qatar Airways....55 C5
- Singapore Airlines....(see 51)

INFORMATION
- Al-Maktoum Hospital....56 D4
- Deira Post Office....57 B3
- DTCM Office....58 C3
- Emirates Bank International....59 C6
- Emirates Bank International....60 B3
- Etisalat....(see 6)
- HSBC....61 C3
- Kuwaiti Consulate....62 C5
- New Dubai Hospital....63 G3
- Police Station....64 C2
- Polyglot Language Institute....65 C4
- Thomas Cook Al-Rostamani....66 B3

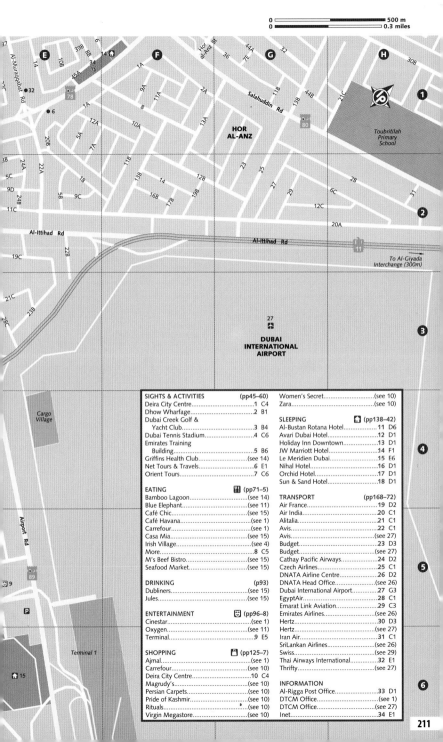

0		500 m
0		0.3 miles

HOR AL-ANZ

Salahuddin Rd

Toubritilah Primary School

Al-Ittihad Rd

To Al-Giyada Interchange (300m)

DUBAI INTERNATIONAL AIRPORT

Cargo Village

Airport Rd

Terminal 1

BUR DUBAI (NORTH)

A	B	C
SIGHTS & ACTIVITIES (pp45–60)	India House.................................22 F4	Panorama Hotel............................34 E4
Ali bin Abi Taleb Mosque.....................1 G3	Kan Zaman................................(see 28)	Ramada Hotel...............................35 E5
Bastakia Quarter.....................................2 G4	Kwality..23 E3	Regal Plaza Hotel.........................36 F5
Bin Suroor Mosque.................................3 F2	Mr Chow.....................................24 E4	Regent Palace Hotel.....................37 F6
Danat Dubai Cruises.............................4 H6	Spinney's.....................................25 E6	Time Palace Hotel........................38 F3
Diwan...5 G4	Spinney's.....................................26 F5	XVA..39 G4
Dubai Museum.......................................6 G4	Troyka...27 E4	
Grand Mosque.......................................7 G4	Yakitori....................................(see 27)	**TRANSPORT** (pp168–70)
Heritage & Diving Villages..................8 G2		Bur Dubai Abra Station................40 F3
House Of Chi & House Of Healing......9 F5	**DRINKING** (pp92–3)	Bur Dubai Bus Station..................41 F3
Majlis Gallery.......................................10 G4	Bollywood Café.......................(see 36)	Deira Old Souq Abra Station........42 H3
Nautilus Academy..............................(see 9)	Rock Bottom Café...................(see 37)	Dubai Old Souq Abra Station.......43 G3
Scuba International.............................(see 8)		Malaysia Airlines..........................44 F5
Sheikh Juma al-Maktoum House.......11 G2	**ENTERTAINMENT** (p89)	Oman Air......................................45 E4
Sheikh Saeed al-Maktoum House......12 G2	Fatafeet Café...........................(see 21)	Royal Brunei Airlines....................46 E4
Shindagha Tower.................................13 F3	Kan Zaman...................................28 G2	Sabkha Abra Station.....................47 H4
Shri Nathje Jayate Temple..................14 G4		Thrifty..48 E6
Sikh Gurdwara....................................15 G4	**SHOPPING** (pp117–31)	
Wonder Bus Tours.............................(see 30)	Al Orooba Oriental..................(see 30)	**INFORMATION**
XVA...(see 39)	Bur Dubai Souq............................29 G3	Al-Jalsa Internet Café...................49 F5
	BurJuman Centre..........................30 F6	Al-Musalla Post Office...................50 G4
EATING (pp75–80)	Gulf Greetings.........................(see 30)	Canadian Consulate......................51 F6
Antique Bazaar..................................(see 33)	No Name Shoe Shop................(see 29)	DTCM Office..............................(see 50)
Automatic...16 F5	Tiffany & Co............................(see 30)	Dutch Consulate...........................52 F3
Basta Art Café......................................17 G4		Emirates Bank International..........53 F3
Carrefour..18 F2	**SLEEPING** (pp142–4)	Etisalat...54 F4
Choithrams..19 F4	Astoria Hotel.................................31 F3	HSBC...55 F3
Dôme..20 F6	Capitol Hotel.................................32 A4	Saudi Arabian Consulate..............56 H6
Fatafeet..21 H6	Four Points Sheraton....................33 F5	UK Embassy..................................57 H6

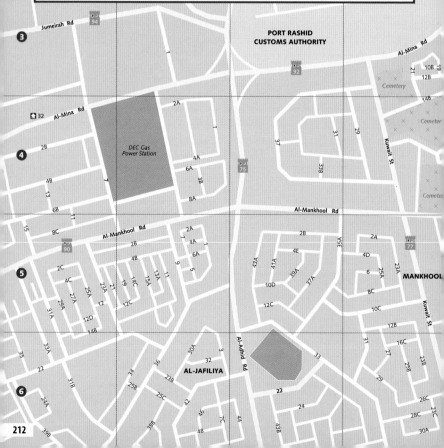

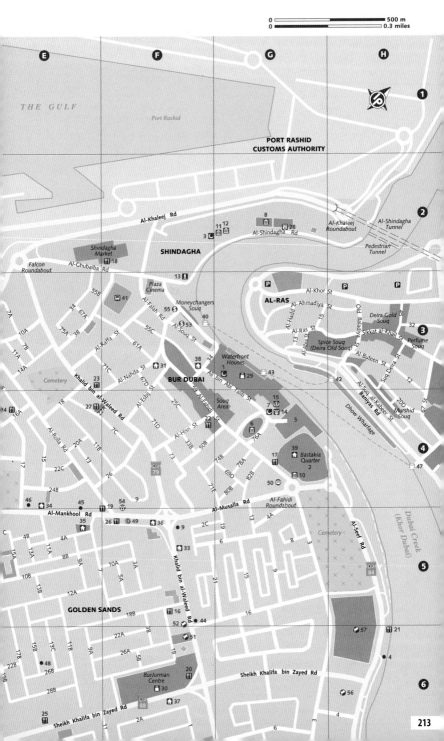

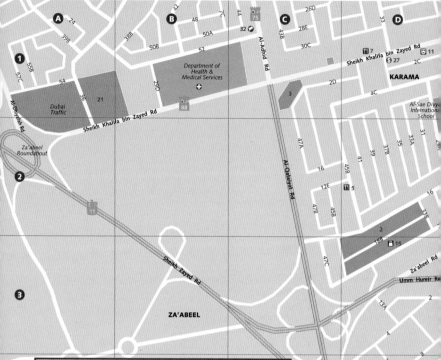

SIGHTS & ACTIVITIES	(pp45–60)
Al-Nasr	(see 8)
Big Bus Company	(see 22)
Cleopatra's Spa	(see 17)
Creekside Park	1 G5
Karama Shopping Centre	2 D2
Pharaohs Club	(see 17)
Scubatec Diving Centre	3 C1

EATING	🍴 (pp75–80)
Asha's	(see 17)
Carter's	(see 17)
Chhappan Bhog	4 E1
Elements Café	(see 17)
Food Castle	5 D2
Karachi Darbar	(see 15)
Lemongrass	6 D4
Medzo	(see 17)
Seville's	(see 17)
Thai Chi	(see 17)
Union Co-op Society	7 D1

DRINKING	(pp92–4)
Carter's	(see 22)
Ginseng	(see 17)
Vintage	(see 17)

ENTERTAINMENT	🎫 (pp87–98)
Al-Nasr Leisureland	8 E4
Alliance Française	9 D5
Lamcy Cinema	10 D4
Maharlika	11 D1
Movies Under the Stars	(see 17)
Peanut Butter Jam	(see 17)
Planetarium	(see 17)
Strand	12 G1

SHOPPING	🛍 (pp127–31)
2000 Horizon Antique	(see 15)
City Shoes	(see 15)
Damas Jewellery	(see 17)

Five Green	13 F3
Flamingo Gifts	(see 15)
Gift Land	(see 15)
Gifts & Souvenirs	(see 15)
Goodies	(see 22)
Ibn Al Saada	(see 15)
Karama Centre	14 E2
Karama Shopping Centre	15 D3
Los Angeles In Dubai	(see 15)
Ohm Records	16 F1
Rafi Frame Store	(see 15)
Sayed Mohammed Ali al-Hashemi	(see 15)
Seven Art Fashion	(see 15)
Splash Boutique	(see 15)
Tetsa Trading	(see 15)
Wafi City Mall	17 D6

SLEEPING	🏠 (p143)
Mövenpick Hotel Bur Dubai	18 D4

TRANSPORT	(p168)
KLM	19 E5

INFORMATION	
Al-Wasl Hospital	20 D6
Department of Immigration & Naturalisation	21 A1
DTCM Office	22 D6
Egyptian Consulate	23 G1
German Consulate	24 G1
Indian Consulate	25 G1
Jordanian Consulate	26 G1
Kanoo Travel	27 D1
Lebanese Consulate	28 G1
Main Post Office	29 E2
Omani Consulate	30 G1
Pakistani Consulate	31 G1
Qatari Consulate	32 C1
Rashid Hospital	33 F4
South African Consulate	(see 24)
Yemeni Consulate	34 G1

0 ————————————————— 500 m
0 ————————————————— 0.3 miles

E

4 ■

Ministry of Health

2B

21

4B

F

2A

16 ■

4A

Khalid bin al-Waleed Rd

24

G

23
31   11
30
26
6
34
7B
25
28
8
3

H

1

84

13A

6A

8B
8A
9A

A'ishat Intermediate School

Al-Karama Kindergarten

12A

16B

16A

Iranian School

12
ℹ

Kuwait St

10C

10B
13B

7A
12B

2

14 ■

18A
20A

Sheikha Latifa bint Hamdan School

Islamic Studies College

77

Za'abeel Rd

24

Karama Park

27A

29

Umm Hureir Rd

13 ■

2

10

Dubai TV

Al-Maktoum Bridge

3

Dubai Courts

12A

8

14B

Oud Metha Rd

33

79

15B

14

4

13

Dubai English Speaking School

Riyadh St

Creekside Park

1

Dubai Creek (Khor Dubai)

5

19

Rashid Hospital

20

81

6

26

Dubai Creek Golf Course

A   **B**   **C**   **D**

SIGHTS & ACTIVITIES (pp45–60)
Al-Boom Diving	1 F5
Dubai Zoo	2 C5
Green Art Gallery	3 D5
Iranian Mosque	4 F5
Jumeirah Mosque	5 F4
Public Beach	6 E4

EATING 🍴 (pp82–6)
Al Qasr	(see 17)
Automatic	(see 10)
Bella Donna	(see 13)
Café Gerard	(see 22)
Coconut Grove	(see 23)
Il Rustico	(see 23)
Japengo Café	(see 15)
Lime Tree Café	7 F4
Ravi's	8 H6
Spinney's	9 E4
Spinney's	(see 13)
Thai Bistro	(see 17)

DRINKING (pp92–4)
Aussie Legends Bar	(see 23)
El Malecon	(see 17)
Sho Cho's	(see 17)

ENTERTAINMENT (p95)
Boudoir	(see 17)

SHOPPING 🛍 (pp132–4)
Al Areej	(see 13)
Beach Centre	10 D5
Jumeirah Centre	11 E5
Jumeirah Plaza	12 E5
Mercato Mall	13 A5
Music Master	(see 15)
One	14 F4
Palm Strip	15 F4
Persian Carpet House & Antiques	(see 13)
Red Sea Exhibitions	(see 10)
Town Centre	16 A5
Virgin Megastore	(see 13)

SLEEPING 🏠 (p146)
Dubai Marine Beach Resort & Spa	17 H3

INFORMATION
Berlitz Language School	18 C5
Dubai London Clinic	19 A6
Formula One	(see 15)
General Medical Centre	(see 22)
Internet Café	20 H5
Iranian Consulate	21 E5
Manchester Clinic	(see 10)

OTHER
Magrudy's Shopping Centre	22 E4
Rydges Plaza Hotel	23 H6

THE GULF

Jumeirah Rd

Al-Wasl Rd

Jumeirah Kindergarten